Endorsed by
Ron McIntosh

This book describes the manifold blessings of God available to the individual through the redemptive work of Jesus Christ on the cross of Calvary. Dr Rajan has thoroughly unfolded the potential of that place of "Great Xchange".

"The Great Xchange" will challenge mindsets, provoke discussion, reveal the heart of God and provide a way forward into a greater experience of the provisions of redemptive power.

"The Great Xchange" reinforces the covenant that was made on the cross of Calvary for each one of us. It describes in detail the benefits and the necessity of applying the blood of Jesus Christ to our lives and those of our household every day.

The fact that the cross provides total care and provision is a surety for us that we can walk in liberty and freedom, knowing that everything we need for life and godliness is met in the cross of Calvary.

We are accepted, forgiven, healed and provided for by the blood of Jesus Christ.

Dr Rajan's deep faith and understanding of the redemptive work of Christ is displayed throughout this book.

Ron McIntosh
President of Ron McIntosh Ministries and I.M.P.A.C.T
Executive Director of Victory Bible Institute,
Tulsa, Oklahoma, USA

The Great Xchange

WestBow
PRESS
A DIVISION OF THOMAS NELSON

The Great Xchange

What happened to you @ the Cross

by

Dr Rajan Thiagarajah

Mighty Living Waters Life Fellowship

ISBN: 978-1-4497-3830-3 (e)
ISBN: 978-1-4497-3831-0 (sc)

Library of Congress Control Number: 2012901473

Published by Mighty Living Waters Life Fellowship, in conjunction with WestBow Press. WestBow Press books may be ordered through booksellers or by contacting:

WestBow Press
A Division of Thomas Nelson
1663 Liberty Drive
Bloomington, IN 47403
www.westbowpress.com
1-(866) 928-1240

Mighty Living Waters Life Fellowship
P O Box 183, Willetton
Western Australia 6955
Phone: +61 – 8 9457 6611
Fax: +61 – 8 9457 6951
Email: admin@lifeinthespirit.info
www.lifeinthespirit.info

Because of the dynamic nature of the Internet, any web addresses or links contained in this book may have changed since publication and may no longer be valid. The views expressed in this work are solely those of the author and do not necessarily reflect the views of the publisher, and the publisher hereby disclaims any responsibility for them.

Certain stock imagery © Thinkstock.
Any people depicted in stock imagery provided by Thinkstock are models, and such images are being used for illustrative purposes only.

Unless otherwise indicated, scripture taken from the King James Version.

Scripture quotations marked (AMP) are taken from the Amplified Bible, Copyright © 1954, 1958, 1962, 1964, 1965, 1987 by The Lockman Foundation. Used by permission.

Printed in the United States of America

WestBow Press rev. date: 2/01/2012

WestBow
PRESS
A DIVISION OF THOMAS NELSON

 oreword

Rev. Dr. Colton S Wickramaratne

As I glance through the manuscript of this book, *The Great XChange*, I see two vital truths that stand out visibly. These truths are the core teachings of the Bible: the atoning blood of the Lord Jesus Christ and the Lord Jesus Christ, the Person.

The emphasis on the efficacy of the sinless blood of the Lord is vividly shown through its power in relation to the great work of our own redemption and the manifestation of this power in many areas of life.

Concerning the Person of the Lord Jesus Christ, there is much material here that will help the reader know the uniqueness of Jesus Christ as the Son of Man and also as the eternal Son of God—as eternal as God the Father.

It is a good book that shows us the "Great Exchange"—how divinity became humanity, to bring humanity to divinity. It is very difficult to summarize the material of this book in a few sentences. I recommend that the reader carefully scrutinize and glean the divine truths recorded in it. It will enrich your life and help you in your Christian walk.

Rev. Dr. Colton S. Wickramaratne
Founder Pastor, PEOPLE'S CHURCH, ASSEMBLY OF GOD

Foreword

Dr. Wayde Goodall

This powerful book is full of faith-producing, life-changing and encouraging truths that will give courage and wisdom to the follower of Christ. Dr. Rajan Thiagarajah's devotion to the Scripture and his powerful presentation of the critical issues concerning our Christian faith are hope-producing and spiritually inspiring. Few are better than Dr. Rajan in providing answers from God's Word for the eternal principles of dynamic faith while living in a very confused world.

The Great Exchange (Xchange) gives the reader a guide through the Scripture concerning the wonderful truths of who we are in Christ and the privileges we have because of Him. This book will impact your life.

Dr. Wayde Goodall
President, Worldwide Family
Author of several bestselling books

Rev. Dr. Prince Guneratnam

The Great Xchange is a book that comes from a heart of a pastor-teacher who desires all believers to fully understand, appreciate and appropriate the blessings that come from Jesus' sacrifice of love on the cross.

The book consistently reminds us of the powerful truth that it is only through the cross that man can have peace with God and enjoy the peace of God. It is the finished work of the cross that disarmed and defeated Satan and enables us to be victorious over the flesh and the works of the enemy.

The principles addressed in this book make it an invaluable resource to those who are in ministry and will greatly enhance their effectiveness.

As Paul says in 1 Corinthians 1:18: "...the message of the cross is foolishness to those who are perishing, but to us who are being saved, it is the power of God."

Dr. Rajan Thiagarah has written a book that will bring great encouragement, victory and joy to those who will apply the biblical truths and principles so ably and clearly presented.

Rev. Dr. Prince Guneratnam
Senior Pastor, Calvary Church, Kuala Lumpur, Malaysia
Chairman, World Pentecostal Fellowship

Dedication

I would like to specially dedicate this book to the blessed Holy Spirit who continues to lead and guide me in the ways of the Lord.

My sincere thanks to my darling wife, Ruby, and son, Josiah, for their love and continued support to the work of the ministry.

To Pastor Kam and Christine Achari and Pastor Ala and Dorah Altraide for their encouragement and support over the years to me and my family.

To Pastor Dariel Forlong, Marlene Wilkinson and Dywen Lauren for their assistance and for allowing the Lord to use their talents in bringing this book to print.

To all the faithful saints of Mighty Living Waters Life Fellowship, whose prayers and support have given me the strength and courage to soldier on in the great work and service of the Lord.

Preface

While in prayer, the Lord began to deposit the value and the gravity of the scriptures in Isaiah 53:4–6:

"Surely He has borne our griefs and carried our sorrows; yet we esteemed Him stricken, smitten by God and afflicted. But He was wounded for our transgressions, He was bruised for our iniquities; the chastisement for our peace was upon Him, and by His stripes we are healed. All we like sheep have gone astray; we have turned, every one, to his own way; and the Lord has laid on Him the iniquity of us all."

I began to realize through the Spirit of God that all God's blessings have come to us because of the finished work of Calvary.

Today many children of God lead a defeated life, even though Christ has given us the victory through His death and resurrection. Children of God, as well as sinners, must be exposed to the knowledge of the great exchange that took place on the cross of Calvary for the human race.

It is the plan and purpose of the heavenly Father to see His redeemed children appropriate all the goodness, blessings and victory that He provided for us through His Son on the cross of Calvary.

I was deeply moved by the Spirit to share with every human being the Savior's love and the ultimate price He paid for each of us on the cross of Calvary. It is my utmost God-given responsibility to share this truth with you and to see you prosper in every aspect of your life.

> 3 John 2,
> *"Beloved I pray that you may prosper in all things and be in health, just as your soul prospers."*

During one of my recent ministry trips to Milan in Europe, as I was meditating and waiting on the Lord, He began to speak to me about the cross and Christ. He brought my attention to this scripture:

> Colossians 1:20
> *"And by Him to reconcile all things to Himself, by Him, whether things on earth or things in heaven, having made peace through the blood of His cross."*

The blessed Holy Spirit began to explain to me that it was upon the cross that our Lord shed His blood. The blood of Jesus became valuable to every human soul because it was shed on the cross. It is only through the blood of Jesus that the Holy Spirit reveals to us the power of the finished work of the cross.

It is the source and the foundation upon which we can lead a victorious life. There are many aspects to the Gospel, such as mercy, grace, life, prosperity, abundance, work of the Holy Spirit, etc. We can only appropriate them because of Christ's death on the cross and His ascension.

I pray that as you journey through this book you will allow my greatest co-author, the Holy Spirit, to reveal the truth about the great exchange that took place for you and me on the cross. Let this truth take effect in your life, so that you will walk in freedom and liberty and be a light in the world for others to know the saving power of Christ in Jesus' name. Amen.

CONTENT

The Great Xchange

INTRODUCTION

The One Who Died for Us

SECTION ONE

The Cross of Calvary Provides Us with a Divine Exchange

SECTION TWO

The Cross of Calvary Provides Protection

SECTION THREE

The Cross of Calvary Provides Us with a Challenge

SECTION FOUR

The Cross of Calvary Reveals God's Unconditional Love to Us

SECTION FIVE

The Cross of Calvary Provides Us with a New Covenant

The Blessing of the New Covenant

INTRODUCTION

The Power of the Cross

As we proceed through this journey we are going to learn about the cross, the One who hung on the cross, and the divine exchange that took place between God and man.

There is a wonderful, divine exchange that took place. We traded something when we entered into the covenant with God through Jesus Christ—there was an exchange that took place at Calvary.

Before we go any further, I want you know that there is a separation in the Church today. There are those who have rejected the cross and those who cling to the cross. Without the cross of Christ there is no hope for the world. Without the cross there is no hope for humanity. It is from the cross of Christ that we receive all the benefits. It is at Calvary that God won the victory for us.

Some have rejected the cross; they do not proclaim or preach the cross anymore, nor do they declare the blood of Christ, and without the blood there is no remission of sin.

It is time for us to get back to the foundation and the reality of what Jesus did for us and know that salvation came through Jesus—the Son of the living God.

Now let us build a foundation and go deeper into what the Word says about what the cross of Jesus has done for us and will continue to do for us.

1. The cross of Christ is the power of God.

> *1 Corinthians 1:17–18*
> *For Christ did not send me to baptize, but to preach the gospel, not with wisdom of words, lest the cross of Christ should be made of none effect. For the message of the cross is foolishness to those who are perishing, but to us who are being saved it <u>is the power</u> of God.*

The word gospel means "good news." There is no other "good news" except Christ crucified and resurrected.

2. The cross of Christ is an offense to some.

For some people, the preaching of the gospel causes offense.

> *Galatians 5:11*
> *And I, brethren, if I still preach circumcision, why do I still suffer persecution? Then the <u>offense</u> of the cross has ceased.*

We see from the Word of God that the cross of Christ has power; the cross of Christ is an offense, or a stumbling block, to some.

3. The cross of Christ brings persecution.

> *Galatians 6:12*
> *As many as desire to make a good showing in the flesh, these would compel you to be circumcised, only that they may not suffer <u>persecution</u> for the cross of Christ.*

We see in this verse that the cross of Christ brings persecution. You may say, "God, I do not want to be persecuted." If you stand for the cross, persecution will come your way. We need to look at the promises Jesus gave us.

> *Mark 10:29b–30*
> *There is no one who has left house or brothers or sisters or*
> *father or mother or wife or children or lands, for My sake*
> *and the gospel's, who shall not receive a hundredfold now in*
> *this time—houses and brothers and sisters and mothers and*
> *children and lands, with persecutions—and in the age to*
> *come, eternal life.*

You will receive a hundredfold NOW! He did not say, "When you get to heaven you will receive a hundredfold"—but NOW in this lifetime. When we get to heaven we will have everything, but God has promised we shall receive one hundredfold NOW IN THIS TIME! He says you will have houses, brothers, sisters, mothers, children and lands—with persecutions.

4. The cross of Christ brings glory.

> *Galatians 6:14*
> *ut God forbid that I should boast [glory] except in the cross of*
> *our Lord Jesus Christ, by whom the world has been crucified*
> *to me, and I to the world.*

Paul says he wants to glory in the cross. What does he mean? He means he wants to glory in what the cross has done for him. All the benefits and all the blessings that God has placed upon you and me have come through the cross of Calvary. If you want to boast, boast in the finished work of the cross of Calvary.

Jesus Christ, the Son of the living God, spoke in:

> *John 16:14*
> *He will glorify Me, for He will take of what is Mine and*
> *declare it to you.*

God the Father and God the Son are the owners of everything. They own all things in heaven and on earth; all things under the earth belong to God. He is highly exalted above everything. So the owners of everything are God the Father and God the Son, and the Holy Spirit is the "gatekeeper" of all God's treasures.

If you want God's treasures, if you want God's blessings, then you must know the "gatekeeper"—the Holy Spirit. The key to open the door to all God's treasures is the cross of Calvary.

When you know the "gatekeeper," He will reveal the power of the cross to you, and it is there that we receive all God's blessings.

Before we proceed any further, I want you to answer the following questions:

- Who owns everything?
  Answer: God the Father

- Who is the "gatekeeper"?
  Answer: The Holy Spirit

- What is the key
  Answer: The cross of Calvary

Jesus made a statement in:

John 12:32–33
"And I, if I am lifted up from the earth, will draw all peoples to Myself." This He said, signifying by what death He would die.

In other words He said, "I will draw all men to Myself." He did not say, "I will draw all men to a denomination." He did not say, "I will draw all men to a certain place." He said, "I will draw all men to Me, Jesus."

What we have done is to lift up Jesus, but we want the people to come to us. Jesus said, "When I am lifted up, I will draw all men to Myself." By saying this, He signified that He is the author and finisher of our faith.

His death and resurrection are like a magnet to the soul. Whenever the cross is presented and Christ crucified and resurrected is preached, it satisfies the parched and dry soul. Every soul is longing to know God.

You may be saying, "The world is not coming to church." The world will not come to church, but they do want to come to Jesus. Every soul is longing to be in touch with their Maker. Why do you think today there are more fortune-tellers, more tarot card readers, and more witches? People want to find themselves in a supernatural realm, and the Church has gone far away from the foundation of the cross, so they have lost the power. Do not blame things from outside. We have to get back to the cross of Jesus Christ—that is where the power is.

Jesus said that His death and resurrection would draw the souls of human beings to Himself. No man ever died for you except Jesus Christ.

You may be following this Swami, or some other man, and you can go and find their tombs, but you cannot find the tomb of Jesus because He not only died but He rose again. He did not just say, "I love you," but He acted on it and went to the cross for you. That is why Jesus said this to Nicodemus in:

John 3:14
And as Moses lifted up the serpent in the wilderness, even so must the Son of Man be lifted up, that whoever believes in Him should not perish but have eternal life.

5. The cross of Christ has reconciled us to God.

Ephesians 2:16
And that He might <u>reconcile</u> them both to God in one body through the cross, thereby putting to death the enmity.

In other words, today God my Father, the Almighty, the Creator of the universe, is my heavenly Father because of the cross of Calvary.

In the Old Covenant, the people could not go to God—they worshipped from afar, but today, "the hour has come," Jesus said. Now you can worship God any place and any time and enter into the Holy of Holies through the blood of Jesus and say "heavenly Father" because of the cross.

My God is my heavenly Father because I have been reconciled to my God through the death of Christ on the cross.

Colossians 1:20
And by Him to reconcile all things to Himself, by Him, whether things on earth or things in heaven, having made peace through the blood of His cross.

He has reconciled ALL things to God. The cross of Christ not only is the power and the offense to some, it brings persecution, it is glorious, and it has also reconciled us to God.

6. The cross of Christ has enemies.

Philippians 3:18
For many walk, of whom I have told you often, and now tell you even weeping, that they are the <u>enemies</u> of the cross of Christ.

The cross of Christ has enemies. Today, if you stand up for the cross of Calvary, people will persecute and ridicule you. The cross has enemies—the devil hates the cross because that is where he was defeated. This was where the great exchange took place. Jesus became poor so we could become rich, He was wounded so we would be healed, He was rejected so we would be accepted, He took our shame so we can partake in His glory, and He bore our curse so we would be blessed with the blessings of heaven. There was an exchange that took place on the cross of Calvary.

7. The cross of Christ has eliminated everything that is contrary toward you and has given you the victory.

Colossians 2:14-15 AMP

> *Having cancelled and blotted out and wiped away the handwriting of the note (bond) with its legal decrees and demands, which was in force and stood against us (hostile to us). This [note with its regulations, decrees, and demands] He set aside and cleared completely out of our way by nailing it to [His] cross. [God] disarmed the principalities and powers that were ranged against us and made a bold display and public example of them, in triumphing over them in Him and in it [the cross].*

There were things that were against us, things said against us, but God has blotted them all out. They are cancelled. The devil has no legal authority over us.

When the enemy brings accusation against you, take him to the above scripture. Remind him there is no record against us; it has been cancelled, blotted out. The demons know their legal rights very well—they are like lawyers. That is why this verse talks about "legal decrees" that have been removed by nailing them to the cross.

Christ on the Cross

Matthew 27:22
Pilate said to them, "What then shall I do with Jesus who is called Christ?" They all said to him, "Let Him be crucified!"

Pilate asked a question that day, and the Holy Spirit is asking the same question today: What are you going to do with Jesus today? Your destiny, future, and eternity depend on your answer.

On the cross Pilate wrote an inscription:

Matthew 27:37
And they put up over His head the accusation written against Him: THIS IS JESUS THE KING OF THE JEWS.

This inscription was written in three languages. These were the languages spoken in the world at that time. Pilate wanted everyone to read it so no one would miss it.

When the Jews looked at the note, they looked at it through the eyes of "religion." They looked at it from the soul. How can He be the Son of God because the scripture says, "Cursed is he that hangs on a tree?"

Deuteronomy 21:22–23
If a man has committed a sin deserving of death, and he is put to death, and you hang him on a tree, his body shall not remain overnight on the tree, but you shall surely bury him that day, so that you do not defile the land which the Lord your God is giving you as an inheritance; for he who is hanged is accursed of God.

Galatians 3:13
Christ has redeemed us from the curse of the law, having become a curse for us (for it is written, "Cursed is everyone who hangs on a tree")..

Jesus became a curse for us. When Adam sinned, he brought a curse not only upon himself, but upon the whole earth. The last Adam (Jesus) knew no sin, but He hung on a cross and bore the curse Himself, so that whoever believes in Him could go free and be blessed with the blessings of heaven. The opposite of a curse is blessing. The Jews could not see it. They looked through the eyes of "religion" and rejected the cross. It was a stumbling block to the Jews.

The Romans came and said, "He says He is a King, but He dies on a cross." Kings were the ones who were supposed to bring victory. This was a stumbling block to the Romans. But what they did not know was that through His death, He brought life.

No other man who has walked on the face of the earth has ever said, "I am the first and the last." No man apart from Jesus has said, "I have the keys of death and hell." But the Romans could not see it. They looked at it from the natural point of view. They did not realize that unless someone dies, no life can come forth. Through His death, He would overcome death and have the victory. To a Roman it became a stumbling block.

For the Greek, it was all about philosophy because the Greeks used their minds. All things had to be beautiful, especially the gods and goddesses. The Greeks asked, if Jesus was the King, why was He not beautiful? The Bible says that He has no beauty that we should desire Him. He was whipped for you and for me. The cross became a stumbling block to the Greeks.

If you lift Jesus up and present Christ crucified, it will draw all men to Him.

1 Corinthians 1:23–24
But we preach Christ crucified, to the Jews a stumbling block and to the Greeks foolishness, but to those who are called, both Jews and Greeks, Christ the power of God and the wisdom of God.

Christ is the power and the wisdom of God. Christ without the cross is no Messiah at all.

Freedom and liberty comes only through the finished work of the cross.

The Cross of Christ

- The cross of Christ is the throne of heaven.
- The cross of Christ is the center of humanity.
- The cross of Christ is the seat of power.
- The cross of Christ is the seat of authority.
- The cross of Christ is the seat of love.
- The cross of Christ is the seat of grace.

All the blessing that is upon you is because of what Jesus has done.

Let us keep our eyes upon Jesus and the finished work of the cross.

Hebrews 12:2
Looking unto Jesus, the author and finisher of our faith, who for the joy that was set before Him endured the cross, despising the shame, and has sat down at the right hand of the throne of God.

Luke 14:27
And whoever does not bear his cross and come after Me cannot be My disciple.

You cannot live your life how you want. You cannot just do your own thing. We must live according to His Word to appropriate His blessings.

The Man on the Cross

All the blessings that you enjoy today as a Christian, you enjoy because of the finished work of the cross of Calvary.

> *Isaiah 40:11*
> *He will feed His flock like a shepherd; He will gather the lambs with His arm, and carry them in His bosom, and gently lead those who are with young.*

- **Total care**

  "He will feed His flock like a shepherd." We need to understand that we are His flock. You need to be able to "see" how God takes care of you. Even the hairs on your head are numbered. That is how much He cares for you. Total care!

- **Total provision**

  All the provision that you will ever need comes through the cross of Calvary. The world is saying that there is not going to be enough money, that we will suffer inflation, and that jobs are going to fail. That is the cycle of the world. This does not belong to us. The children of God prosper because the Kingdom of God always reigns.

Deuteronomy 30:9
The LORD your God will make you abound in all the work of
your hand, in the fruit of your body, in the increase of your
livestock, and in the produce of your land for good. For the
Lord will again rejoice over you for good as He rejoiced over
your fathers.

What He is saying is that He will "make your hand prosperous" for good. In other words, God is going to bless you. The world may go into a dark realm, but as far as the children of God are concerned, God said, "It will be good." Total provision—continuous supply.

Everything that you need now and for the future, for all the days of your life, is already supplied in total for you.

• Total health

Deuteronomy 7:13–15
And He will love you and bless you and multiply you; He will
also bless the fruit of your womb and the fruit of your land,
your grain and your new wine and your oil, the increase
of your cattle and the offspring of your flock, in the land
of which He swore to your fathers to give you. You shall be
blessed above all peoples; there shall not be a male or female
barren among you or among your livestock. And the Lord
will take away from you all sickness, and will afflict you with
none of the terrible diseases of Egypt which you have known,
but will lay them on all those who hate you.

God did not only say He would bless you, but He said "I will love you." God has placed a mark on your life—you belong to Him. That mark says that you are blessed above all people. People who are not walking with the Lord will say to you, "I have lost my job, I do not have the money to pay my bills, yet you are prospering."

God will remove all sickness, whether it is a headache or toothache. Whatever the sickness, God says He will remove it. Not only does He say He will remove the sickness, but He will not put any diseases upon us.

God in Christ has promised to provide total care, total provision, and total health.

Now let us look at the person of Christ.

There were others who hung on a cross that day with Jesus. But what makes this cross different is the **One** who hung on this cross, the cross with the inscription, "This is Jesus, King of the Jews." He not only died but He rose again. He did not just die for us, but He died for every human being.

The Holy Spirit spoke to me and said, "Son, you must **know** who it was that died for you on the cross of Calvary." When we know **of** Him, the finished work of the cross and the divine exchange that took place at the cross of Calvary between man and God, then the cross of Calvary becomes a reality to you and to me."

We need to know **Him**, not just **about** Him. There is a great difference between knowing about a person and knowing that person intimately. When we know Him for ourselves, the finished work of the cross of Calvary and the divine exchange that took place between man and God on the cross of Calvary will become a life-giving power in our lives.

He Is Divine

Many say that the One who hung on the cross for you and me was a good man; some say that He was a religious leader, but the holy scripture says He is divine. The word divine means "from God" or "belonging to God." The Word of God is the final authority on everything.

What makes Him "divine"?

1. He is the Son of God.

The Word says that He is the Son of the living God, the One who hung on the cross for you and for me.

Luke 22: 70
Then they all said, "Are You then <u>the Son of God</u>?" So He said to them, "You rightly say that I am."

Remember, it is not the cross, but the One who died on the cross, that made the difference.

2. He is the only begotten Son.

John 1:18
No one has seen God at any time. <u>The only begotten Son</u>, who is in the bosom of the Father, He has declared Him.

When we know Him as divine, then what He accomplished on the cross becomes profitable to us and we will be able to appropriate all our provision through the cross of Calvary.

3. He is the First and the Last.

He is not only the Son of God; He is the only begotten Son of God—the first and the last.

Revelation 1:17
And when I saw Him, I fell at His feet as dead. But He laid His right hand on me, saying to me, "Do not be afraid; I am <u>the First and the Last</u>."

When you know Him as the First and the Last, you will never fear again. Why? He is declaring that "I am supreme in authority; I have everything under My control." When you say to someone, "He is the First and the Last," you are saying He is totally in control of everything.

Isaiah 44:6
  Thus says the Lord, the King of Israel, and his Redeemer, the Lord of hosts: "I am the First and I am the Last; besides Me there is no God."

There is no other God, because He is the First and the Last. The First and the Last died on the cross for you and for me.

4. He is the Alpha and Omega.

Revelation 1:11
  Saying, "I am the Alpha and the Omega, the First and the Last," and, "What you see, write in a book and send it to the seven churches which are in Asia: to Ephesus, to Smyrna, to Pergamos, to Thyatira, to Sardis, to Philadelphia, and to Laodicea."

He is the first letter and the last letter of the alphabet.

He is the One who wrote history. The past, present and future is in His hand.

5. He is the Holy One.

He is Divine because the scripture calls Him the Holy One.

Acts 3:14
  But you denied the Holy One and the Just, and asked for a murderer to be granted to you..

Jesus Christ, the Son of the living God, is the Holy One. The world does not know that He is the Holy One. For many He is just a man, a religious leader. God is not religious - He is the Truth. Man has taken the Truth and made a religion out of it. He is the only Truth. Jesus said "You shall know the truth and the truth shall set you free."

6. He is the Lord

Christ's Lordship is over all.

Acts 4:26
   The kings of the earth took their stand, and the rulers were gathered together against <u>the</u> Lord and against his Christ.

7. He is the Lord of Glory

Psalm 24:8–10
   Who is this King of glory? The Lord strong and mighty, the Lord mighty in battle. Lift up your heads, O you gates! Lift up, you everlasting doors! And the King of glory shall come in. Who is this King of glory? The Lord of hosts, He is <u>the King of glory</u>. Selah.

Selah means stop and think. The scripture says that Jesus, who died on the cross for you and for me, is the King of glory who knows no defeat, who never fails.

Thomas declared Jesus Christ to be his Lord and his God.

John 20:28
   And Thomas answered and said to Him, "My Lord and my God!"

Yes, He is our Lord and our God.

Now I want you to know the attributes of the Divine One.

i. **He is omnipotent.** He is all powerful, the King of glory, mighty in deed.

John 5:25
> *Most assuredly, I say to you, the hour is coming, and now is, when the dead will hear the voice of the Son of God; and those who hear will live*

The Lord Jesus has not only power and authority over the living, but also over the dead, because He never changes and His promises do not change.

Matthew 28:18 AMP
> *Jesus approached and, breaking the silence, said to them, All authority(all power of rule)in heaven and on earth has been given to Me.*

ii. **He is omniscient.** He knows all things. He knows and perceives all our thoughts. He stood before a Samaritan woman and knew the story of her life.

John 4:16–19
> *Jesus said to her, "Go, call your husband, and come here." The woman answered and said, "I have no husband." Jesus said to her, "You have well said, 'I have no husband,' for you have had five husbands, and the one whom you now have is not your husband; in that you spoke truly." The woman said to Him, "Sir, I perceive that You are a prophet."*

She did not have to tell Jesus anything—He knew all about her. We do things and we think that God does not see. How foolish we are. He knows everything. You may hide things from your parents or anyone else, but I want you to know that God sees and knows everything. You may have done things in secret, there may be skeletons in the closet, but He knows. You cannot hide anything from the Lord. He knows all things.

iii. He is omnipresent.

Matthew 18:20
For where two or three are gathered together in My name,
I am there in the midst of them.

When you shake hands with another believer and you say, "We are meeting in the name of Jesus," expect Jesus to be there. Why? Because He says, "Where two or three gather in My name, I will be there." He is everywhere.

iv. He is eternal.

John 1:1
In the beginning was the Word, and the Word was with God, and the Word was God.

God does not live in eternity. Eternity dwells in Him. God does not have time; He stands outside of time. That is why He is able to see the past, the present, and the future. Physicists say in the realm of time, things are consumed. When there is no time, or absence of time, things cannot be consumed. That is why when Moses saw the burning bush, he was surprised that the bush was not consumed. God stands outside of time. God does not have to face tomorrow, but tomorrow has to face God. If we are in Christ Jesus, we do not have to face tomorrow; tomorrow has to face us.

v. He never changes.

Hebrews 13:8
Jesus Christ is the same yesterday, today, and forever.

God never changes; He never changes His mind. Aren't you glad that our Jesus is not like the politicians? Aren't you glad that our Jesus is not like the economists? Our Lord never changes. What He did yesterday, He will do today and tomorrow. His Word is still the same.

vi. He is the fullness of God.

Colossians 2:9
For in Him dwells all the fullness of the Godhead bodily.

Everything of God dwells in Him. The totality of God in its fullness and glory resides in Christ Jesus.

vii. He is the express image of God.

Hebrews 1:3
Who being the brightness of His glory and the express image of His person, and upholding all things by the word of His power, when He had by Himself purged our sins, sat down at the right hand of the Majesty on high.

He is not only the fullness of God; He is the express image of God. That is why God does not want you to have any other image. He is the One who died for you on the cross of Calvary. If you see Him, you have seen God. He is the only image that you should have in your heart, life, and mind.

Who is the Son of God who died on the cross for you and me?

1. He is the creator.

John 1:3
All things were made through Him, and without Him nothing was made that was made.

Colossians 1:16
For by Him all things were created that are in heaven and that are on earth, visible and invisible, whether thrones or dominions or principalities or powers. All things were created through Him and for Him.

All things were created by Him. We were created by Him, for Him, and for His pleasure.

When an individual does not have a living relationship with the living God, then his or her soul will never be satisfied. Why? Because every human being was created by God for God.

2. He upholds all things by the power of His Word.

Not only is He your Creator, but He holds everything in His hands by the power of His Word.

Hebrews 1:3
Who being the brightness of His glory and the express image of His person, and upholding all things by the word of His power, when He had by Himself purged our sins, sat down at the right hand of the Majesty on high.

Matthew 28:18
And Jesus came and spoke to them, saying, "All authority has been given to Me in heaven and on earth."

All power, authority, and dominion belong to Him.

3. He has the power to forgive.

Not only does He hold everything by the power of His Word, but He has the power to forgive. Nobody is able to forgive sin except Jesus Christ, the Son of the living God.

Mark 2:5–11
When Jesus saw their faith, He said to the paralytic, "Son, your sins are forgiven you." And some of the scribes were sitting there and reasoning in their hearts, "Why does this Man speak blasphemies like this? Who can forgive sins but God alone?" But immediately, when Jesus perceived in His spirit that they reasoned thus within themselves, He said to them, "Why do you reason about these things in your hearts? Which is easier, to say to the paralytic, 'Your sins are forgiven you,' or to say, 'Arise, take up your bed and walk?' But that you may know that the Son of Man has power on earth to forgive sins" --He said to the paralytic. "I say to you, arise, take up your bed, and go to your house."

Jesus Christ, the Son of the living God, has the power to forgive sin.

4. He has the power to raise the dead.

John 6:39
This is the will of the Father who sent Me, that of all He has given Me I should lose nothing, but should raise it up at the last day.

Remember, He has all power.

5. He also has the power to give eternal life.

John 10:28
And I give them eternal life, and they shall never perish;
neither shall anyone snatch them out of My hand.

As you watch the Olympics, you can see how hard the athletes work for the medals. But when you come to Jesus, the medal you get is eternal life. When those athletes perish, they cannot take their medals with them, but what God gives you and me is everlasting; it is eternal.

The word eternal is one of the words in the Scriptures everybody thinks they understand.

Very few realize the deep and glorious truth that is contained in this word. If I ask you what eternal means, you will say, "Something that always continues, something that has no end." That is partially correct, but it does not tell us the nature and being of eternal. Everything that exists in time has a beginning and an end and is subject to the law of increase and decrease, becoming and decaying.

So how does something that is eternal differ?

Anything that is eternal has no beginning and no end, knows no change, and does not decay or diminish. Why? Because it has in itself a life that is independent of time, a life always glorious and endlessly present. It has the life of Christ in it. He has given you and me eternal life through His death on the cross of Calvary.

6. He will judge every human being.

Every human being will stand before the Lord one day, and He will judge them. He has the power and authority to judge because He is the Creator.

2 Timothy 4:1
I charge you therefore before God and the Lord Jesus Christ,
who will judge the living and the dead at His appearing and
His kingdom..

7. He is the lover of my soul.

There is no one who loves with an unconditional love like the Son of God.

John 3:16–17
For God so loved the world that He gave His only begotten
Son, that whoever believes in Him should not perish but have
everlasting life. For God did not send His Son into the world
to condemn the world, but that the world through Him might
be saved.

He loved us so much that He was prepared to leave heaven and come to this earth to walk this dusty road and hang on the cross to die for us. You might say that your wife or husband or children do not love you that much, but I want you to know that the only person you need is Jesus. He is the lover of your soul. He will never leave you or forsake you. He is a friend that stays closer than a brother. He is your faithful husband.

He is the One who died for you and rose again. If you want to know Jesus, just go through the Word of God and find out who Jesus is. Talk to Him. Every book of the Bible contains the Lord Jesus.

Genesis	Seed of the Woman
Exodus	Passover Lamb
Leviticus	High Priest
Numbers	Cloud and Pillar of Fire
Deuteronomy	The Prophet Like Moses
Joshua	Captain of the Host
Judges	Judge and Lawgiver
Ruth	Kinsman Redeemer
1 &2 Samuel	Trusted Prophet of the Lord
1 &2 Kings	Reigning King
1 & 2 Chronicles	Reigning King
Ezra	Faithful Scribe
Nehemiah	Rebuilder of the Walls
Esther	Mordecai
Job	Ever-Living Redeemer
Psalms	Lord Our Shepherd
Proverbs/Ecclesiastes	Our Wisdom
Song of Solomon	Lover and our Bridegroom
Isaiah	Suffering Servant
Jeremiah	Righteous Branch
Lamentations	Weeping Prophet
Ezekiel	Son of Man
Daniel	Fourth Man
Hosea	Faithful Husband
Joel	Baptism with Holy Ghost and Fire
Amos	Burden Bearer
Obadiah	Mighty Savior
Jonah	Forgiving God
Micah	Messenger with Beautiful Feet
Nahum	Avenger of God's Elect

Habakkuk	God's Evangelist Crying for Revival
Zephaniah	Savior and Restorer of the Remnant
Haggai	Owner of the Silver and Gold/ Cleansing Fountain
Zechariah	Pierced Son
Malachi	Son of Righteousness
Matthew	Messiah
Mark	Miracle Worker
Luke	Son of Man
John	Son of God
Acts	Holy Ghost/Ascended Lord
Romans	Justifier
1 Corinthians	Gifts of the Holy Spirit
2 Corinthians	Resurrection
Galatians	Redeems me from the curse of the law
Ephesians	Unsearchable Riches
Philippians	Need Meeter
Colossians	Fullness of God
1 & 2 Thessalonians	Soon-Coming King
1 & 2 Timothy	Mediator
Titus	Faithful Pastor
Philemon	Friend Who Sticks Closer Than a Brother
Hebrews	Blood of the Everlasting Covenant
James	Great Physician
1 & 2 Peter	Chief Shepherd
1, 2, & 3 John	Everlasting Love
Jude	Savior Coming with 10,000 Saints
Revelation	Lord of all Lords and King of all Kings

Revelation 1:17–18
And when I saw Him, I fell at His feet as dead. But He laid
His right hand on me, saying to me, "Do not be afraid; I am
the First and the Last. I am He who lives, and was dead, and
behold, I am alive forevermore. Amen. And I have the keys of
Hades and of Death."

Do you know the One who has the keys of death and hell?
No man has ever walked the face of the earth who has said,
"I have the keys of death and hell," except Jesus Christ.

Meditate upon the One who died on the cross to give us life
and life more abundantly.

The Life of Christ

Let us now look at the life of Christ and what He did to obtain eternal peace for humanity.

The world is crying out for peace. People are running to and fro looking for peace. True peace can only be received from God through Christ.

If you are not following God, then you will not have peace. Today is the day for salvation. The peace that God gives is not just for a moment but will last forever.

Remember, there is no peace for the wicked.

> *Isaiah 48:22*
> *"There is no peace," says the Lord, "for the wicked."*

> *Isaiah 57:21*
> *"There is no peace," says my God, "for the wicked."*

> *Isaiah 66:24*
> *And they shall go forth and look upon the corpses of the men who have transgressed against Me. For their worm does not die, and their fire is not quenched. They shall be an abhorrence to all flesh.*

Isaiah 53 has been called the center of the Word of God. It is very interesting to note that the Word of God contains thirty-nine books of the Old Covenant and twenty-seven books of the New Covenant, totalling sixty-six books. The book of Isaiah contains sixty-six chapters.

If you divide the sixty-six chapters of the book of Isaiah into the first thirty-nine chapters and then the twenty-seven chapters, you will see that the last twenty-seven chapters begins with chapter forty. If you divide the last twenty-seven chapters into three groups of nine, it is divided as follows:

(a) First group of nine contains chapters 40 to 48.

(b) Second group of nine contains chapters 49 to 57.

(c) Third group of nine contains chapters 58 to 66.

The middle chapter is chapter 53, which contains twelve verses, but the suffering of the Lord starts from Isaiah 52:13-15. The total verses add up to fifteen. If you then divide the fifteen verses into sets of three, you will find the center verses are from Isaiah 53:4–6.

> *Isaiah 53:4–6*
> *Surely He has borne our griefs and carried our sorrows; yet we esteemed Him stricken, smitten by God, and afflicted. But He was wounded for our transgressions, He was bruised for our iniquities; the chastisement for our peace was upon Him, and by His stripes we are healed. All we like sheep have gone astray; we have turned, every one, to his own way; and the Lord has laid on Him the iniquity of us all.*

The word surely is there to get our attention. It is saying, "Here is the answer to your problem." The Lord Jesus has borne all our grief and taken all our sorrow upon Himself. The Word says the Lord has laid on Jesus the iniquity of us all—in other words the guilt, the consequences, and the punishment that was due to us was laid on Jesus. The Word of God tells us that "whom the Son sets free, is free indeed." So the guilt, the perversity, the consequences of sin, the punishment, and the death that was due to us was placed upon Jesus. The goodness and the blessing that was due to Jesus have now come upon us. The divine exchange on the cross is what will give you and me eternal peace.

When God created Adam, He created him perfectly.

1 Thessalonians 5:23
Now may the God of peace Himself sanctify you completely; and may your whole spirit, soul, and body be preserved blameless at the coming of our Lord Jesus Christ.

This tells us that we are spirit, soul, and body. The spirit is the real you; the soul is your intellect, your emotion, your affections, and much more. Your body is the part of you that acts. When God created Adam, He created him perfectly in his spirit, soul, and body. When Adam disobeyed God, sin entered, and the consequences of that sin were that his spirit died and he lost his communion with God. His soul became subject to burdens, heaviness, and sorrow. His body became subject to sickness and disease. The good news is that God has made a way for us. He sent His only begotten Son to die on the cross so that you and I would be saved, not only in our spirits but also in our souls and bodies.

Romans 6:23
For the wages of sin is death, but the gift of God is eternal life in Christ Jesus our Lord.

Romans 5:8
But God demonstrates His own love toward us, in that while we were still sinners, Christ died for us.

Romans 3:23–24
For all have sinned and fall short of the glory of God, being justified freely by His grace through the redemption that is in Christ Jesus..

This means that there is not one person walking on the face of the earth who has not sinned. Everyone has come short of the glory of God. The word justified in this passage of scripture means "just as if I had never sinned." We have been justified freely by His grace through the redemption that is in Christ Jesus. It is the cross of Calvary that brought the grace of God to us, and He has given us that grace freely. We cannot earn our salvation; it is given to us freely. We cannot pay for our salvation but Christ has already paid for it. All we need to do is to simply receive it.

> *Ephesians 2:8–9*
> *For by grace you have been saved through faith, and that not of yourselves; it is the gift of God, not of works, lest anyone should boast.*

In order for you to appreciate what Jesus has done for you on the cross of Calvary, we need to talk about the Day of Atonement and the Passover.

The Day of Atonement is also known in Judaism as the Day of Judgement, and the Sabbath of the Sabbath. The Day of Atonement was a very special day. It was a day when the people of Israel were judged.

> *Leviticus 23:26–32*
> *And the Lord spoke to Moses, saying: "Also the tenth day of this seventh month shall be the Day of Atonement. It shall be a holy convocation for you; you shall afflict your souls, and offer an offering made by fire to the Lord. And you shall do no work on that same day, for it is the Day of Atonement, to make atonement for you before the Lord your God. For any person who is not afflicted in soul on that same day shall be cut off from his people. And any person who does any work on that same day, that person I will destroy from among his people. You shall do no manner of work; it shall be a statute forever throughout your generations in all your dwellings. It shall be to you a sabbath of solemn rest, and you shall afflict your souls; on the ninth day of the month at evening, from evening to evening, you shall celebrate your sabbath."*

This Day of Atonement was a day that had been set aside. It was a time when they cleansed themselves by fasting. They fasted in order to afflict their souls. Not only did they refrain from doing things but they reflected and thought about the things they had done. As a church we must fast and pray. Jesus did not say, "if you fast"; He said, "**when** you fast." That means fasting is an integral part of our Christian walk. We live in a society where fasting and prayer are the last things we consider. Fasting and prayer must become the first things we consider. We need to deny our flesh.

Not only did they fast and reflect, but they had to bring an offering. They were not allowed to work on that day. Why? Because they had to concentrate and focus on themselves and God. The children of Israel observed the feast, Christ fulfilled the feast, and we must appropriate it.

The exact procedure taken on The Day of Atonement is outlined in Leviticus 16:11–22. Scholarly writings have recorded additional traditions adopted. For instance, the high priest would set himself apart seven days before the Day of Atonement. There was a room in the temple where he would go and remain alone to examine himself and seek the face of God. After that time, he would wash and change the robes that he was wearing and wear a robe of linen. An ancient writing has it that he would have a chain attached to his feet before he went in to offer an offering for himself and the Levites and enter the Holy of Holies.

The reason for the chain was if the high priest had not dealt correctly in the sight of God when he went into the Holy of Holies, God's judgment would be upon him and he would die. They would need something by which to retrieve his body. God is a holy God.

So now the high priest, with fear and trembling, would enter into the Holy of Holies, and as long as the bells that were hanging from his garment were ringing, they knew that he was still alive. But if they did not hear the bells and they heard a thud, that meant he was dead and they would have to pull him out by the chain tied to his ankle. The high priest had to examine himself so well or it could mean death.

Think of what Jesus has done on the cross of Calvary. During the Day of Atonement only the high priest could go into the Holy of Holies; nobody else could. But today, you and I can go into the Holy of Holies without any fear and with boldness, and say, "Abba Father," because of the blood of Jesus.

One of the obligations of the high priest was that he would take the blood into the mercy seat and sprinkle the blood. The words mercy seat in Hebrew mean "place of atonement," which means "of covering" or "propitiation."

The mercy seat as a place of atonement was not permanent. God knew that He was going to send His Son and He was going to atone for everything once and for all. When the high priest sprinkled the blood on the mercy seat, it was a substitute for what was to come.

Hebrews 9:11–12
But Christ came as High Priest of the good things to come, with the greater and more perfect tabernacle not made with hands, that is, not of this creation. Not with the blood of goats and calves, but with His own blood He entered the Most Holy Place once for all, having obtained eternal redemption.

During the Day of Atonement, the high priest would also take two goats and he would draw lots to see which one of the goats was for the Lord and which one was the scapegoat. When the high priest knew through the drawing of the lots which one he should lay his hand on, he would take that goat and place his hand upon the goat, transferring the sins of the nation upon this goat. Think about this—that means that everything they had done that was not right in the sight of God was now placed upon this scapegoat. They would take this goat outside of the city to wander in the wilderness, never to return. Jewish tradition has it that, to ensure it did not return, the goat would be led to a cliff and be herded off it so that it would die.

So now the sins of the nation and its people were transferred to the scapegoat and sent away forever, the sin-offering goat having already been killed. Similarly, our guilt, our punishment, the consequences of our sin that we should have faced, were placed upon our Lord Jesus on the cross of Calvary.

Declare this: "The guilt, the perversity, the consequences of sin, the punishment, the death that was due to me, has come upon Jesus, and the goodness and the blessing that was due to Jesus has come upon me. I receive it now, in Jesus' name."

When the high priest had laid his hand on and transferred the sins of the nation onto the goat, the people knew their sins were forgiven.

In order for us to know the divine exchange that took place at the cross of Calvary, we need to know the "life of Christ." We need to know what happened to our Lord and Savior on that cross of Calvary. As we journey through the chapters, you will begin to see the truth.

> *Psalm 22:16–18*
> *For dogs have surrounded Me; the congregation of the wicked has enclosed Me. They pierced My hands and My feet; I can count all my bones. They look and stare at Me. They divide My garments among them, and for My clothing they cast lots.*

This was written hundreds of years before Jesus came to earth, but the Word clearly predicts what would happen.

The following scriptures describe the Lord Jesus and His sufferings.

> *Matthew 27:35*
> *Then they crucified Him, and divided His garments, casting lots, that it might be fulfilled which was spoken by the prophet: "They divided My garments among them, and for My clothing they cast lots."*

Proverbs 30:4
Who has ascended into heaven, or descended? Who has gathered the wind in His fists? Who has bound the waters in a garment? Who has established all the ends of the earth? What is His name, and what is His Son's name, if you know?

Solomon writes, "What is His Son's name?" His Son's name is Jesus Christ, the Son of the living God. Thank God we know that name!

Isaiah 53:12
Therefore I will divide Him a portion with the great, and He shall divide the spoil with the strong, because He poured out His soul unto death, and He was numbered with the transgressors, and He bore the sin of many, and made intercession for the transgressors.

Mark 15:27
With Him they also crucified two robbers, one on His right and the other on His left.

Genesis 49:10
The scepter shall not depart from Judah, nor a lawgiver from between his feet, until Shiloh comes; and to Him shall be the obedience of the people.

All these scriptures speak about the Lord Jesus.

His birth was supernatural. We see in Matthew 1:18 and Luke 1:35 that He was born by the power of the Highest. The seed that was planted into Mary's womb by the Holy Ghost was the Word of the Living God.

John 1:14
And the Word became flesh and dwelt among us, and we beheld His glory, the glory as of the only begotten of the Father, full of grace and truth.

The Word is Jesus and this Word became flesh in Mary's womb. I do not think Mary really understood that she was holding the books of the Old Covenant when she held baby Jesus in her arms. It was not Mary holding the child, but the Word was holding Mary. The Word says, "All things are held by the power of His Word." His birth is miraculous, His birth is supernatural, and His childhood is supernatural.

> *Luke 2:40–47*
> *And the Child grew and became strong in spirit, filled with wisdom; and the grace of God was upon Him. His parents went to Jerusalem every year at the feast of the Passover. And when He was twelve years old, they went up to Jerusalem according to the custom of the feast. When they had finished the days, as they returned, the Boy Jesus lingered behind in Jerusalem. And Joseph and His mother did not know it; but supposing Him to have been in the company, they went a day's journey, and sought Him among their relatives and acquaintances. So when they did not find Him, they returned to Jerusalem, seeking Him. Now so it was that after three days they found Him in the temple, sitting in the midst of the teachers, both listening to them and asking them questions. And all who heard Him were astonished at His understanding and answers.*

Jesus was twelve years old. His childhood was an uncommon childhood. He knew all the things of the Law, and the Pharisees were surprised that this twelve-year-old boy knew the Law that they have been studying all their lives. What they did not know was that He was the Word. Not only was His birth supernatural, but His childhood was also.

At the age of thirty He entered His ministry. Under the Law you had to be thirty years old to enter into the priesthood. What nobody knew was that one day this Jesus would be the Great High Priest—forever.

Luke 3:21–22
When all the people were baptized, it came to pass that Jesus also was baptized; and while He prayed, the heaven was opened. And the Holy Spirit descended in bodily form like a dove upon Him, and a voice came from heaven which said, "You are My beloved Son; in You I am well pleased."

The Holy Spirit descended upon Jesus and empowered Him for ministry. As He stepped into the river, John the Baptist made a prophetic statement:

John 1:29
The next day John saw Jesus coming toward him, and said, "Behold! The Lamb of God who takes away the sin of the world!"

We should be glad that He has taken away the sin of the world.

As a carpenter working in His father's shop, handling wood and nails, He would have known that one day nails would pierce His hands and His feet and that He would be nailed to a tree. He would have known that one day He would hang between heaven and earth for humanity. Each Passover when they killed the lamb, He would have known that one day, just like the lamb, He would be killed.

I want you to know His agony did not start at the cross of Calvary; it started long before the cross.

Luke 22:44
And being in agony, He prayed more earnestly. Then His sweat became like great drops of blood falling down to the ground.

The word here translated agony means "tremendous pressure." This agony of the Lord Jesus took place in Gethsemane a word meaning "winepress." Gethsemane is on the edge of the Kidron Valley, which has been called the "Valley of Darkness." At this place, Gethsemane, Jesus' soul became so agonized beyond description that He began to sweat great drops of blood.

But when John saw the Master as described in Revelation Chapter 19, His eyes were like flames of fire and out of His mouth came a two-edged sword. He was clothed in a garment dipped in blood, but it was a triumphant picture of the blood-stained Jesus.

Let us continue to look at the suffering Christ who gave us eternal redemption.

The Suffering of Christ

Isaiah 53:4–6
Surely He has borne our griefs and carried our sorrows; yet
we esteemed Him stricken, smitten by God, and afflicted. But
He was wounded for our transgressions, He was bruised for
our iniquities; the chastisement for our peace was upon Him,
and by His stripes we are healed. All we like sheep have gone
astray; we have turned, every one, to his own way; and the
Lord has laid on Him the iniquity of us all.

These three verses are the heartbeat of salvation. If you understand these verses, they are the key to the storehouse that God has made available for you.

There is not one person on the face of the earth who has not gone astray from God. The Word tells us that all have gone astray; that is why we need God's mercy.

The Hebrew word translated iniquity can also be translated "guilt," "punishment," or "evil consequences." Sin produces death. Many do not realize that sin has consequences. God has laid upon Jesus our guilt and perversity and the evil consequences of our actions.

The guilt, punishment, death, perversity, and evil consequences that were due to us were placed upon Jesus, and the goodness and the blessing that was due to Jesus has come upon us. If you take hold of this, your life will never be the same again. We need to remind ourselves every day what Jesus has done for us—how the divine exchange has taken place. When you declare it, you hear it; when you hear it, you believe it; and when you believe it, you will walk in it. Our spiritual ears need to hear this, because when the devil comes to bring guilt on us, we can then say, "Jesus took it all upon Himself and therefore we are free in Christ."

When you see what God's Son had to bear on the cross of Calvary, then you are able to appropriate and receive the divine exchange that took place at the cross. When you came to Jesus, there was a divine exchange. When you realize this, you can then appropriate this exchange and walk in victory.

His agony and His pain did not start on the cross of Calvary. The Word tells us He was in agony at the Garden of Gethsemane, where our Master knelt and began to pray before He went to the cross of Calvary.

> *Luke 22:40–44*
> *When He came to the place, He said to them, "Pray that you may not enter into temptation." And He was withdrawn from them about a stone's throw, and He knelt down and prayed, saying, "Father, if it is Your will, take this cup away from Me; nevertheless not My will, but Yours, be done." Then an angel appeared to Him from heaven, strengthening Him. And being in agony, He prayed more earnestly. Then His sweat became like great drops of blood falling down to the ground.*

Jesus asked the Father if it was possible to let this cup pass from Him. Nevertheless He was willing to drink it if it was the Father's will, knowing that God was pouring into Him the grief, the pain and the sorrow of the entire human race. Jesus was agonizing over this, but He said, "Not My will, but Yours."

The agony was so great—to the extent that He began to sweat blood. That blood was for you and for me.

> *Isaiah 53:4*
> *Surely He has borne our griefs and carried our sorrows; yet we esteemed Him stricken, smitten by God, and afflicted.*

The word surely is like saying, "Look, you have been searching and here is the answer." The Word of God has the answer to your situation. The answer is Jesus. He has borne all our griefs and sorrows, not just some of them. There has been an exchange—He has taken and removed your grief, your sorrow, and your pain.

From the Garden, Jesus was brought before the Pharisees, the Sadducees, the lawyers, and the high priest, and they accused Him of things He had never done. Here is the Son of God who came to give life, but now He stands accused before the leaders.

Isaiah 53:7
He was oppressed and He was afflicted, yet He opened not His mouth; He was led as a lamb to the slaughter, and as a sheep before its shearers is silent, so He opened not His mouth.

Jesus did not open His mouth to defend Himself.

Matthew 26:62–68
And the high priest arose and said to Him, "Do you answer nothing? What is it these men testify against You?" But Jesus kept silent. And the high priest answered and said to Him, "I put You under oath by the living God: Tell us if You are the Christ, the Son of God!" Jesus said to him, "It is as you said. Nevertheless, I say to you, hereafter you will see the Son of Man sitting at the right hand of the Power, and coming on the clouds of heaven." Then the high priest tore his clothes, saying, "He has spoken blasphemy! What further need do we have of witnesses? Look, now you have heard His blasphemy! What do you think?" They answered and said, "He is deserving of death." Then they spat in His face and beat Him; and others struck Him with the palms of their hands, saying, "Prophesy to us, Christ! Who is the one who struck You?"

He was innocent but they beat Him, and Isaiah tells us that they pulled His beard out. The Jews marred His face, and the Gentiles marred His body. He died for the Jew and the Gentile.

> *Isaiah 52:14*
> *Just as many were astonished at you, so His visage was marred more than any man, and His form more than the sons of men.*

When they saw Him, they could not recognize Him because He was marred beyond recognition. He did this for you and for me. After He had been beaten and spat upon, they bound Him and brought Him before Pilate.

> *Matthew 27:2*
> *And when they had bound Him, they led Him away and delivered Him to Pontius Pilate the governor.*

As He stood before Pilate, Pilate realized that Jesus was a Galilean; therefore he sent Jesus to Herod to be judged. Prior to this incident, Pilate and Herod could not see eye to eye. But because of this issue with Jesus, they became friends that day.

> *Luke 23:12–15*
> *That very day Pilate and Herod became friends with each other; for previously they had been at enmity with each other. Then Pilate, when he had called together the chief priests, the rulers, and the people, said to them, "You have brought this Man to me, as one who misleads the people. And indeed, having examined Him in your presence, I have found no fault in this Man concerning those things of which you accuse Him; no, neither did Herod, for I sent you back to him; and indeed nothing deserving of death has been done by Him."*

Both Pilate and Herod examined Jesus, but neither could find any fault in Him. These events were taking place during the time of the Feast of Passover.

1 Corinthians 5:7
Therefore purge out the old leaven, that you may be a new
lump, since you truly are unleavened. For indeed Christ, our
Passover, was sacrificed for us.

Jesus Christ, the Son of the living God, is our Passover Lamb. In the Old Covenant, the Passover Lamb was kept for a number of days, and they would examine it to make sure that there was no blemish in that lamb. Similarly, Jesus was examined and found to be without fault. He is our Passover Lamb. That is why we can appropriate every blessing of the feast of Passover today.

Pilate asked an important question.

Matthew 27:22–26
Pilate said to them, "What then shall I do with Jesus who is
called Christ? They all said to him, Let Him be crucified!"
Then the governor said, "Why, what evil has He done?" But
they cried out all the more, saying, "Let Him be crucified!"
When Pilate saw that he could not prevail at all, but rather
that a tumult was rising, he took water and washed his hands
before the multitude, saying, "I am innocent of the blood of
this just Person. You see to it." And all the people answered
and said, "His blood be on us and on our children." Then he
released Barabbas to them; and when he had scourged Jesus,
he delivered Him to be crucified.

I believe that the Holy Spirit put these words into the mouth of Pilate, and to this day, the Holy Spirit is asking the same question, "What will you do with Jesus who is called the Anointed One?"

All the people watching said, "Let Him be crucified!" Barabbas was a murderer and a thief, but they asked for him to be released. Barabbas was not a righteous man; he deserved to die. Just like Barabbas, we should have been on the cross, but Jesus took our place.

Pilate sentenced Jesus to be crucified, the Son of God who knew no sin. They brought Jesus to a pole that was about four feet high, and they tied His hands to the pole. The Roman soldier took the whip that had nine leather straps in it; at the end of each strap there was a piece of jagged bone or a nail. The Romans hated the Jews, and now Jesus, the "King of the Jews" was bound to the pole with nowhere to go, His back fully exposed to the Roman soldiers. He stood as a lamb ready to be slaughtered. The Roman soldier then took his whip and, with all of his might and with all of his strength, he began to whip the Master thirty-nine times.

Every time the Roman soldier struck the Master, that whip would wind around His body and the jagged nail would penetrate into His flesh. The soldier retreated, the whip ready for the next stroke that would tear through His flesh.

> *Isaiah 50:6*
> *I gave My back to those who struck Me, and My cheeks to those who plucked out the beard; I did not hide My face from shame and spitting.*

He did this for you and for me. And when He was struck those thirty-nine times, He took every sickness from the face of the earth. The good news is that Jesus bore your sickness.

> *Isaiah 53:5b*
> *And by His stripes we are healed.*

His body was ripped apart. He had already suffered at the hands of the Jews and the suffering continued.

> *Matthew 27:27–34*
> *Then the soldiers of the governor took Jesus into the Praetorium and gathered the whole garrison around Him. And they stripped Him and put a scarlet robe on Him. When they had twisted a crown of thorns, they put it on His head,*

and a reed in His right hand. And they bowed the knee before Him and mocked Him, saying, "Hail, King of the Jews!" Then they spat on Him, and took the reed and struck Him on the head. And when they had mocked Him, they took the robe off Him, put His own clothes on Him, and led Him away to be crucified. Now as they came out, they found a man of Cyrene, Simon by name. Him they compelled to bear His cross. And when they had come to a place called Golgotha, that is to say, Place of a Skull, they gave Him sour wine mingled with gall to drink. But when He had tasted it, He would not drink.

When Adam fell in Genesis, God cursed the earth and said it would bring forth thorns and thistles. That day, when they made the crown of thorns, He was taking on the sins of the entire world. Eastern thornbushes are poisonous. When those thorns penetrated His head, the blood gushed out. Poison talks about demons and devils, but that day His blood took care of every demon, every principality and power. The blood of Jesus has not lost its power.

In some societies, a staff stands for authority and is normally carried by a prominent person. But they gave Jesus a reed to signify that He did not have authority and was weak. Reeds are symbolic of weakness. They were saying that Jesus was weak and that He was not a king. But He took our weakness, so that we would have strength. That day they mocked Him and spat on Him. You may have been ridiculed by family and friends, but 2,000 years ago He took that ridicule upon Himself so that we can be free. I want you to see the divine exchange.

Roman soldiers took that reed and beat Him, but He opened not His mouth.

Despite what Jesus had been through, He still had the strength and determination to walk to the cross. As He began to walk toward Calvary, something happened. He turned around and saw the women who were weeping and crying.

Luke 23:27–31

And a great multitude of the people followed Him, and women who also mourned and lamented Him. But Jesus, turning to them, said, "Daughters of Jerusalem, do not weep for Me, but weep for yourselves and for your children. For indeed the days are coming in which they will say, 'Blessed are the barren, wombs that never bore, and breasts which never nursed!' Then they will begin to say to the mountains, 'Fall on us!' and to the hills, 'Cover us!' For if they do these things in the green wood, what will be done in the dry?"

Jesus' words to these women were, "Do not weep for Me; weep for yourselves." His eyes and His heart were not upon Himself. He was not looking for sympathy. He looked beyond; His heart was to bring redemption to humanity.

Luke 23:32-42

There were also two others, criminals, led with Him to be put to death. And when they had come to the place called Calvary, there they crucified Him, and the criminals, one on the right hand and the other on the left. Then Jesus said, "Father, forgive them, for they do not know what they do." And they divided His garments and cast lots. And the people stood looking on. But even the rulers with them sneered, saying, "He saved others; let Him save Himself if He is the Christ, the chosen of God." The soldiers also mocked Him, coming and offering Him sour wine, and saying, "If You are the King of the Jews, save Yourself." And an inscription also was written over him in letters of Greek, Latin, and Hebrew: THIS IS THE KING OF THE JEWS. Then one of the criminals who were hanged blasphemed Him, saying, "If You are the Christ, save Yourself and us." But the other, answering, rebuked him, saying, "Do you not even fear God, seeing you are under the same condemnation? And we indeed justly, for we receive the due reward of our deeds; but this Man has done nothing wrong." Then he said to Jesus, "Lord, remember me when You come into Your kingdom."

He was crucified at nine in the morning, and He hung on the cross until three in the afternoon—six hours till it was "finished." Why six hours? God created and made everything in six days.

As He hung on the cross of Calvary, He said to His Father, "Forgive them for they know not what they do." He did not accuse anyone. Look at the forgiving heart of the Son of God. Because our Lord is a forgiving God, we are forgiven.

He never lets you go. If you cry out to the Master, He will never forsake you.

> *Luke 23:43*
> *And Jesus said to him, "Assuredly, I say to you, today you will be with Me in Paradise."*

A thief who was crucified alongside Jesus looked across at Jesus hanging there, covered in spittle and blood, and he said, "Master, remember me." Even in the state that Jesus was in, He looked across, reached out to the thief, and said to him, "You will be with Me in Paradise."

> *John 19:26–27*
> *When Jesus therefore saw His mother, and the disciple whom He loved standing by, He said to His mother, "Woman, behold your son!" Then He said to the disciple, "Behold your mother!" And from that hour that disciple took her to his own home.*

Jesus' earthly mother was the last human connection of His life and He said, "I give My mother to you." He forsook everything for humanity. You may say, "I do not have a father or a mother," but in Christ you have a father and a mother. He forsook everything so that you might have life and life more abundantly.

> *Matthew 27:46*
> *And about the ninth hour Jesus cried out with a loud voice, saying, "Eli, Eli, lama sabachthani?" that is, "My God, My God, why have You forsaken Me?"*

When Jesus asked His Father why He had forsaken Him, it was pitch dark. The Father had turned His face because He could not look at sin. Jesus, the Son of God, was rejected so that you and I could be accepted.

> *John 19:28*
> *After this, Jesus, knowing that all things were now accomplished, that the Scripture might be fulfilled, said, "I thirst!"*

Look at the humanity of the Master. He cried out that He was thirsty. He became thirsty so that whoever thirsts can come to Him and they will never be thirsty again.

> *John 19:30*
> *So when Jesus had received the sour wine, He said, "It is finished!" And bowing His head, He gave up His spirit.*

It is finished!

> *Luke 23:46*
> *And when Jesus had cried out with a loud voice, He said, "Father, 'into Your hands I commit My spirit.'" Having said this, He breathed His last.*

In other words, Jesus laid His life down. He gave it willingly for you and for me. There is no one else who loves you that much that they would die for you. There is only one person who willingly gave His life for you—His name is Jesus.

During the Passover when the priest would cut the throat of the Passover lamb offered for all Israel at three o'clock in the afternoon, he would say, "It is finished." When Jesus said, "It is finished," He had become the perfect sacrificial lamb for you and for me.

Today, you and I can approach God through the blood of Jesus and say, "Abba Father," all because of the perfect sacrifice of Jesus on the cross.

Luke 18:17
Assuredly, I say to you, whoever does not receive the kingdom
of God as a little child will by no means enter it.

A child has the ability to receive with a believing heart. We must be the same. Whatever circumstances you are going through, all you have to do is to come as a little child and receive what has been done for you on the cross of Calvary. When you receive, He wants you to thank Him, and when you thank Him, He wants you to act on the divine exchange.

Consider Calvary:
It Is Perfect in Every
Aspect and Respect.

Section One

The Cross of Calvary Provides Us with a Divine Exchange

The Divine Exchange

The cross of Calvary is where a divine exchange took place between God and man. Consider Calvary, which is perfect in every respect. Our answers are found in Calvary where Jesus died for you and for me.

1. God placed our guilt and punishment upon Him.

God put upon Jesus our guilt, our perversity, the consequences of our sin, our punishment, and our death so that we could receive His goodness and blessings.

Isaiah 53:4–6
Surely He has borne our griefs and carried our sorrows; yet we esteemed Him stricken, smitten by God, and afflicted. But He was wounded for our transgressions, He was bruised for our iniquities; the chastisement for our peace was upon Him, and by His stripes we are healed. All we like sheep have gone astray; we have turned, every one, to his own way; and the Lord has laid on Him the iniquity of us all.

2. He was punished that we could be forgiven.

The punishment that brought peace to us was upon Him. Because He was punished we receive our peace. He was punished so that we could be forgiven.

If the enemy reminds you of your past, remember your past is forgotten and blotted out under the blood of Jesus. If God does not remember, why should you? There are people who are physically sick because they are still carrying the guilt of the past. Jesus bore your punishment so that you would have forgiveness.

Ephesians 2:14–17
For He Himself is our peace, who has made both one, and has broken down the middle wall of separation, having abolished in His flesh the enmity, that is, the law of commandments contained in ordinances, so as to create in Himself one new man from the two, thus making peace, and that He might reconcile them both to God in one body through the cross, thereby putting to death the enmity. And He came and preached peace to you who were afar off and to those who were near.

Every wall that separated us from God has been broken down. The cross has reconciled us to God.

Colossians 1:19–20
For it pleased the Father that in Him all the fullness should dwell, and by Him to reconcile all things to Himself, by Him, whether things on earth or things in heaven, having made peace through the blood of His cross.

Through the cross He has reconciled all things. Reconciliation has given us access to the Holy of Holies.

Remember, we have an eternal relationship with God having been redeemed by the cross of Calvary. Psalm 107 says, "Let the redeemed of the Lord say so." We need to declare and confess that we are redeemed and there has been a divine exchange.

3. He was wounded that we could be healed.

Isaiah 53:4
Surely He has borne our griefs and carried our sorrows; yet
we esteemed Him stricken, smitten by God, and afflicted. But
He was wounded for our transgressions, He was bruised for
our iniquities; the chastisement for our peace was upon Him,
and by His stripes we are healed.

He has borne all our sicknesses, diseases, and pain, so we
can be free. This is part of the great exchange that took
place at the cross of Calvary.

Exodus 15:23–25
Now when they came to Marah, they could not drink the
waters of Marah, for they were bitter. Therefore the name
of it was called Marah. And the people complained against
Moses, saying, "What shall we drink?" So he cried out to the
Lord, and the Lord showed him a tree. When he cast it into
the waters, the waters were made sweet. There He made a
statute and an ordinance for them, and there He tested them.

You may be saying that life has dealt you a cruel blow, a
bitter experience, similar to the experience the Israelites
had. But here is the answer. God said to His servant Moses,
"Take the branch, and when the branch touches the water,
the water will be sweet." So when your life comes in contact
with the cross, it will become sweet. Why? Because there has
been a divine exchange.

Which is a better option—divine healing or divine health? I
am sure you will say "walking in divine health." The divine
exchange will give you divine health. Money cannot buy this
exchange.

Matthew 8:16–17
When evening had come, they brought to Him many who
were demon-possessed. And He cast out the spirits with a
word, and healed all who were sick, that it might be fulfilled
which was spoken by Isaiah the prophet, saying: "He Himself
took our infirmities and bore our sicknesses."

1 Peter 2:24
Who Himself bore our sins in His own body on the tree, that
we, having died to sins, might live for righteousness—by
whose stripes you were healed.

God heals us so that we can continue to walk in divine health.
We need to proclaim this over our lives and appropriate it for
ourselves. God's promise is that every child of God should
walk in divine health.

4. He was made sin with our sinfulness so we may be clothed with His righteousness.

Isaiah 53:10
Yet it pleased the Lord to bruise Him; He has put Him to
grief. When you make His soul an offering for sin, He shall
see His seed, He shall prolong His days, and the pleasure of
the Lord shall prosper in His hand.

He was made sin with our sinfulness. The exchange was made
when He bore our sin and He gave us His righteousness.
That is why today we are in right standing with God. We can
go to our heavenly Father and ask Him anything, and He will
hear us and answer us. Why? We are in right standing with
God because of what Jesus has done for us at the cross of
Calvary.

2 Corinthians 5:21
For He made Him who knew no sin to be sin for us, that we
might become the righteousness of God in Him.

Barabbas should have died on the cross. Barabbas is a type of you and me. He was a murderer and a thief, but Jesus took his place. He took our place. He bore our sins; that is why we have peace. Do you know what it means to be in right standing with God? Sometimes we go through the motions of attending church, but we have forgotten what Jesus has done for us.

Isaiah 61:10–11
I will greatly rejoice in the Lord, my soul shall be joyful in my God; for He has clothed me with the garments of salvation, He has covered me with the robe of righteousness, as a bridegroom decks himself with ornaments, and as a bride adorns herself with her jewels. For as the earth brings forth its bud, as the garden causes the things that are sown in it to spring forth, so the Lord God will cause righteousness and praise to spring forth before all the nations.

He has clothed us with the righteousness of God. He bore our sin and He gave us His righteousness. He was made sin with our sinfulness that we would be made righteous with His righteousness. That is why there is no condemnation to them who are in Christ Jesus.

5. He died our death that we might have life and life more abundantly.

Hebrews 2:9
But we see Jesus, who was made a little lower than the angels, for the suffering of death crowned with glory and honor, that He, by the grace of God, might taste death for everyone.

You must see Jesus. You must see what He has done for you on the cross of Calvary. He tasted death for you and for me. He died our death that we might have life and life more abundantly. Jesus did not die on the cross for us to merely exist. God wants you to enjoy your life. Everything that you received from God came through the grace of God. Whenever you see the words grace of God, it means you cannot earn it. It is freely given. If it is not freely given, then it is not grace. People try to earn things from God, but God clearly says that you cannot earn anything from Him. The basis of grace is the cross.

Ephesians 2:8
For by grace you have been saved through faith, and that not of yourselves; it is the gift of God.

Every blessing that comes to you is found in the cross of Calvary. The grace that came to us came through Jesus.

John 1:17
For the law was given through Moses, but grace and truth came through Jesus Christ.

You cannot have the grace of God any other way, but by Jesus. That grace is made available to us because of the cross. We appropriate that grace by faith.

6. He was made a curse for us so that we will receive heaven's blessings.

Galatians 3:13–14
Christ has redeemed us from the curse of the law, having become a curse for us (for it is written, "Cursed is everyone who hangs on a tree,") that the blessing of Abraham might come upon the Gentiles in Christ Jesus, that we might receive the promise of the Spirit through faith.

The word redemption is a legal word. It means that someone has paid the price for you. The opposite of "curse" is "blessing." The word curse is mentioned three times in the above passage of scripture.

Deuteronomy 21:22–23

If a man has committed a sin deserving of death, and he is put to death, and you hang him on a tree, his body shall not remain overnight on the tree, but you shall surely bury him that day, so that you do not defile the land which the Lord your God is giving you as an inheritance; for he who is hanged is accursed of God.

The Old Covenant says that if you hung on a cross, you were cursed. Galatians 3:13 tells us that Jesus hung on the cross and became a curse for us so that the blessing of Abraham might come to the Gentiles through Him. When He hung on that cross, He made available to us all the blessings of Abraham.

Galatians 3:16

Now to Abraham and his Seed were the promises made. He does not say, "And to seeds," as of many, but as of one, "And to your Seed," who is Christ.

The promise was made to Abraham and his seed. This is singular. The seed is Christ. God had to institute the law because of sin. Then Jesus came to fulfil the law.

Remember, God had to institute the Law.

Galatians 3:17–18 AMP

This is my argument: The Law, which began 430 years after the covenant [concerning the coming Messiah], does not and can not annul the covenant previously established (ratified) by God, so as to abolish the promise and make it void [Exod. 12:40.] For if the inheritance [of the promise depends on observing] the Law [as these false teachers would like you to believe], it no longer [depends] on the promise; however, God gave it to Abraham [as a free gift solely] by virtue of His promise.

Because of the death and resurrection of Christ we now live under grace not under the law. The moment the sinner accepts Jesus he is in Christ.

Galatians 3:9 AMP
So then, those who are people of faith are blessed and made happy and favored by God [as partners in fellowship] with the believing and trusting Abraham.

Galatians 3:29 AMP
And if you belong to Christ [are in Him, Who is Abraham's Seed], then you are Abraham's offspring and [spiritual] heirs according to promise.

This is the covenant promise: that we are able to appropriate Abraham's blessings.

I would like to take some time and talk to you about the curse. Many are under a curse and do not know how to be free.

What is a curse? A curse is a dark shadow that follows you. Sometimes you are about to make a breakthrough, and a dark hand comes and stops it. Some people go through their lives with a curse following them. Every time people think they are progressing, a dark hand comes and stops it. That is the curse. For example, some people struggle with emotional disorders; they have no freedom from it. They get prayed for, but they never break the cycle. There is a continual pattern. In some families you can see a pattern of suicide, divorce, miscarriage, accident, poverty, certain sickness, etc. These things are passed on through generations. Strengths and weakness are passed on through generations, as well.

I have seen on some occasions that a curse needs to be broken before we pray for healing. Until the curse is broken, the person is not ready to receive their healing. Some chronic sicknesses stay with people; they never get over the sickness.

Deuteronomy 28 is the best place to read about blessings and curses. Jesus took that curse upon Himself. There was a divine exchange that took place on the cross. He bore your curse so that you might go free and have abundant life.

The curse needs to be broken for freedom and healing to come.

Deuteronomy 5:9

You shall not bow down to them nor serve them. For I, the Lord your God, am a jealous God, visiting the iniquity of the fathers upon the children to the third and fourth generations of those who hate Me.

Some curses follow from one generation to another. That is why you need to break the curse so it will not follow on to your seed. There are also familiar spirits. This will be explained in another chapter.

People say it is all right to go and visit fortune-tellers, mediums, etc. When individuals entertain mediums, fortune-telling, and tarot card reading, they open a door for evil spirits to take a legal hold upon their lives.

Deuteronomy 18:9–13

When you come into the land which the Lord your God is giving you, you shall not learn to follow the abominations of those nations. There shall not be found among you anyone who makes his son or his daughter pass through the fire, or one who practices witchcraft, or a soothsayer, or one who interprets omens, or a sorcerer, or one who conjures spells, or a medium, or a spiritist, or one who calls up the dead. For all who do these things are an abomination to the Lord, and because of these abominations the Lord your God drives them out from before you. You shall be blameless before the Lord your God.

Divination is fortune-telling. God said it is cursed if you do these things. These strongholds must be broken. If you have visited a spiritualist, witches, or fortune-tellers, you have to renounce these things because these familiar spirits will begin to follow and harass you due to their legal hold on you.

Jesus became our curse so that we can be free to walk in an abundant life.

Luke 18:17
Assuredly, I say to you, whoever does not receive the kingdom of God as a little child will by no means enter it.

You must receive what Jesus has done for you like a child. Remember, He has already done it all for you and me.

Seven ways to be free

i. Appropriate, acknowledge, and declare the divine exchange that has taken place for you on the cross.

ii. Renounce the curses. You know the things that hinder you. You have to break the cycle. Renounce those acts that you have committed that God says in His Word are an abomination and ask forgiveness.

iii. Break the curse upon your life and your household in the name of Jesus and through the blood of Jesus. The legality must be broken. Now declare that Jesus Christ is Lord of your life and your household.

iv. Command the curses to leave your life and your household in Jesus' name. Do not just break and leave them, but command them to never return to your house again.

v. Yield your vessel as a living sacrifice to the Holy Spirit. Ask the Spirit of God to come and fill you.

vi. Thank Him; give Him praise for delivering you and your household.

vii. Begin to declare the Word of God. Declare "whom the Son sets free is free indeed."

7. Jesus became poor so that we will become rich.

2 Corinthians 8:9 AMP
For you are becoming progressively acquainted with and recognizing more strongly and clearly the grace of our Lord Jesus Christ (His kindness, His gracious generosity, His undeserved favor and spiritual blessing), [in] that though He was [so very] rich, yet for your sakes He became [so very] poor, in order that by His poverty you might become enriched (abundantly supplied).

As I was writing, the blessed Holy Spirit spoke to me and said, "Son, many are in poverty. Explain to them from the Word of God how they can break the cycle of poverty and appropriate the blessings from the finished work of the cross."

I am going to take your through some tremendous truths from His Word that you can use in your day-to-day living.

The world is facing tremendous financial crisis. God has eliminated poverty through His Son, Jesus, on the cross of Calvary. God wants to break the spirit of poverty over His people.

Poverty is a curse—it is not God's way to live.

Deuteronomy 28:47–48
Because you did not serve the Lord your God with joy and gladness of heart, for the abundance of everything, therefore you shall serve your enemies, whom the Lord will send against you, in hunger, in thirst, in nakedness, and in need of everything; and He will put a yoke of iron on your neck until He has destroyed you.

God wants us to serve Him with joy and gladness. Jesus suffered hunger, thirst, and nakedness, and He was in need of everything as He hung on the cross.

Psalm 23:1
The Lord is my shepherd; I shall not want.

A spirit of poverty has been released on the earth, but at the cross there was a divine exchange. Jesus became poor for us so that we could become rich in Christ Jesus

2 Corinthians 8:9
For you know the grace of our Lord Jesus Christ, that though He was rich, yet for your sakes He became poor, that you through His poverty might become rich.

Remember, it is through your belief and confession that the blessings will come upon you.

2 Corinthians 9:8 AMP
And God is able to make all grace (every favor and earthly blessing) come to you in abundance, so that you may always and under all circumstances and whatever the need be self-sufficient [possessing enough to require no aid or support and furnished in abundance for every good work and charitable donation].

The world may be in darkness, but God is able to make His grace, favor, and blessing flow to you. The word self-sufficient means "possessing enough to require no aid or support."

There is a difference between insufficiency, sufficiency, and abundance. God has said that He will not just meet your needs, but that you will have abundance. Let me explain: Your grocery bill is $150 but you only have $100—that is insufficient. Your grocery bill is $150 and you have $150—that is sufficient. Your grocery bill is $150 and you have $200—that is abundance. You have $50 dollars above what you need and so you are able to bless others. There are no conditions placed on God's abundance. We belong to God's Kingdom and we operate by a different system from that of the world.

Matthew 6:25–26

> *Therefore I say to you, do not worry about your life, what you will eat or what you will drink; nor about your body, what you will put on. Is not life more than food and the body more than clothing? Look at the birds of the air, for they neither sow nor reap nor gather into barns; yet your heavenly Father feeds them. Are you not of more value than they?*

This passage of Scripture clearly states that you are valuable in the sight of God. He cares for you.

Signs of the Times

Matthew 24:1–8, 14

> *Then Jesus went out and departed from the temple, and His disciples came up to show Him the buildings of the temple. And Jesus said to them, "Do you not see all these things? Assuredly, I say to you, not one stone shall be left here upon another, that shall not be thrown down." Now as He sat on the Mount of Olives, the disciples came to Him privately, saying, "Tell us, when will these things be? And what will be the sign of Your coming, and of the end of the age?" And Jesus answered and said to them, "Take heed that no one deceives you. For many will come in My name, saying, 'I am the Christ,' and will deceive many. And you will hear of wars and rumors of wars. See that you are not troubled; for all these things must come to pass, but the end is not yet. For nation will rise against nation, and kingdom against kingdom. And there will be famines, pestilences, and earthquakes in various places. All these are the beginning of sorrows. And this gospel of the kingdom will be preached in all the world as a witness to all the nations, and then the end will come."*

When Jesus was walking on the earth, people asked, "What will be the sign of the times? When will all this end?" Today the same questions are being asked. Man's heart and mind has not changed.

The heartbeat of God is to get the Good News out to people. As long as you and I are getting the Good News out, God will continue to supply our needs. You will lack nothing.

The world is not only facing financial crisis, but it is facing famine. There is famine that is sweeping the earth, and there will be a food crisis. When you put all this together, it is going to be a catastrophe.

As I was in prayer, the Lord began to show me the following. I will call it:

Seven things God wants us to know

1. People think that the worst has come and gone, but the worst is yet to come because the truth has not been told.

2. The money is still there, but the supply has stopped. But those who know how to find it will prosper. God will give you the keys. This is the hour for the transfer of wealth.

3. The foundation of the financial world is sinking. Sooner or later it is going to collapse. God shows us things to come because He loves us.

   Amos 3:7
   Surely the Lord God does nothing, unless He reveals His secret to His servants the prophets.

4. The enemy has released certain spirits upon the earth— the spirit of fear, the spirit of confusion, and the spirit of poverty. That is why the Lord wants to break the spirit of poverty.

5. Governments do not know what to do. They are all making decisions on the run. Nobody has the answers except the Church. This is our finest hour because the world is looking for answers.

6. The heart of man will fail because there is no hope. All over the world people are saying the same thing: What is going to happen? We should rejoice because our God still reigns.

7. Remember, the situation is not going to get better.

Isaiah 60:1–3
Arise, shine; for your light has come! And the glory of the Lord is risen upon you. For behold, the darkness shall cover the earth, and deep darkness the people; but the Lord will arise over you, and His glory will be seen upon you. The Gentiles shall come to your light, and kings to the brightness of your rising.

There will be gross darkness upon the earth, but they will not have the answer. They will come to you and me to find the answer. The answer lies in and with the Church.

To the Church

God has put all things under His feet for you and me.

Ephesians 1:22
And He put all things under His feet, and gave Him to be head over all things to the church..

By the Church

God will manifest His wisdom only through you and me.

Ephesians 3:10
To the intent that now the manifold wisdom of God might be made known by the church to the principalities and powers in the heavenly places..

God has said He will reveal His wisdom through the Church. The answer lies in the hands of His people, and we need to be prepared.

In the Church

Ephesians 3:21
To Him be glory in the church by Christ Jesus to all generations, forever and ever. Amen.

God has said He would manifest His glory in the church in us, through us and for us.

God is interested and concerned about your finances and needs.

Matthew 6:25–26, 31–34
Therefore I say to you, do not worry about your life, what you will eat or what you will drink; nor about your body, what you will put on. Is not life more than food and the body more than clothing? Look at the birds of the air, for they neither sow nor reap nor gather into barns; yet your heavenly Father feeds them. Are you not of more value than they? Therefore do not worry, saying, 'What shall we eat?' or 'What shall we drink?' or 'What shall we wear?' For after all these things the Gentiles seek. For your heavenly Father knows that you need all these things. But seek first the kingdom of God and His righteousness, and all these things shall be added to you. Therefore do not worry about tomorrow, for tomorrow will worry about its own things. Sufficient for the day is its own trouble.

When we seek the Kingdom of God and His righteousness, then everything we need for life will follow us.

Matthew 10:29–30
Are not two sparrows sold for a copper coin? And not one of them falls to the ground apart from your Father's will. But the very hairs of your head are all numbered.

Our Father in heaven knows everything—He knows what is happening in your life.

Psalm 35:27
Let them shout for joy and be glad, who favor my righteous cause; and let them say continually, "Let the Lord be magnified, who has pleasure in the prosperity of His servant."

God delights in your prosperity!

Isaiah 48:17
Thus says the Lord, your Redeemer, the Holy One of Israel: "I am the Lord your God, Who teaches you to profit, Who leads you by the way you should go."

This is current; it is in the present tense. God is teaching you how to profit.

Mark 10:30
Who shall not receive a hundredfold now in this time—houses and brothers and sisters and mothers and children and lands, with persecutions—and in the age to come, eternal life.

You shall receive one hundredfold now. At the cross of Calvary the great exchange took place where Jesus became poor so that you and I can become rich.

Rich means you have more than enough to meet your needs and to be able to give to the Gospel.

God showed me keys to prosper, and I would now like to place these keys in your hand.

These master keys can be used in any area of your life.

Seven Master Keys

Master  Number One

Ask Me for Wisdom

In this time of uncertainty, we need to ask the Lord for His wisdom.

James 1:5 AMP
If any of you is deficient in wisdom, let him ask of the giving God [Who gives] to every one liberally and ungrudgingly, without reproaching or faultfinding, and it will be given him.

God says if you want wisdom, then ask. When you ask it will be freely given to you. We are to ask Him for wisdom because God knows His wisdom carries power. When we talk about wisdom, we frequently connect wisdom to King Solomon. He built the temple through the wisdom of God. When the Queen of Sheba came to receive wisdom from King Solomon, she did not come empty-handed. We are told that she came with gifts worth more than four million dollars. She came to get advice. Wisdom has power.

Genesis 41:47–49, 53–57
Now in the seven plentiful years the ground brought forth abundantly. So he gathered up all the food of the seven years which were in the land of Egypt, and laid up the food in the cities; he laid up in every city the food of the fields which surrounded them. Joseph gathered very much grain, as the sand of the sea, until he stopped counting, for it was immeasurable. Then the seven years of plenty which were in the land of Egypt ended, and the seven years of famine began to come, as Joseph had said. The famine was in all lands,

but in all the land of Egypt there was bread. So when all the land of Egypt was famished, the people cried to Pharaoh for bread. Then Pharaoh said to all the Egyptians, "Go to Joseph; whatever he says to you, do." The famine was over all the face of the earth, and Joseph opened all the storehouses and sold to the Egyptians. And the famine became severe in the land of Egypt. So all countries came to Joseph in Egypt to buy grain, because the famine was severe in all lands.

They all came to Joseph because he had the answer. He became prime minister of the land through the wisdom of God.

Genesis 41:38
And Pharaoh said to his servants, "Can we find such a one as this, a man in whom is the Spirit of God?"

The wisdom of God gave Joseph the power to manage the resources in his hands. Joseph was different from everyone else because the Spirit of God was in him.

1 Kings 3:9–14
"Therefore give to Your servant an understanding heart to judge Your people, that I may discern between good and evil. For who is able to judge this great people of Yours?" The speech pleased the Lord, that Solomon had asked this thing. Then God said to him: "Because you have asked this thing, and have not asked long life for yourself, nor have asked riches for yourself, nor have asked the life of your enemies, but have asked for yourself understanding to discern justice, behold, I have done according to your words; see, I have given you a wise and understanding heart, so that there has not been anyone like you before you, nor shall any like you arise after you. And I have also given you what you have not asked: both riches and honor, so that there shall not be anyone like you among the kings all your days. So if you walk in My ways, to keep My statutes and My commandments, as your father David walked, then I will lengthen your days."

a. Wisdom produces divine power.

God asked Solomon what he wanted. Solomon asked God for wisdom so he would be able to judge God's people, and his request pleased God. God wants us to understand His mind and heart. What is wisdom? Wisdom is knowing what is true coupled with just judgment. Wisdom not only reveals the truth, but it will tell you what to do with that truth.

What is knowledge?

Knowledge is facts or a state of knowing. It is a perception of truth, clear and certain.

What is understanding?

Understanding is knowing or perceiving the meaning of truth. Wisdom not only gives you the ability to know the truth, but it also gives you understanding.

God gave Solomon not only what he asked for—wisdom and understanding—but He also gave him wealth and honor.

Colossians 2:3
In whom are hidden all the treasures of wisdom and knowledge.

Isaiah 11:2
The Spirit of the Lord shall rest upon Him, the Spirit of wisdom and understanding, the Spirit of counsel and might, the Spirit of knowledge and of the fear of the Lord.

In Christ all wisdom and knowledge can be found. The Holy Spirit is the Spirit of wisdom, knowledge and understanding, counsel, might, and the fear of the Lord. The Holy Spirit is the Spirit of Jesus. If you have the Spirit of Jesus in you, you have all of these things.

b. Wisdom has the ability to reveal and discern.

1 Kings 3:16–28

Now two women who were harlots came to the king, and stood before him. And one woman said, "O my lord, this woman and I dwell in the same house; and I gave birth while she was in the house. Then it happened, the third day after I had given birth, that this woman also gave birth. And we were together; no one was with us in the house, except the two of us in the house. And this woman's son died in the night, because she lay on him. So she arose in the middle of the night and took my son from my side, while your maidservant slept, and laid him in her bosom, and laid her dead child in my bosom. And when I rose in the morning to nurse my son, there he was, dead. But when I had examined him in the morning, indeed, he was not my son whom I had borne." Then the other woman said, "No! But the living one is my son, and the dead one is your son." And the first woman said, "No! But the dead one is your son, and the living one is my son." Thus they spoke before the king. And the king said, "The one says, 'This is my son, who lives, and your son is the dead one'; and the other says, "No! But your son is the dead one, and my son is the living one."' Then the king said, "Bring me a sword." So they brought a sword before the king. And the king said, "Divide the living child in two, and give half to one, and half to the other." Then the woman whose son was living spoke to the king, for she yearned with compassion for her son; and she said, "O my lord, give her the living child, and by no means kill him!" But the other said, "Let him be neither mine nor yours, but divide him." So the king answered and said, "Give the first woman the living child, and by no means kill him; she is his mother." And all Israel heard of the judgment which the king had rendered; and they feared the king, for they saw that the wisdom of God was in him to administer justice.

God's wisdom gave Solomon the ability to discern correctly.

c. Divine wisdom imparts "uncommon" wisdom.

Uncommon wisdom is wisdom that cannot be obtained through natural means. It is wisdom that you cannot receive at the best universities that are available to you. It only comes from the "University of Heaven." No earthly source is able to provide "uncommon" wisdom.

1 Kings 4:21–34
So Solomon reigned over all kingdoms from the River to the land of the Philistines, as far as the border of Egypt. They brought tribute and served Solomon all the days of his life. Now Solomon's provision for one day was thirty kors of fine flour, sixty kors of meal, ten fatted oxen, twenty oxen from the pastures, and one hundred sheep, beside deer, gazelles, roebucks, and fatted fowl. For he had dominion over all the region on this side of the River from Tiphsah even to Gaza, namely over all the kings on this side of the River; and he had peace on every side all around him. And Judah and Israel dwelt safely, each man under his vine and his fig tree, from Dan as far as Beersheba, all the days of Solomon. Solomon had forty thousand stalls of horses for his chariots, and twelve thousand horsemen. And these governors, each man in his month, provided food for King Solomon and for all who came to King Solomon's table. There was no lack in their supply. They also brought barley and straw to the proper place, for the horses and steeds, each man according to his charge. And God gave Solomon wisdom and exceedingly great understanding, and largeness of heart like the sand on the seashore. Thus Solomon's wisdom excelled the wisdom of all the men of the East and all the wisdom of Egypt. For he was wiser than all men—than Ethan the Ezrahite, and Heman, Chalcol, and Darda, the sons of Mahol; and his fame was in all the surrounding nations. He spoke three thousand proverbs, and his songs were one thousand and five. Also he spoke of trees, from the cedar tree of Lebanon even to the hyssop that springs out of the wall; he spoke also of animals, of birds, of creeping

things, and of fish. And men of all nations, from all the kings of the earth who had heard of his wisdom, came to hear the wisdom of Solomon.

Divine wisdom will always bring peace and rest. Solomon had "uncommon," or divine, wisdom. We see in verse 25 that everyone in his kingdom prospered. When you operate in "uncommon" wisdom, everyone in your household will prosper. Uncommon wisdom brought great fame to Solomon, and it can bring great opportunities for us today.

Divine wisdom imparts to us "uncommon" wisdom. Uncommon wisdom is given to uncommon people. You may think that you are just an ordinary person—that you do not possess anything special.

1 Peter 2:9
But you are a chosen generation, a royal priesthood, a holy nation, His own special people, that you may proclaim the praises of Him who called you out of darkness into His marvelous light..

You are not an ordinary person if you are a child of God. You are part of a chosen generation, a royal priesthood, a holy nation, a peculiar people. You are a special person, a candidate to receive uncommon wisdom.

d. Divine and uncommon wisdom can only be found in Christ.

God said if you want wisdom, you should turn to Him. God, who owns all wisdom, has made this available to us through His Son, Jesus. The basis of this wisdom is grace because Jesus died so that you would have all the blessings. Grace is something that cannot be earned, but it is given to us freely through Jesus. Wisdom comes by grace, but we must appropriate it by faith.

Colossians 2:3
In whom are hidden all the treasures of wisdom and
knowledge.

How does God impart this divine uncommon wisdom to us?

God imparts this divine uncommon wisdom by His Spirit to our spirits.

God is able to use different channels to impart His wisdom and instruction into our lives.

1. Dreams

   Job 33:14–16
   For God may speak in one way, or in another, yet man
   does not perceive it. In a dream, in a vision of the night,
   when deep sleep falls upon men, while slumbering on
   their beds, then He opens the ears of men, and seals their
   instruction.

2. Visions

   Acts 10:19
   While Peter thought about the vision, the Spirit said to
   him, "Behold, three men are seeking you."

3. Circumstances

   Genesis 24:14
   Now let it be that the young woman to whom I say, 'Please
   let down your pitcher that I may drink,' and she says,
   'Drink, and I will also give your camels a drink'—let her
   be the one You have appointed for Your servant Isaac.
   And by this I will know that You have shown kindness to
   my master.

Abraham's servant asked God for certain signs so that he would know the right damsel for his master's son.

4. The Word of God

Deuteronomy 4:6
Therefore be careful to observe them; for this is your wisdom and your understanding in the sight of the peoples who will hear all these statutes, and say, "Surely this great nation is a wise and understanding people."

5. Gifts of the Holy Spirit—Word of wisdom

1 Corinthians 12:8
For to one is given the word of wisdom through the Spirit, to another the word of knowledge through the same Spirit..

Wisdom from God can come in the form of a word.

6. His still, small voice

1 Kings 19:11–12
The He said, "Go out, and stand on the mountain before the Lord." And behold, the Lord passed by, and a great and strong wind tore into the mountains and broke the rocks in pieces before the Lord, but the Lord was not in the wind; and after the wind an earthquake, but the Lord was not in the earthquake; and after the earthquake a fire but the Lord was not in the fire; and after the fire a still small voice.

7. The audible voice of God

Luke 3:21–22
When all the people were baptized, it came to pass that Jesus also was baptized; and while He prayed, the heaven was opened. And the Holy Spirit descended in bodily form like a dove upon Him, and a voice came from heaven

which said, "You are My beloved Son; in You I am well pleased."

God is able to put uncommon wisdom into your heart through all these channels. We must be open to Him and not put limits on how God will speak to us.

Let us take another look at King Solomon.

1 Kings 3:24
Then the king said, "Bring me a sword." So they brought a sword before the king.

Solomon had a dispute to settle between two women. Solomon was just an ordinary person in the midst of a dispute, but God began to speak into his spirit. He listened to the complaint and suddenly the wisdom of God came. He asked for a sword. This is an example of uncommon wisdom. This uncommon wisdom uncovered the truth. We need to see ourselves as uncommon people.

e. The wisdom in Christ knows all things.

Colossians 2:3
In whom are hidden all the treasures of wisdom and knowledge..

Jesus has knowledge of everything. He knows the past, the present, and the future. He knows the thoughts of man, your comings and goings. He knows your circumstances and your situation.

The wisdom in Christ knows where, how, and when. If you know the answer to where, how, and when; that is uncommon wisdom.

Matthew 17:24–27

When they had come to Capernaum, those who received the temple tax came to Peter and said, "Does your Teacher not pay the temple tax?" He said, "Yes." And when he had come into the house, Jesus anticipated him, saying, "What do you think, Simon? From whom do the kings of the earth take customs or taxes, from their sons or from strangers?" Peter said to Him, "From strangers." Jesus said to him, "Then the sons are free. Nevertheless, lest we offend them, go to the sea, cast in a hook, and take the fish that comes up first. And when you have opened its mouth, you will find a piece of money; take that and give it to them for Me and you."

We see these things in the scripture passage above:

1. Jesus knew what Peter was thinking. When you are faced with a situation, Jesus cares.

2. He told Peter he belonged to a different Kingdom and he was free, but as long as we are here on earth we should honor and not offend.

3. Jesus told Peter where to find the money, how to get the money, and when to get it. The wisdom of God told him how to pay the bills.

> The wisdom in Christ had knowledge of where, how, and when.
>
> Where—the sea
> How—cast a hook
> When—when you catch the first fish

4. The Lord gave specific instructions.

   When His wisdom leads you to find the treasure, the treasure will be more than sufficient for you.

Luke 5:1–11

So it was, as the multitude pressed about Him to hear the word of God, that He stood by the lake of Gennesaret, and saw two boats standing by the lake; but the fishermen had gone from them and were washing their nets. Then He got into one of the boats, which was Simon's, and asked him to put out a little from the land. And He sat down and taught the multitudes from the boat. When He had stopped speaking, He said to Simon, "Launch out into the deep and let down your nets for a catch." But Simon answered and said to Him, "Master, we have toiled all night and caught nothing; nevertheless at Your word I will let down the net." And when they had done this, they caught a great number of fish, and their net was breaking. So they signalled to their partners in the other boat to come and help them. And they came and filled both the boats, so that they began to sink. When Simon Peter saw it, he fell down at Jesus' knees, saying, "Depart from me, for I am a sinful man, O Lord!" For he and all who were with him were astonished at the catch of fish which they had taken; and so also were James and John, the sons of Zebedee, who were partners with Simon. And Jesus said to Simon, "Do not be afraid. From now on you will catch men." So when they had brought their boats to land, they forsook all and followed Him.

When Peter answered the Lord in verse 5, he did not understand that the "wisdom of Christ knows." The Master tells Peter where, how, and when to access the flow.

You may be asking, What must I do?

i.   Be in Christ.

He is the source of wisdom.

ii. Ask.

Ask God for wisdom according to the Word (James 1:5) in the

iii. Receive it by faith and thank Him for the wisdom.

iv. Yield to the leading of the Spirit of God.

v. Trust God to show you when, where, and how.

Jesus Christ is the same yesterday, today, and forever.

Master  Number Two

Prayer and Fasting
for a Specific Purpose

Prayer and fasting are like two hands. One hand is prayer, in which we take hold of the invincible promises of God. The other hand is fasting; in which we lose all the things that hold us back from taking hold of the promises. The two go hand in hand. We need to pray as well as fast. Jesus did not say "if" you fast; He said "when" you fast. Fasting must become an integral part of your life.

Let me remind you of some of the important principles about prayer.

1. We are to pray without ceasing.

> *1 Thessalonians 5:17*
> *Pray without ceasing.*

2. Pray in the Spirit.

> *Romans 8:26*
> *Likewise the Spirit also helps in our weaknesses. For we do not know what we should pray for as we ought, but the Spirit Himself makes intercession for us with groanings which cannot be uttered.*

Often we do not know what to pray, but the Spirit knows what to pray.

3. Our prayers must be accompanied by faith.

Mark 11:24
Therefore I say to you, whatever things you ask when you pray, believe that you receive them, and you will have them.

When you pray, you have to believe that you already have what you are praying for—that is faith.

4. Keep a clear conscience and a clean heart.

Mark 11:25
And whenever you stand praying, if you have anything against anyone, forgive him, that your Father in heaven may also forgive you your trespasses.

Prayer is communicating with God. There are many ways in which we can communicate with God.

Isaiah 1:18
Come now, and let us reason together," says the Lord, "Though your sins are like scarlet, they shall be as white as snow; though they are red like crimson, they shall be as wool.

God is giving us an invitation to come and reason with Him. Some people call this "holy reasoning," and some call it "holy pleading." It is passionately presenting to God our petitions with reasons that are based on the Word of God as to why God should grant us our requests. That is reasoning. In other words, it is like going before a judge and saying, "Here are the facts; this is why you should have this case resolved in my favor."

Isaiah 63:15–19 NIV
Look down from heaven and see from your lofty throne, holy and glorious. Where are your zeal and your might? Your tenderness and compassion are withheld from us. But you are our Father, though Abraham does not know us or Israel acknowledge us; you, O Lord, are our Father, our Redeemer from of old is your name. Why, O Lord, do you make us wander from your ways and harden our hearts so we do not revere you? Return for the sake of your servants, the tribes that are your inheritance. For a little while your people possessed your holy place, but now our enemies have trampled down your sanctuary. We are yours from of old; but you have not ruled over them, they have not been called by your name.

Here Isaiah is "reasoning" with God. Look at the way he is reasoning with God. What Isaiah is saying is, "If You do not look down and do something, who will?" He is coming to God and reasoning, in holy pleading with God.

Psalm 119:126 NIV
It is time for you to act, O Lord; your law is being broken.

Psalm 79:9 NIV
Help us, O God our Savior, for the glory of your name; deliver us and forgive our sins for your name's sake.

The psalmist comes to God and reasons with Him, telling Him He should act now.

When we approach God, we must come with a right attitude and with reverential fear as the following scripture states.

Isaiah 57:15
For thus says the High and Lofty One who inhabits eternity, whose name is Holy: "I dwell in the high and holy place, with him who has a contrite and humble spirit, to revive the spirit of the humble, and to revive the heart of the contrite ones."

Let us go through some ways to reason our case before God.

1. Plead or appeal to the greatness of His name.

Joshua 7:9 NIV
The Canaanites and the other people of the country will hear about this and they will surround us and wipe out our name from the earth. What then will you do for your own great name?

Joshua appealed to His great name. There is no greater name than His name.

Jeremiah 14:7 NIV
Although our sins testify against us, O Lord, do something for the sake of your name. For our backsliding is great; we have sinned against you.

He asked this of God because he knew that God would always honor His name.

2. Reason on the basis of your relationship with God.

Isaiah 63:15–19 NIV
Look down from heaven and see from your lofty throne, holy and glorious. Where are your zeal and your might? Your tenderness and compassion are withheld from us. But you are our Father, though Abraham does not know us or Israel acknowledge us; you, O Lord, are our Father, our Redeemer from of old is your name. Why, O Lord, do you make us wander from your ways and harden our hearts so we do not revere you? Return for the sake of your servants, the tribes that are your inheritance. For a little while your people possessed your holy place, but now our enemies have trampled down your sanctuary. We are yours from of old; but you have not ruled over them, they have not been called by your name.

Tell God who He is to you. When you come to God, ask God on the basis of your relationship, having confidence that you will receive.

3. Reason toward His attributes.

Nehemiah 9:32
Now therefore, our God, the great, the mighty, and awesome God, who keeps covenant and mercy: Do not let all the trouble seem small before You that has come upon us, our kings and our princes, our priests and our prophets, our fathers and on all Your people, from the days of the kings of Assyria until this day.

God reveals His attributes to His people. The Lord God is merciful, gracious, and long-suffering, and abundant in goodness and truth. As you get to know God, you know immediately you look at Him that He is merciful and gracious. It is something that you perceive and know in your heart.

Nehemiah pleads toward God's attributes and says, "You are merciful, You are great, and You are mighty. Our God is a faithful God; He is a covenant-keeping God and His compassion never fails."

4. Reason based on His promises and the Word of God.

1 Chronicles 17:23 NIV
And now, Lord, let the promise you have made concerning your servant and his house be established forever. Do as you promised..

God honors His Word and wants us to bring His promises before Him.

2 Chronicles 6:16
Therefore, Lord God of Israel, now keep what You promised
Your servant David my father, saying, "You shall not fail to
have a man sit before Me on the throne of Israel, only if your
sons take heed to their way, that they walk in My law as you
have walked before Me."

Solomon came to God and said, "This is what You told my father; You promised him, and I want You to do this."

Here is another verse that states clearly that God wants His children to prosper.

Proverbs 13.22
A good man leaves an inheritance to his children's children,
but the wealth of the sinner is stored up for the righteous.

God has said that we will be blessed above all people.

5. Declare the all-powerful blood of Jesus.

Hebrews 10:19
Therefore, brethren, having boldness to enter the Holiest by
the blood of Jesus..

A great man of God once said, "Many keys open many doors, but there is one master key that opens all doors, and that key is the blood of Jesus." Every time you plead the blood of Jesus, God's heart is touched, and the Father stops to listen to what you have to say.

6. Reason for the sake of His people.

When God sees your heart, God will grant your request.

1 Kings 3:9 NIV
*So give your servant a discerning heart to govern your people
and to distinguish between right and wrong. For who is able
to govern this great people of yours?*

Solomon calls the children of Israel a "great people;" therefore
he needed great wisdom to govern them. Whenever you ask
on behalf of His children, it touches the heart of God.

1 Kings 8:30 NIV
*Hear the supplication of your servant and of your people
Israel when they pray towards this place. Hear from heaven,
your dwelling place, and when you hear, forgive.*

7. Recognize the power of thanksgiving.

John 6:11 NIV
*Jesus then took the loaves, gave thanks, and distributed to
those who were seated as much as they wanted. He did the
same with the fish.*

All Jesus did was give thanks and the multiplication came.
This made such an impression in John's life that he recorded
it again in verse 23:

John 6:23
*However, other boats came from Tiberias, near the place
where they ate bread after the Lord had given thanks--*

After Jesus gave thanks, there was a great miracle. Giving
thanks to God is a great key.

John 11:41
*Then they took away the stone from the place where the dead
man was lying. And Jesus lifted up His eyes and said, "Father,
I thank You that You have heard Me."*

Jesus thanked the Father for having heard Him, and then He called Lazarus forth from the grave. When Jesus prayed, He was very specific; He called Lazarus by name. Giving thanks is very powerful and produces the miracle. Giving thanks must become a natural part of your walk with God.

Fasting

The Master said when you fast, not if you fast. Fasting must become an integral part of your walk with God.

Fasting does not change God. He is the same yesterday, today, and forever. Fasting changes us.

Let us look at the importance of fasting.

Judges 20:18–28
Then the children of Israel arose and went up to the house of God to inquire of God. They said, "Which of us shall go up first to battle against the children of Benjamin?" The LORD said, "Judah first!" So the children of Israel rose in the morning and encamped against Gibeah. And the men of Israel went out to battle against Benjamin, and the men of Israel put themselves in battle array to fight against them at Gibeah. Then the children of Benjamin came out of Gibeah, and on that day cut down to the ground twenty-two thousand men of the Israelites. And the people, that is, the men of Israel, encouraged themselves and again formed the battle line at the place where they had put themselves in array on the first day. Then the children of Israel went up and wept before the LORD until evening, and asked counsel of the LORD, saying, "Shall I again draw near for battle against the children of my brother Benjamin?" And the LORD said, "Go up against him." So the children of Israel approached the children of Benjamin on the second day. And Benjamin went out against them from Gibeah on the second day, and cut down to the ground eighteen thousand more of the children of Israel; all

> *these drew the sword. Then all the children of Israel, that is,*
> *all the people, went up and came to the house of God and*
> *wept. They sat there before the* LORD *and fasted that day*
> *until evening; and they offered burnt offerings and peace*
> *offerings before the* LORD. *So the children of Israel inquired*
> *of the* LORD *(the ark of the covenant of God was there in*
> *those days, and Phinehas the son of Eleazar, the son of Aaron,*
> *stood before it in those days), saying, "Shall I yet again go*
> *out to battle against the children of my brother Benjamin,*
> *or shall I cease?" And the* LORD *said, "Go up, for tomorrow I*
> *will deliver them into your hand."*

God said, "Go," and twenty-two thousand people died! They inquired of the Lord a second time, and God said, "Go." This time eighteen thousand men died. Now there are forty thousand men of Israel dead. They had heard from God, and God said, "Go." What happened here? The next time they inquired of the Lord, they wept and fasted. Previously when they inquired of God, He said, "Go"—but they never inquired when.

Fasting fine-tunes your ear to hear from God, not only in the area of finances, but in every area of life. It makes us hear God's instructions clearly.

The specific reason God wants us to fast and pray at this time is because He wants us to prosper. Prayer and fasting helps us to perceive, know, and recognize. The word *perceive* means "to gain awareness of" or "to discover." God wants you to discover the things that you have not seen or known before. Those who walk with the Lord will perceive. The word *know* means "to have a strong conviction within you." To recognize means to identify. When you identify something, you know what is yours.

The Great Xchange

Reasons why you should pray and fast

1. To <u>perceive</u> that this is your appointed time. Do not look at the situation, but know that this is God's appointed time for you.

2. To <u>know</u> that you are God's end-time vessel for the end-time harvest and for the transfer of the end-time wealth into the hand of the just.

3. To <u>recognize</u> that God will bring divine opportunities across your path. You must identify these opportunities and take hold of them so you can walk in His blessings.

> *1 Kings 17:4–9*
> *"And it will be that you shall drink from the brook, and I have commanded the ravens to feed you there." So he went and did according to the word of the LORD, for he went and stayed by the Brook Cherith, which flows into the Jordan. The ravens brought him bread and meat in the morning, and bread and meat in the evening; and he drank from the brook. And it happened after a while that the brook dried up, because there had been no rain in the land. Then the word of the LORD came to him, saying, "Arise, go to Zarephath, which belongs to Sidon, and dwell there. See, I have commanded a widow there to provide for you."*

God has already spoken His Word over us and said, "I want to meet your needs." That means total provision and continuous supply. When the provision ran out, God told Elijah that He had already spoken and his needs would be met. The widow was a heathen woman. Elijah had to perceive that it was time for him to go to this appointed place. If he had stayed at the brook, God would not have met his needs.

Elijah had to know that he was the child of the Most High God. He had to realize that God had make a way for him. Elijah had *to recognize and identify* the woman.

90

When you perceive, know, and recognize, something happens to you. Even the world will recognize that God is with you. God used Elijah to solve the woman's financial crisis. But God used this woman's resources to meet Elijah's needs. God is going to bring divine opportunities across your path. God is going to make available the resources of the world for you.

Master Number Three

Make Giving the Center of Your Life

The heartbeat of heaven is giving. God gave us His very best to redeem us. In John 3:16 we know that God so loved the world that *He gave*. Those who learn to give are blessed.

> *Luke 6:38*
> *Give, and it will be given to you: good measure, pressed down, shaken together, and running over will be put into your bosom. For with the same measure that you use, it will be measured back to you.*

Jesus issues a command and says "Give." After commanding us to give He presents a promise—it shall be given back to you. When the children of Israel left Egypt, God told them to go and ask for the gold and silver from their neighbors. Their neighbors had no option but to give them what they asked for. So it was man that gave them the silver and gold. We see from God's Word that the channel God uses to bring in the harvest is man.

> *Exodus 12:35–36*
> *Now the children of Israel had done according to the word of Moses, and they had asked from the Egyptians articles of silver, articles of gold, and clothing. And the LORD had given the people favor in the sight of the Egyptians, so that they granted them what they requested. Thus they plundered the Egyptians.*

Let us look at what Jesus said about giving:

1. He commanded us to give.

2. He promised we would reap a harvest.

3. He explained the size of the harvest.

4. He said that man would give it to us.

5. With what measure we give, that is what will come back.

The apostle Paul shared this truth:

> *2 Corinthians 9:6*
> *But this I say: He who sows sparingly will also reap sparingly, and he who sows bountifully will also reap bountifully.*

> *Proverbs 3:9–10 NIV*
> *Honor the LORD with your wealth, with the firstfruits of all your crops; then your barns will be filled to overflowing, and your vats will brim over with new wine.*

When you honor God, do not bring Him the leftovers. Honoring Him with your substance and the first fruits of all of your increase brings the promise for your barns to be filled with plenty.

Here is an event that took place in the Word of God. It is very similar to the crisis the world is facing today. The important factor is what the man of God did in the midst of the crisis.

> *Genesis 26:1–5*
> *There was a famine in the land, besides the first famine that was in the days of Abraham. And Isaac went to Abimelech king of the Philistines, in Gerar. Then the LORD appeared to him and said: "Do not go down to Egypt; live in the land of which I shall tell you. Dwell in this land, and I will be with you and bless you; for to you and your descendants I give all these lands, and I will perform the oath which I swore to Abraham your father. And I will make your descendants multiply as the stars of heaven; I will give to your descendants all these lands; and in your seed all the nations of the earth shall be blessed; because Abraham obeyed My voice and kept My charge, My commandments, My statutes, and My laws."*

I want you to give attention to what God's instructions were to Isaac. Isaac was walking in a time of famine, and God instructed him not to go down to Egypt. Egypt is a type of the world and its systems. God does not want us to get entangled with the system of the world because the world does not have the answer.

God told Isaac to stay where he was—it was there that God blessed him. All the promises in the Word of God are ours in Christ Jesus. God will give you all the resources, because He holds all the resources in His hands.

> *Genesis 26:12*
> *Then Isaac sowed in that land, and reaped in the same year a hundredfold; and the LORD blessed him.*

Faith is a fact, but it also must act. Isaac began to sow, and everyone knew that there was a famine, but God made sure that Isaac reaped in the same year. Why? Because God wants to show that His children reap when the world is sinking, and they will know that He is the great "I am." For every dollar Isaac invested, he got one hundred dollars back. God knows the situation and the circumstances you are in, and the harvest will come your way at the same time that you begin to plant.

> *1 Chronicles 29:11*
> *Yours, O LORD, is the greatness, the power and the glory, the victory and the majesty; for all that is in heaven and in earth is Yours; Yours is the kingdom, O LORD, and You are exalted as head over all.*

Everything belongs to God. Even what the heathens have belongs to God. That is why He said in His Word that He would take it and give it to you. Just as God used Elijah to provide for the widow's need, so He will use you and me to solve the world's crisis. God will give us the resources of the earth because the resources belong to Him.

Isaiah 55:11 NIV
*So is my word that goes out from my mouth: It will not return
to me empty, but will accomplish what I desire and achieve
the purpose for which I sent it.*

Numbers 23:19 NIV
*God is not a man, that he should lie, nor a son of man, that
he should change his mind. Does he speak and then not act?
Does he promise and not fulfill?*

If God said it, He will do it.

The key to this is sowing. There is a universal law that God has
put in place. There is a seed time and a harvest time. The harvest
in your life will depend on the seed that you have planted.

Genesis 8:22
*While the earth remains, seedtime and harvest, cold and
heat, winter and summer, and day and night shall not cease.*

1. You must choose the best seed.

If you sow, then you can reap. But the harvest will depend
on the seed that you plant. When a farmer wants a good
harvest, he will choose the best seed. He would have saved
the best seed from the previous harvest. When you come to
God, give Him the very best seed that you have.

Genesis 14:20
*"And blessed be God Most High, who has delivered your
enemies into your hand." And he gave him a tithe of all.*

Abraham gave a tithe of all. He did not keep back any for
himself. Some say that this is due under the Old Covenant,
but Abraham brought his tithe before the law was even
given.

Galatians 3:9 and Galatians 3:29 tell us that we are blessed with the blessing of Abraham.

God made sure through the law that tithing continued so that the children of Israel would continue to be blessed. The word tithe means "one-tenth."

It has also been said to be a means of learning to give.

Remember, everything belongs to God

Leviticus 27:30–33
And all the tithe of the land, whether of the seed of the land or of the fruit of the tree, is the LORD's. It is holy to the LORD. If a man wants at all to redeem any of his tithes, he shall add one-fifth to it. And concerning the tithe of the herd or the flock, of whatever passes under the rod, the tenth one shall be holy to the LORD. He shall not inquire whether it is good or bad, nor shall he exchange it; and if he exchanges it at all, then both it and the one exchanged for it shall be holy; it shall not be redeemed.

In Proverbs 3:9 God tells us, "Honor Me with your substance." When you come to God with your tithe, you are honoring Him.

Deuteronomy 14:22
You shall truly tithe all the increase of your grain that the field produces year by year.

2. The soil must be fertile.

The farmer does not scatter his seed. He will make sure that the ground is fertile because he wants the best possible harvest. We must plant our seed in the right soil. God gives us instruction as to where to plant our seed.

Malachi 3:10
"Bring all the tithes into the storehouse, that there may be food in My house, and try Me now in this," says the LORD of hosts, "if I will not open for you the windows of heaven and pour out for you such blessing that there will not be room enough to receive it."

Deuteronomy 14:22–23
You shall truly tithe all the increase of your grain that the field produces year by year. And you shall eat before the LORD your God, in the place which He chooses to make His name abide, the tithe of your grain and your new wine and your oil, of the firstborn of your herds and your flocks, that you may learn to fear the LORD your God always.

God chose the place to bring the tithe. He chose the storehouse, the local church where you are nourished by the Word of God; where they watch over your soul and where they pray for you. It is the local church that takes care of you. Some people scatter their seed, and they do not know where the harvest is or even if there is a harvest.

3. The seed needs protection.

Genesis 14:18
Then Melchizedek king of Salem brought out bread and wine; he was the priest of God Most High. And he blessed him and said: "Blessed be Abram of God Most High, Possessor of heaven and earth; and blessed be God Most High, who has delivered your enemies into your hand." And he gave him a tithe of all. Now the king of Sodom said to Abram, "Give me the persons, and take the goods for yourself." But Abram said to the king of Sodom, "I have raised my hand to the LORD, God Most High, the Possessor of heaven and earth, that I will take nothing, from a thread to a sandal strap, and that I will not take anything that is yours, lest you should say, 'I have made Abram rich'--"

A farmer takes great care to protect his seed. This is often why the person who tithes has lack in their life—they do not protect the seed. When the offering bag comes around, people just "dump" in their offering. But when you bring something to God, it should be fresh, it has to be new, it has to be sanctified and presented to God. Every time you sow, make sure that you sanctify that seed. Not only must the seed be sanctified, but it must be offered to the Great High Priest, and He will protect it. Hebrews 4:14 tells us that Jesus is our Great High Priest.

Hebrews 5:6
You are a priest forever according to the order of Melchizedek.

Melchizedek is a type of Jesus.

Poverty was broken at the cross of Calvary. When you are partaking of His body and His blood, <u>one of the things</u> you are declaring is that "I no longer live under poverty; I am under heaven's blessing." Melchizedek gave Abraham bread and wine, and in return Abraham gave him tithes of all because he honored <u>him as</u> the priest <u>of God Most High</u>.

When you take the body and the blood and you offer your seed to the Great High Priest, He will make sure that you are blessed by heaven. Abraham said that he did not want anyone to think that man had made him rich. He wanted everyone to know that it was God who made him rich.

4. The seed must have direction.

For a seed to have direction means it must have an assignment. If a farmer planted corn and got bananas, he would not be happy. The direction is the assignment that you place upon the seed in Jesus' name. Speak to the seed and tell the seed what it should accomplish. The harvest will depend on the seed that you plant. When our seed is sanctified and we declare that Jesus Christ is the Great High

Priest, and then the seed is given an assignment, the power of heaven gives that seed direction to fulfill its assignment.

5. The seed needs nourishment.

I nourish the seed through prayer, faith, and expectation. Some people will say, "I give it to God and I do not expect anything." What would you say if the farmer planted his seed and did not expect a harvest? I am sure you would say that he was a foolish farmer. When you plant your seed, expect a harvest. Jesus said, "Give and it shall be given to you." Faith must expect because it is impossible to please God without faith. Those who come to God must believe that He is the Rewarder of those who diligently seek Him. In other words, you must expect Him to reward you.

6. The seed needs to be watered.

Deuteronomy 30:9
The LORD your God will make you abound in all the work of your hand, in the fruit of your body, in the increase of your livestock, and in the produce of your land for good. For the LORD will again rejoice over you for good as He rejoiced over your fathers.

Deuteronomy 7:14
You shall be blessed above all peoples; there shall not be a male or female barren among you or among your livestock.

I water the seed by the Word of God. Every time I speak the Word over it, I water the seed.

Proverbs 13:22
A good man leaves an inheritance to his children's children, but the wealth of the sinner is stored up for the righteous.

These promises are ours in Christ Jesus.

2 Corinthians 9:8
*And God is able to make all grace abound toward you, that
you, always having all sufficiency in all things, may have an
abundance for every good work.*

In any situation or circumstance <u>God is able</u> to make all grace
abound so that you will always have sufficiency to meet your
needs and have some leftover to give to good works.

7. Every seed must produce fruit.

Genesis 1:11
*Then God said, "Let the earth bring forth grass, the herb that
yields seed, and the fruit tree that yields fruit according to its
kind, whose seed is in itself, on the earth"; and it was so.*

God wants that seed to grow and produce fruit. The seed
must produce after its own kind. That is why we give an
assignment to the seed. If you eat the seed, God will not
give you any more. Do not consume the seed; give it to
God.

Luke 16:10
*He who is faithful in what is least is faithful also in much;
and he who is unjust in what is least is unjust also in much.*

God will see your faithfulness with the small things, and
when you are faithful with the little, the Lord will continue to
expand and enlarge your territory.

Remember, the seed that multiplies is the seed that is in the
Master's hand.

Master  Number Four

Confession Is
Our Profession

The word *confession* means "to say the same thing" or "to affirm." Our confession is to say the same as the Word of God says. The Word of God is the final authority. Profession means "an act of declaration."

Let me share with you these principles about confession:

1. Our confession is our profession.

Hebrews 3:1
Therefore, holy brethren, partakers of the heavenly calling, consider the Apostle and High Priest of our confession, Christ Jesus..

We activate the office of the Great High Priest upon our confession.

Hebrews 4:14 NIV
Therefore, since we have a great high priest who has gone through the heavens, Jesus the Son of God, let us hold firmly to the faith we profess.

2. Confess and express it.

Psalm 107:2
Let the redeemed of the LORD say so, whom He has redeemed
from the hand of the enemy..

Hold fast your confession. It is upon our confession that He becomes our High Priest.

3. Know what to confess.

Isaiah 55:11
So shall My word be that goes forth from My mouth; it shall
not return to Me void, but it shall accomplish what I please,
and it shall prosper in the thing for which I sent it.

We confess the same things God has said in His Word because we know that God's Word has power; it is infallible and impregnable. It will do what God said it will do. We must know the Word of God or we will fail.

Matthew 4:1–11
Then Jesus was led up by the Spirit into the wilderness to be
tempted by the devil. And when He had fasted forty days and
forty nights, afterward He was hungry. Now when the tempter
came to Him, he said, "If You are the Son of God, command
that these stones become bread." But He answered and said,
"It is written, 'Man shall not live by bread alone, but by
every word that proceeds from the mouth of God.'" Then the
devil took Him up into the holy city, set Him on the pinnacle
of the temple, and said to Him, "If You are the Son of God,
throw Yourself down. For it is written: 'He shall give His
angels charge over you,' and, 'In their hands they shall bear
you up, lest you dash your foot against a stone.'" Jesus said to
him, "It is written again, 'You shall not tempt the LORD your
God.'" Again, the devil took Him up on an exceedingly high
mountain, and showed Him all the kingdoms of the world

and their glory. And he said to Him, "All these things I will give You if You will fall down and worship me." Then Jesus said to him, "Away with you, Satan! For it is written, 'You shall worship the LORD your God, and Him only you shall serve.'" Then the devil left Him, and behold, angels came and ministered to Him.

Here, Jesus was making His confession His profession. He was saying the same thing that God had already said: "It is written..."

The more you know your legal rights, the more you know what to say, because upon confession of the Word, Jesus your Messiah becomes your High Priest.

Deuteronomy 8:3
So He humbled you, allowed you to hunger, and fed you with manna which you did not know nor did your fathers know, that He might make you know that man shall not live by bread alone; but man lives by every word that proceeds from the mouth of the LORD.

Experience does not count; it is the Word of the living God that will stand.

Deuteronomy 6:16
You shall not tempt the LORD your God as you tempted Him in Massah.

Deuteronomy 6:13
You shall fear the LORD your God and serve Him, and shall take oaths in His name.

Jesus knew the Word of God. He is the Word of God, and He confessed the Word. When the enemy knocks on your door, confess the Word of God. The enemy had to leave Jesus. Jesus overcame the enemy by the confession of His mouth.

The Word of God must become prominent in your life. There is power in the Word of God.

4. Understand why we confess the Word of God.

The Word can do what God can do. If you rely on His Word, you are relying on God.

Numbers 23:19
God is not a man, that He should lie, nor a son of man, that He should repent. Has He said, and will He not do? Or has He spoken, and will He not make it good?

5. His Word is eternal.

John 1:1–5, 9, 12, 14, 16
In the beginning was the Word, and the Word was with God, and the Word was God. He was in the beginning with God. All things were made through Him, and without Him nothing was made that was made. In Him was life, and the life was the light of men. And the light shines in the darkness, and the darkness did not comprehend it. That was the true Light which gives light to every man coming into the world. But as many as received Him, to them He gave the right to become children of God, to those who believe in His name. And the Word became flesh and dwelt among us, and we beheld His glory, the glory as of the only begotten of the Father, full of grace and truth. And of His fullness we have all received, and grace for grace.

Facts about the Word of God:

a. The Word of God is the pre-existing Word.

b. The Word of God is a personal Word to us.

c. The Word of God is creative.

d. The Word of God is life-giving.

e. The Word of God is light-giving.

f. The Word of God has the power to illuminate your life.

g. The Word of God has the power to save.

h. The Word of God is the incarnate Word of God.

This is why God said, "Make your confession your profession."

6. Confession produces results.

Mark 1:15
And saying, "The time is fulfilled, and the kingdom of God is at hand. Repent, and believe in the gospel."

To repent means to change direction. Repentance is vital because God said we have all been rebellious.

Romans 10:9–10
That if you confess with your mouth the Lord Jesus and believe in your heart that God has raised Him from the dead, you will be saved. For with the heart one believes unto righteousness, and with the mouth confession is made unto salvation.

When we believe, we come into right standing with God. When you confess, there is a destination unto salvation. We need both, believing and confession.

Let me share some principles that the blessed Holy Spirit taught me with regard to confession and how to incorporate it in my prayer life. The Lord wanted me to include this section for the benefit of His children.

This is how I pray:

I thank You, Lord, that the blood of Jesus speaks and intercedes for me and my household.

Hebrews 12:24
> *To Jesus the Mediator of the new covenant, and to the blood of sprinkling that speaks better things than that of Abel*

I thank You, Lord, that the blood of Jesus has redeemed me and my household from the powers of darkness and translated us into the Kingdom of Jesus.

Colossians 1:14
> *In whom we have redemption through His blood, the forgiveness of sins.*

I thank You, Lord, that His blood has redeemed me and my household from sickness and disease and brought us into divine health.

I thank You, Lord, that the blood of Jesus has redeemed me and my household from poverty and brought us into prosperity.

The blood of Jesus has redeemed me and my household from calamity and brought us to peace.

The blood of Jesus has redeemed me and my household from the curse and brought us to the blessing of God.

I thank You, Lord, that the guilt, perversity, and punishment that was due to me and my household was laid on Jesus, and the blessings and the goodness that was due to Jesus now rest on me and my household.

We must also confess who Jesus Christ, the Son of the living God, is to us. This activates the blessing and authority that follows from the respective attributes of the office of Christ.

Let me remind you of the attributes of His office so that you may begin to confess and declare these attributes.

Attributes of Jesus

➤ Jesus Christ is our Great High Priest.

Hebrews 4:14–16
Seeing then that we have a great High Priest who has passed through the heavens, Jesus the Son of God, let us hold fast our confession. For we do not have a High Priest who cannot sympathize with our weaknesses, but was in all points tempted as we are, yet without sin. Let us therefore come boldly to the throne of grace, that we may obtain mercy and find grace to help in time of need.

➤ Jesus Christ is our intercessor.

Romans 8:34
Who is he who condemns? It is Christ who died, and furthermore is also risen, who is even at the right hand of God, who also makes intercession for us.

When Jesus prays, nothing can go wrong. He is on our side.

➤ Jesus Christ is our mediator.

Hebrews 9:15
And for this reason He is the Mediator of the new covenant,
by means of death, for the redemption of the transgressions
under the first covenant, that those who are called may receive
the promise of the eternal inheritance.

Start confessing "Jesus Christ is my mediator" right now.

➤ Jesus Christ is our advocate.

1 John 2:1
My little children, these things I write to you, so that you may
not sin. And if anyone sins, we have an Advocate with the
Father, Jesus Christ the righteous.

You have a king's counsel who has never lost a case yet.

➤ Jesus Christ is our jubilee.

Luke 4:18–19
The Spirit of the Lord is upon Me, because He has anointed
Me to preach the gospel to the poor; He has sent Me to heal
the brokenhearted, to proclaim liberty to the captives and
recovery of sight to the blind, to set at liberty those who are
oppressed; to proclaim the acceptable year of the Lord.

When I declare that Jesus is my jubilee, the enemy has to
return everything he has stolen from me. Jesus Christ is the
great restorer.

➤ Jesus Christ is our Messiah.

Luke 9:20
He said to them, "But who do you say that I am?" Peter
answered and said, "The Christ of God."

When you declare Jesus as the Messiah, you are appropriating His anointing upon your life.

Proverbs 18:21
Death and life are in the power of the tongue, and those who love it will eat its fruit.

If we want to eat the wonderful fruit of God's promises, watch what you are declaring. God said that He wanted to bless His people abundantly.

Seven Ways God Wants to Bless Us

1. Abundance

Isaiah 41:18
I will open rivers in desolate heights, and fountains in the midst of the valleys; I will make the wilderness a pool of water, and the dry land springs of water.

2. Assurance

Genesis 26:3
Dwell in this land, and I will be with you and bless you; for to you and your descendants I give all these lands, and I will perform the oath which I swore to Abraham your father.

All the promises given to Isaac have become ours in Christ Jesus.

3. Confidence

2 Corinthians 9:8
And God is able to make all grace abound toward you; that ye, always having all sufficiency in all things, may abound to every good work:

That is the confidence that God has given us.

4. Favor

Psalm 5:12
For You, O Lord, will bless the righteous; with favor You will surround him as with a shield.

We are righteous in Christ Jesus, and this promise belongs to us. Wherever we go we have a shield and it is called "favor."

5. Rest

Proverbs 3:24
When you lie down, you will not be afraid; yes, you will lie down and your sleep will be sweet.

6. Provision

Deuteronomy 28:3–4
Blessed shall you be in the city, and blessed shall you be in the country. Blessed shall be the fruit of your body, the produce of your ground and the increase of your herds, the increase of your cattle and the offspring of your flocks.

7. Riches

Isaiah 45:3
I will give you the treasures of darkness and hidden riches of secret places, that you may know that I, the Lord, who call you by your name, am the God of Israel.

Do not waver; hold fast to your confession.

Master  Number Five

Abraham's Blessings
Are Ours in Christ

God has promised to supply our needs with total provision and continuous supply. Our source is God and God alone. He has made provision for all our needs through the finished work of the cross.

Let me give you three scriptures that confirm God's provision:

1. Everything we possess and own belongs to God.

1 Chronicles 29:11
Yours, O Lord, is the greatness, the power and the glory, the victory and the majesty; for all that is in heaven and in earth is Yours; Yours is the kingdom, O Lord, and You are exalted as head over all.

2. Giving is not the problem; it is the solution to your problem.

Luke 6:38
Give, and it will be given to you: good measure, pressed down, shaken together, and running over will be put into your bosom. For with the same measure that you use, it will be measured back to you.

3. God's will and purpose is to prosper you.

3 John 2
Beloved, I pray that you may prosper in all things and be in health, just as your soul prospers.

There is a law in the Word that says that seedtime and harvest will never cease.

Genesis 8:22
While the earth remains, seedtime and harvest, cold and heat, winter and summer, and day and night shall not cease.

The law is called sowing and reaping. The source of our income is God, and the Kingdom of Heaven has no lack.

God's thoughts toward us are for good. His mind and His will are to bless us.

Jeremiah 29:11
For I know the thoughts that I think toward you, says the Lord, thoughts of peace and not of evil, to give you a future and a hope.

The word blessing encompasses God's goodness. His goodness is unlimited. When God revealed Himself to Moses, He said, "I am merciful, gracious, long-suffering, and abundant in goodness." When God says He will bless us, He is saying, "I am pouring on you the abundance of My goodness." The goodness of God includes His favor and His gifts.

Galatians 3:13–14
Christ has redeemed us from the curse of the law, having become a curse for us (for it is written, "Cursed is everyone who hangs on a tree"), that the blessing of Abraham might come upon the Gentiles in Christ Jesus, that we might receive the promise of the Spirit through faith.

Jesus has redeemed us from the curse. When the exchange took place, He became a curse so that we could be blessed.

When Abraham walked on the face of the earth, he was not under the law because the law had not yet been given. He believed God, and it was counted unto him as righteousness. From Abraham to Jacob, there was no law, but God had to introduce the law because the children of Israel had departed from the ways of God.

Galatians 3:16–19
Now to Abraham and his Seed were the promises made. He does not say, "And to seeds," as of many, but as of one, "And to your Seed," who is Christ. And this I say, that the law, which was four hundred and thirty years later, cannot annul the covenant that was confirmed before by God in Christ, that it should make the promise of no effect. For if the inheritance is of the law, it is no longer of promise; but God gave it to Abraham by promise. What purpose then does the law serve? It was added because of transgressions, till the Seed should come to whom the promise was made; and it was appointed through angels by the hand of a mediator.

God had already given promises to Abraham.

Genesis 12:1–3
Now the Lord had said to Abram: "Get out of your country, from your family and from your father's house, to a land that I will show you. I will make you a great nation; I will bless you and make your name great; and you shall be a blessing. I will bless those who bless you, and I will curse him who curses you; and in you all the families of the earth shall be blessed."

When God makes a promise, it is already settled. In these verses we see that God has already destined Abraham's blessing. The enemy can come, but God has said that this was where Abraham was going to finish.

Galatians 3:8
And the Scripture, foreseeing that God would justify the Gentiles by faith, preached the gospel to Abraham beforehand, saying, "In you all the nations shall be blessed."

Jesus came and fulfilled the Law. He met every requirement of the Law so that whoever believes in Him can walk in His blessing.

When all the negative reports come, remember you are destined to be blessed.

Galatians 3:9
So then those who are of faith are blessed with believing Abraham.

Every promise that was given to Abraham belongs to us.

Galatians 3:29
And if you are Christ's, then you are Abraham's seed, and heirs according to the promise.

You are an heir to receive the promises. When God gives us promises, it leads us to God's blessing, and God's blessing opens the door to God's riches.

Isaiah 45:3
I will give you the treasures of darkness and hidden riches of secret places, that you may know that I, the Lord, who call you by your name, am the God of Israel.

"Treasures" means accumulated or stored wealth. "Riches" means abundance of provision and wealth. It is wisdom in Christ that brings the light needed to see the treasure. All you have to do is to ask God for wisdom every morning and that wisdom will show you where the treasures are.

We find the riches by sowing. When you sow, God said He would command the harvest and the harvest will come out of the secret places. He knows where the blessings are. All you have to do is to obey and know that you are destined to be blessed.

Master  Number Six

Prove Me

Malachi 3:10–12
"Bring all the tithes into the storehouse, that there may be
food in my house, and try Me now in this," says the Lord of
hosts, "if I will not open for you the windows of heaven and
pour out for you such blessing that there will not be room
enough to receive it. And I will rebuke the devourer for your
sakes, so that he will not destroy the fruit of your ground, nor
shall the vine fail to bear fruit for you in the field," says the
Lord of hosts;, "and all nations will call you blessed, for you
will be a delightful land," says the Lord of hosts.

God is giving a challenge here—"prove Me." This is the only
place in scripture we are allowed to prove God. God said He
would open the windows of heaven. In the Scriptures, "gates"
and "doors" speak about strength and authority. It has been
said "windows" talk about permitting. Windows in a house
permit light. God is saying He will permit heaven's wealth to be
given to us.

Blessings that come from giving:

→ The windows will open.

→ He will pour out.

→ You will not have enough room to store it.

→ The devourer will be stopped.

→ Nothing will affect the fruit of your labor.

→ All nations shall call you blessed.

Master  Number Seven

Godly Counsel

1. Live within your means.

You cannot expect to borrow to the hilt and have God come and rescue you. If you have made a mistake, repent and ask forgiveness.

Deuteronomy 28:12
The Lord will open to you His good treasure, the heavens, to give the rain to your land in its season, and to bless all the work of your hand. You shall lend to many nations, but you shall not borrow.

2. Do not act hastily.

Isaiah 52:12
For you shall not go out with haste, nor go by flight; for the Lord will go before you, and the God of Israel will be your rear guard.

3. Do not make impulse decisions.

4. Make sure there is agreement between husband and wife.

Matthew 18:19
Again I say to you that if two of you agree on earth concerning anything that they ask, it will be done for them by My Father in heaven.

5. Be wise and faithful with the provision that you have.

Proverbs 6:6
Go to the ant, you sluggard! Consider her ways and be wise..

6. Take godly counsel.

Job 33:14–16
For God may speak in one way, or in another, yet man does not perceive it. In a dream, in a vision of the night, when deep sleep falls upon men, while slumbering on their beds, then He opens the ears of men, and seals their instruction.

7. Remember to look to Jesus our Lord and what He accomplished on the cross of Calvary for us.

Hebrews 12:2
Looking unto Jesus, the author and finisher of our faith, who for the joy that was set before Him endured the cross, despising the shame, and has sat down at the right hand of the throne of God.

Seven Great Exchanges

1. The guilt, punishment, and evil consequences that were due to us were placed upon Jesus, and the goodness and the blessings of Jesus have come upon us.

2. Jesus was punished so we can be forgiven.

3. Jesus was wounded so we can be healed.

4. Jesus became sin with our sinfulness so we can be made righteous in Him.

5. Jesus died our death so we can have life and life more abundantly.

6. Jesus bore our curse so that we can be blessed with heaven's blessing.

7. Jesus became poor so that we can become rich.

Every day meditate upon what Jesus accomplished for you on the cross of Calvary. Declare it and make it your prayer for you and your household.

Consider Calvary:
It Is Perfect in Every
Aspect and Respect.

The Cross of Calvary
Provides Protection

Christ on the Cross Disarmed and Defeated the Devil

One day I was driving to my workplace. As usual, I was praying in the car. As I drew closer to a bridge, the Lord spoke to me. This is what He said:

"Son, I know all things. I am fully aware of the enemy's plans and tactics." Then He went on to say, "You cannot visit the enemy's camp, but I can because I am all-powerful and I have all authority. I want you to know what the enemy is planning."

What the Enemy Has Planned

God wants us to know what the enemy is planning and show us what is to come.

> *John 16:13*
> *However, when He, the Spirit of truth, has come, He will guide you into all truth; for He will not speak on His own authority, but whatever He hears He will speak; and He will tell you things to come.*

> *Acts 11:28*
> *Then one of them, named Agabus, stood up and showed by the Spirit that there was going to be a great famine throughout all the world, which also happened in the days of Claudius Caesar.*

There is not only going to be a financial crisis, but famine, and not one nation on the earth is going to be excluded. The enemy's plan is to cover the world with a spirit of poverty, a spirit of fear, and the spirit of confusion. We do not have to be subject to these spirits. God has destroyed the work of the enemy on the cross of Calvary.

Fear brings torment, fear paralyzes, and fear sees the negative, but faith sees the positive. The enemy's strategy is to fill the minds and hearts of God's people with fear through circumstances and suggestions. When you know the enemy's strategy, you are able to overcome. The enemy targets the heart and the mind because the inner recess of your heart is where the Word of God takes root and faith is born.

If your mind and heart is full of fear, you will be unable to receive the promises of God. Without faith it is impossible to please Him. If the enemy can fill the innermost recess with fear, and if faith is not born, then you cannot take hold of the promises of God. This is the strategy of the enemy. We must put our trust in the Word of God.

The heart is the innermost being, where God's Word dwells and faith is born. That is why the devil targets your heart.

Hebrews 11:6
But without faith it is impossible to please Him, for he who comes to God must believe that He is, and that He is a rewarder of those who diligently seek Him.

The first time the enemy tempted Jesus, it was a physical temptation. The next temptation was psychological, and the third temptation was spiritual. The enemy always comes with a suggestion. He is a liar from the very beginning.

John 8:44
You are of your father the devil, and the desires of your father
you want to do. He was a murderer from the beginning, and
does not stand in the truth, because there is no truth in him.
When he speaks a lie, he speaks from his own resources, for he
is a liar and the father of it.

Everything that comes out of the enemy's mouth is a lie; there is
no truth in him. The enemy works in two ways. He may whisper
in your ear himself, or he may send somebody else with the bad
news. The moment you listen, you open the door. If you do not
have the Word of God in your heart, you will listen and allow the
enemy to put fear and doubt in your heart. But if you have the
Word of God in your heart, you will be like Jesus and say, "It is
written," and the Holy Spirit will bring to remembrance what He
has taught you.

Hebrews 12:2
Looking unto Jesus, the author and finisher of our faith,
who for the joy that was set before Him endured the cross,
despising the shame, and has sat down at the right hand of
the throne of God.

The Word of God is commanding us to look to Jesus. What He
started in you He has the power to finish. When you are looking
unto Jesus, fear cannot come and settle on you because there
is no gate for the enemy to enter. That is why you guard your
heart with all diligence, because out of it flow the issues of life.

2 Timothy 1:7
For God has not given us a spirit of fear, but of power and of
love and of a sound mind.

God has given us power to overcome and power to make the
right decisions. Never make a decision out of fear. Fear will
cause you to make the wrong decision.

Isaiah 43:1–2
But now, thus says the Lord, who created you, O Jacob, and
He who formed you, O Israel: "Fear not, for I have redeemed
you; I have called you by your name; you are Mine. When you
pass through the waters, I will be with you; and through the
rivers, they shall not overflow you. When you walk through the
fire, you shall not be burned, nor shall the flame scorch you."

This scripture is applicable right now. God is saying fear not now because He has taken you out of the powers of darkness and translated you into the Kingdom of God. In the Kingdom of God, there is no fear; remember, God will be with you.

When Jesus told Peter to come to Him on the water, everything went well while Peter's eyes were on Jesus. When he took his eyes off Jesus, he began to sink. When you are drowning, there is no time for big prayers. Peter said, "Lord, save me." Jesus reached out, and, hand in hand, they walked back to the boat because now Peter kept his eyes on Jesus and he walked on the Word. When Jesus said, "Come," Peter walked on the Word while he kept his eyes on Jesus.

The enemy is flooding governments and financial institutions with confusion. The reason the enemy is bringing confusion is because it will destroy people's hope. As long as we are in Christ Jesus, we have hope. Weeping lasts for a night, but joy comes in the morning. The darkest hour is just before dawn. Just around the corner is your miracle.

1 Timothy 1:1
Paul, an apostle of Jesus Christ, by the commandment of God
our Savior and the Lord Jesus Christ, our hope..

This is a strong, steadfast hope. We know that our God is able.

Romans 15:13
Now may the God of hope fill you with all joy and peace in
believing, that you may abound in hope by the power of the
Holy Spirit.

Hope always brings joy and peace. God wants you to abound in hope through the power of the Holy Spirit.

The enemy wants to cover the world with a spirit of fear and uncertainty. His strategy is to keep everyone in bondage, but Jesus said He came to set the captives free. On the cross of Calvary, every yoke was destroyed. We need to tell the enemy to get out of our territory because he was defeated on the cross of Calvary. Do not entertain the enemy. He has no legal right to touch you. Know your legal rights. Say, "It is written... I am redeemed by the blood of Jesus." God has redeemed us from the powers of darkness.

> *Isaiah 10:27*
> *It shall come to pass in that day that his burden will be taken away from your shoulder, and his yoke from your neck, and the yoke will be destroyed because of the anointing oil.*

Bondages have been broken on the cross of Calvary, and today we can walk free.

The Name of Jesus

Let us look at the name of Jesus before we go any further. The Holy Spirit wants me to bring the name of Jesus to our remembrance. A person's name represents the person, along with their ability, their authority, and their accomplishments.

> *Hebrews 1:4*
> *Having become so much better than the angels, as He has by inheritance obtained a more excellent name than they.*

1. The name of Jesus is an excellent name.

There is no other name like the name of Jesus.

2. His name is above every name.

Philippians 2:5–9
Let this mind be in you which was also in Christ Jesus, who,
being in the form of God, did not consider it robbery to be
equal with God, but made Himself of no reputation, taking
the form of a bondservant, and coming in the likeness of
men. And being found in appearance as a man, He humbled
Himself and became obedient to the point of death, even the
death of the cross. Therefore God also has highly exalted Him
and given Him the name which is above every name.

3. His name has power not only in this world, but in the world to come.

Ephesians 1:20–22
Which He worked in Christ when He raised Him from the
dead and seated Him at His right hand in the heavenly
places, far above all principality and power and might and
dominion, and every name that is named, not only in this
age but also in that which is to come. And He put all things
under His feet, and gave Him to be the head over all things
to the church..

4. Jesus is called the Son of the Highest.

Luke 1:32
He will be great, and will be called the Son of the Highest;
and the Lord God will give Him the throne of His father
David. And He will reign over the house of Jacob forever, and
of His kingdom there will be no end.

5. His name has all power.

Matthew 28:18
And Jesus came and spoke to them, saying, "All authority has been given to Me in heaven and on earth."

Revelation 1:17–18
And when I saw Him, I fell at His feet as dead. But He laid His right hand on me, saying to me, "Do not be afraid; I am the First and the Last. I am He who lives, and was dead, and behold, I am alive forevermore. Amen. And I have the keys of Hades and of Death."

Jesus said that all power was given unto Him in heaven and on earth. If you know the power that God has invested in that name, you will never be defeated.

6. His name is the Word.

Revelation 19:13
He was clothed with a robe dipped in blood, and His name is called The Word of God.

He is the Word of God.

7. In that name we have unlimited power of attorney.

Luke 9:1–2
Then He called His twelve disciples together and gave them power and authority over all demons, and to cure diseases. He sent them to preach the kingdom of God and to heal the sick.

Jesus gave the disciples power and authority to cast out demons and heal the sick. He gave them power of attorney.

John 14:14
If you ask anything in My name, I will do it.

That means you can use this unlimited power of attorney any time and in any place.

2 Corinthians 10:4–5
For the weapons of our warfare are not carnal but mighty in God for pulling down strongholds, casting down arguments and every high thing that exalts itself against the knowledge of God, bringing every thought into captivity to the obedience of Christ..

God gave us an imagination so that we could picture what wonderful things the Word has done for us. You must use your imagination toward God, not toward what the enemy can do. Everything God has given, the enemy wants to pervert. People are depressed because they have let their minds loose with negative imaginations and thoughts. God has given you a name that is above every name—**the name of Jesus**.

Satan Disarmed and Defeated

~ PART ONE ~

The enemy was disarmed and defeated at the cross of Calvary. We must realize that there are two spiritual kingdoms, God's Kingdom and Satan's kingdom.

> *Colossians 1:13–14*
> *He has delivered us from the power of darkness and conveyed us into the kingdom of the Son of His love, in whom we have redemption through His blood, the forgiveness of sins.*

> *Matthew 12:26–28*
> *If Satan casts out Satan, he is divided against himself. How then will his kingdom stand? And if I cast out demons by Beelzebub, by whom do your sons cast them out? Therefore they shall be your judges. But if I cast out demons by the Spirit of God, surely the kingdom of God has come upon you.*

Jesus describes the two kingdoms. In Satan's kingdom there is a hierarchy.

Satan's Kingdom

> *Ephesians 6:12*
> *For we do not wrestle against flesh and blood, but against principalities, against powers, against the rulers of the darkness of this age, against spiritual hosts of wickedness in the heavenly places.*

This scripture verse indicates to us the Kingdom's hierarchical system.

1. Demon spirits

The Word states that we do not wrestle against flesh and blood. Therefore we wrestle against demonic spirits.

2. Principalities

The word translated principalities means "chief rulership over certain regions or territories, having certain authority and power."

3. Power

The word translated power means "delegated authority." The rulers control and give the orders of what is to be done. It is like the major, the sergeant, and the battalion. Every country has a demonic ruler, and the enemy has agents on the face of the earth who fulfill his desires and plans.

4. Rulers of darkness of this world

These are the devil's agents who are being controlled and used by the devil and his demon spirits on the face of the earth.

5. Spiritual wickedness in high places

These are spiritual forces of iniquity in the heavens, or "fallen angels."

Ephesians 2:1–3
And you He made alive, who were dead in trespasses and sins, in which you once walked according to the course of this world, according to the prince of the power of the air, the spirit who now works in the sons of disobedience, among

whom also we all once conducted ourselves in the lusts of our flesh, fulfilling the desires of the flesh and of the mind, and were by nature children of wrath, just as the others.

If you are not in the Kingdom of God, you are in Satan's kingdom, and all the people who are in this kingdom walk in disobedience. Disobedience produces unrighteousness, and unrighteousness produces sin. The kingdom of Satan is dominated by sin.

Romans 6:16–18 AMP
Do you not know that if you continually surrender yourselves to any one to do his will, you are the slaves of him whom you obey, whether that be to sin, which leads to death, or to obedience which leads to righteousness (right doing and right standing with God)? But thank God, though you were once slaves of sin, you have become obedient with all your heart to the standard of teaching in which you were instructed and to which you were committed. And having been set free from sin, you have become the servants of righteousness (of conformity to the divine will in thought, purpose, and action).

Satan rebelled against God, and anyone in his kingdom is a rebel. If you surrender to the enemy, you will be a slave to that kingdom. Sin dominates the kingdom of Satan. Sin produces guilt.

People who are in Satan's kingdom are filled with guilt; that is how he operates, and eventually sin produces death.

Romans 6:23
For the wages of sin is death, but the gift of God is eternal life in Christ Jesus our Lord.

Now let us look at the Kingdom of God.

The Kingdom of God has a King, and He is no ordinary King. He is the King of all kings and the Lord of all lords.

Matthew 4:17
From that time Jesus began to preach and to say, "Repent, for the kingdom of heaven is at hand."

To live in the Kingdom of God, we must turn from our wicked ways and repent. Jesus comes to rule and reign in your life. This Kingdom is the Kingdom of light, hope, and love; it is the Kingdom of grace, provision, and prosperity.

Luke 9:1–2
Then He called His twelve disciples together and gave them power and authority over all demons, and to cure diseases. He sent them to preach the kingdom of God and to heal the sick.

Jesus has given us all power over sickness and the enemy. The Kingdom of God does not have sickness, but it sets the captive free so that people can walk in freedom and liberty.

Revelation 19:16
And He has on His robe and on His thigh a name written: KING OF KINGS AND LORD OF LORDS.

In any kingdom there are legal and illegal citizens, but in the heavenly Kingdom there is only one type of citizen, and they are called the sons and daughters of the Most High God.

Galatians 4:6
And because you are sons, God has sent forth the Spirit of His Son into your hearts, crying out, "Abba, Father!"

The heavenly Father is highly exalted and dearly beloved.

Matthew 28:18
And Jesus came and spoke to them, saying, "All authority has been given to Me in heaven and on earth.

The Kingdom of God has all power and authority.

Revelation 1:17–18
And when I saw Him, I fell at his feet as dead. But He laid His right hand on me, saying to me, "Do not be afraid; I am the First and the Last. I am He who lives, and was dead, and behold, I am alive forevermore. Amen. And I have the keys of Hades and of Death."

The characteristics of the Kingdom of heaven are righteousness, peace, and joy.

Romans 14:17
For the kingdom of God is not eating and drinking, but righteousness and peace and joy in the Holy Spirit.

Colossians 1:13–14
He has delivered us from the power of darkness and conveyed us into the kingdom of the Son of His love, in whom we have redemption through His blood, the forgiveness of sins.

God sent His Son to die on the cross of Calvary and pay the price for us, to redeem us from the kingdom of darkness into the Kingdom of Jesus. The Kingdom of God is more powerful than the kingdom of darkness. The defeat of Satan is irreversible.

Luke 11:17–18, 21–22
But He, knowing their thoughts, said to them: "Every kingdom divided against itself is brought to desolation, and a house divided against a house falls. If Satan also is divided against himself, how will his kingdom stand? Because you say I cast out demons by Beelzebub. When a strong man, fully

*armed, guards his own palace, his goods are in peace. But
when a stronger than he comes upon him and overcomes him,
he takes from him all his armor in which he trusted, and
divides his spoils."*

In the above scripture, Jesus is the stronger man. A person may
be a "strong man" when that person has everything under his
control, but when a stronger man comes:

1. He will overcome him—meaning, He will subdue him.

2. He will take away all his armor—meaning, He will destroy
   and remove all his protection.

3. He will divide the spoils—meaning, He will take away all his
   possessions and distribute them to others.

Let us now look at the following scriptures in which Jesus Christ
explains how the demon spirits operate in the kingdom of
darkness.

> *Luke 11:24–26*
> *"When an unclean spirit goes out of a man, he goes through
> dry places, seeking rest; and finding none, he says, 'I will
> return to my house from which I came.' And when he comes,
> he finds it swept and put in order. Then he goes and takes
> with him seven other spirits more wicked than himself, and
> they enter and dwell there; and the last state of that man is
> worse than the first."*

Even though demons have no bodies, they have certain personality traits.

1. They have a will.

Luke 11:24
When an unclean spirit goes out of a man, he goes through dry places, seeking rest; and finding none, he says, "I will return to my house from which I came."

2. They have emotions.

James 2:19
You believe that there is one God. You do well. Even the demons believe—and tremble!

3. They have intellect.

Mark 1:24
Saying, "Let us alone! What have we to do with You, Jesus of Nazareth? Did You come to destroy us? I know who you are—the Holy One of God!"

4. They have self-awareness.

Mark 5:9
Then He asked him, "What is your name?" And he answered, saying, "My name is Legion; for we are many."

5. They have the ability to speak.

Mark 5:9
Then He asked him, "What is your name?" And he answered, saying, "My name is Legion; for we are many."

6. They travel.

Mark 5:9
*When an unclean spirit goes out of a man, he goes through
dry places, seeking rest; and finding none, he says, "I will
return to my house from which I came."*

7. They seek to find a living vessel.

Mark 5:12
*So all the demons begged Him, saying, "Send us to the swine,
that we may enter them."*

Luke 11:24
*When an unclean spirit goes out of a man, he goes through
dry places, seeking rest; and finding none, he says, "I will
return to my house from which I came."*

When a demon is cast out, it will come back to see how the
house is—it calls it "MY house." The reason the demon calls
it "my house" is because its ownership was never broken
over that house and so the demon has a legal right over
it. Demons know their legal rights very well. You must also
know your legal position in Jesus Christ.

God provided the cross of Calvary as the way for people to
come out of the kingdom of darkness into the Kingdom of
God. Without the cross, there is no crossing over into the
Kingdom of God. It is the cross that made provision for all
to come into the Kingdom of God. The price was paid with
Jesus' life.

Acts 13:38–39
*Therefore let it be known to you, brethren, that through this
Man is preached to you the forgiveness of sins; and by Him
everyone who believes is justified from all things from which
you could not be justified by the law of Moses.*

Colossians 2:13–15
And you, being dead in your trespasses and the uncircumcision of your flesh, He has made alive together with Him, having forgiven you all trespasses, having wiped out the handwriting of requirements that was against us, which was contrary to us. And He has taken it out of the way, having nailed it the cross. Having disarmed principalities and powers, He made a public spectacle of them, triumphing over them in it.

The cross not only made a way for us to cross over into the Kingdom of God, but it disarmed and defeated the enemy. It took care of the past, and God made provision to take care of the future.

Your enemy is disarmed and defeated.

Satan Disarmed and Defeated

~ PART TWO ~

The damage the cross of Calvary did to the enemy is irreversible.

In order to appropriate this truth, we must understand the divine process that occurred when we entered into the Kingdom of God.

> *Romans 10:9–10*
> *That if you confess with your mouth the Lord Jesus and believe in your heart that God has raised Him from the dead, you will be saved. For with the heart one believes unto righteousness, and with the mouth confession is made unto salvation.*

Many people confess that Jesus is Lord but do not believe. Then again, we must not only believe but also confess.

> *Romans 5:8*
> *But God demonstrates His own love toward us, in that while we were still sinners, Christ died for us.*

Jesus identified Himself with us. When we come to Jesus, we must identify ourselves with Him and His death.

Before we proceed any further, I would like to explain to you the process that takes place when you believe and confess that Jesus is Lord and accept Him as your personal Savior.

1. We are crucified with Christ.

Romans 6:6
Knowing this, that our old man was crucified with Him, that the body of sin might be done away with, that we should no longer be slaves of sin.

We have been crucified with Christ and no longer serve sin.

2. We died with Him.

Romans 6:8
Now if we died with Christ, we believe that we shall also live with Him.

If we have been crucified with Christ, we have died with Him. We need to know that the "old man" is dead.

The Law has no dominion over you.

It is important for us to understand that we died with Christ and the life that we live, we live in and through Christ. This truth will give us the ability to overcome the enemy that was defeated and disarmed at the cross of Calvary.

Romans 10:4
For Christ is the end of the law for righteousness to everyone who believes.

Leviticus 16:34
"This shall be an everlasting statute for you, to make atonement for the children of Israel, for all their sins, once a year." And he did as the Lord commanded Moses.

God did not say the law was only for a time. Everlasting means forever. God does not change His mind.

Does that mean we have to continue making sacrifices?

You will immediately say that Jesus paid the price, and you do not have to sacrifice anymore. Yes, it is true, but this is only partially correct.

Matthew 5:17
Do not think that I came to destroy the Law or the Prophets. I did not come to destroy but to fulfill.

Jesus did not come to abolish the law but to fulfill it. The law says that if you break the law you have committed a sin and the wages of sin is death. The law and sin go hand in hand.

1 Corinthians 15:56
The sting of death is sin, and the strength of sin is the law.

This is how the law of sin and death work together. Jesus is sinless; He never broke the law yet He paid the price in full. So for whom did He pay the price? For you and for me.

Remember, the law still exists, even though we have died with Christ. The law was not abolished, but we died in Christ Jesus. The law has no effect on us because we are dead in Christ. What a glorious truth.

Galatians 3:17–19
And this I say, that the law, which was four hundred and thirty years later, cannot annul the covenant that was confirmed before by God in Christ, that it should make the promise of no effect. For if the inheritance is of the law, it is no longer of promise; but God gave it to Abraham by promise. What purpose then does the law serve? It was added because of transgressions, till the Seed should come to whom the promise was made; and it was appointed through angels by the hand of a mediator.

The moment a person comes to Christ, he is crucified and dies with Christ. The law is still there, but those who are in Christ Jesus are free from the law.

Galatians 2:20
I have been crucified with Christ; it is no longer I who live, but Christ lives in me; and the life which I now live in the flesh I live by faith in the Son of God, who loved me and gave Himself for me.

Romans 6:14
For sin shall not have dominion over you, for ye are not under law but under grace.

Romans 7:6
But now we have been delivered from the law, having died to what we were held by, so that we should serve in the newness of the Spirit and not in the oldness of the letter.

We are now delivered from the law. Christianity is not living by a set of rules; we live by grace. We are dead in Christ, and the law has no dominion over us.

Romans 4:3–5
For what does the Scripture say? "Abraham believed God, and it was accounted to him for righteousness." Now to him who works, the wages are not counted as grace but as debt. But to him who does not work but believes on Him who justifies the ungodly, his faith is accounted for righteousness..

Abraham believed God, and it was counted to him as righteousness, even though he made mistakes. He went where he was not supposed to go; he lied; and then he tried to help God out. Even with the mistakes he made, he believed God.

Romans 4:22–25
And therefore "it was accounted to him for righteousness." Now it was not written for his sake alone that it was imputed to him, but also for us. It shall be imputed to us who believe in Him who raised up Jesus our Lord from the dead, who was delivered up because of our offenses, and was raised because of our justification.

Abraham believed God would make a way for him. So we must believe God and walk with Him by His grace.

3. We are buried with Him.

Romans 6:4
Therefore we were buried with Him through baptism into death, that just as Christ was raised from the dead by the glory of the Father, even so we also should walk in newness of life.

4. We are quickened by the Spirit of God.

Romans 8:11
But if the Spirit of Him who raised Jesus from the dead dwells in you, He who raised Christ from the dead will also give life to your mortal bodies through His Spirit who dwells in you.

5. We are raised together with Christ.

Romans 6:9
Knowing that Christ, having been raised from the dead, dies no more. Death no longer has dominion over Him.

6. We are seated in heavenly places with Christ.

Ephesians 2:6
And raised us up together, and made us sit together in the heavenly places in Christ Jesus..

Jesus has triumphed; he is seated in heavenly places. We are seated with Christ in heavenly places. You are not just observing, but you are actually there with Christ.

God has disarmed principalities and powers. Jesus made a bold display and triumphed over Satan.

Colossians 2:14–15

Having wiped out the handwriting of requirements that was against us, which was contrary to us. And He has taken it out of the way, having nailed it to the cross. Having disarmed principalities and powers, He made a public spectacle of them, triumphing over them in it.

God's Armor

God has clothed us with His armor, and He provides us with the necessary weapons to walk on this earth.

> *2 Corinthians 10:4–5* AMP
> *For the weapons of our warfare are not physical [weapons of flesh and blood], but they are mighty before God for the overthrow and destruction of strongholds, [Inasmuch as we] refute arguments and theories and reasonings and every proud and lofty thing that sets itself up against the [true] knowledge of God; and we lead every thought and purpose away captive into the obedience of Christ (the Messiah, the Anointed One)..*

The weapons that God has provided are not of this world. You cannot buy these weapons; they are created and formed by God Himself.

The weapons God has given us:

1. His name

> *John 14:14*
> *If you ask anything in My name, I will do it.*

2. His blood

Colossians 1:13–14
He has delivered us from the power of darkness and conveyed us into the kingdom of the Son of His love, in whom we have redemption through His blood, the forgiveness of sins.

It is this blood that has translated us from the kingdom of darkness into the Kingdom of Light. It has given us forgiveness.

Revelation 12:11
And they overcame him by the blood of the Lamb and by the word of their testimony, and they did not love their lives to the death.

The blood has given us the ability to overcome. We overcome by testifying what the blood has done for us. The blood has justified and redeemed us, forgiven us and reconciled us to God. The blood has redeemed us from bondage and the curse, and gives us freedom.

3. The Word

Hebrews 4:12
For the word of God is living and powerful, and sharper than any two-edged sword, piercing even to the division of soul and spirit, and of joints and marrow, and is a discerner of the thoughts and intents of the heart.

Jeremiah 23:29
"Is not My word like a fire?" says the Lord, "And like a hammer that breaks the rock in pieces?"

His Word is not only sharp, but it is like a fire and a hammer and can break anything.

2 Corinthians 10:4–5
For the weapons of our warfare are not carnal but mighty in God for pulling down strongholds, casting down arguments and every high thing that exalts itself against the knowledge of God, bringing every thought into captivity to the obedience of Christ.

The enemy comes and bombards your thoughts. When you do not deal with these thoughts, they lodge in your conscious mind. God has given you the weapons to pull down all strongholds. You need to take your authority in Christ and break these strongholds. Remember, you are armed and dangerous to the devil because Christ has clothed you with His victory on the cross of Calvary.

Ephesians 6:11–17
Put on the whole armor of God, that you may be able to stand against the wiles of the devil. For we do not wrestle against flesh and blood, but against principalities, against powers, against the rulers of the darkness of this age, against spiritual hosts of wickedness in the heavenly places. Therefore take up the whole armor of God, that you may be able to withstand in the evil day, and having done all, to stand. Stand therefore, having girded your waist with truth, having put on the breastplate of righteousness, and having shod your feet with the preparation of the gospel of peace; above all, taking the shield of faith with which you will be able to quench all the fiery darts of the wicked one. And take the helmet of salvation, and the sword of the Spirit, which is the word of God.

The armor that God supplied can never be penetrated or defeated. You must always be clothed with the armor of God. Paul was comparing the armor of a soldier to God's armor.

Belt of truth: holds the garment in position, holds things in place.

Truth is needed to know our position in Christ.

What is our position in Christ?

1. We are redeemed.

Colossians 1:13–14
He has delivered us from the power of darkness and conveyed us into the kingdom of the Son of his love, in whom we have redemption through His blood, the forgiveness of sins.

2. We are seated in heavenly places.

Ephesians 1:3
Blessed be the God and Father of our Lord Jesus Christ, who has blessed us with every spiritual blessing in the heavenly places in Christ.

3. We are joint heirs with Jesus Christ.

Galatians 4:6
And because you are sons, God has sent forth the Spirit of His Son into your hearts, crying out, "Abba, Father."

4. Greater is He that is in us than he that is in the world.

1 John 4:4
You are of God, little children, and have overcome them, because He who is in you is greater than he who is in the world.

5. As He is, so are we.

1 John 4:17
Love has been perfected among us in this: that we may have boldness in the day of judgment; because as He is, so are we in this world.

Breastplate: Your heart needs to know that you are in right standing in Christ.

Jesus became sin with our sinfulness that we can be made righteous with His righteousness.

2 Corinthians 5:21
For He made Him who knew no sin to be sin for us, that we might become the righteousness of God in Him.

Romans 3:22
Even the righteousness of God, through faith in Jesus Christ, to all and on all who believe. For there is no difference.

Feet: A soldier needs the correct shoes; otherwise he cannot march far, nor plant his feet firm. Likewise, we need the Gospel, the good news, to stand firm knowing that we belong to the Kingdom of God.

Romans 14:17
For the kingdom of God is not eating and drinking, but righteousness and peace and joy in the Holy Spirit.

Shield of Faith: You must have faith. Without faith, it is impossible to please God. We live by faith, and faith is trusting in the ability of God.

Hebrews 11:6
But without faith it is impossible to please Him, for he who comes to God must believe that He is, and that He is a rewarder of those who diligently seek Him.

Romans 1:17
For in it the righteousness of God is revealed from faith to faith; as it is written, "The just shall live by faith."

Helmet of Salvation: We must understand and know that when God saved us, it was a total salvation: spirit, soul, and body.

1 Thessalonians 5:23
Now may the God of peace Himself sanctify you completely; and may your whole spirit, soul, and body be preserved blameless at the coming of our Lord Jesus Christ.

On the cross of Calvary, salvation was provided for our spirit, soul, and body.

Sword: The sword is a defensive weapon. The sword of the Spirit is the Word of God.

Hebrews 4:12
For the word of God is living and powerful, and sharper than any two-edged sword, piercing even to the division of soul and spirit, and of joints and marrow, and is a discerner of the thoughts and intents of the heart.

Matthew 4:4
But He answered and said, "It is written, 'Man shall not live by bread alone, but by every word that proceeds from the mouth of God.'"

God has supplied us with His armor. Nothing can penetrate this armor.

Having established the fact that God has given us all the necessary weapons and armor to live a victorious life, now let us go deeper to understand the victory that was provided on the cross of Calvary for you and for me.

Flesh and Witchcraft

There are two major weapons the enemy uses against us:

1. Guilt

2. Witchcraft

Christ has set us free from guilt.

> *Romans 8:1*
> *There is therefore now no condemnation to those who are in Christ Jesus, who do not walk according to the flesh, but according to the Spirit.*

> *Galatians 3:1–5*
> *O foolish Galatians! Who has bewitched you that you should not obey the truth, before whose eyes Jesus Christ was clearly portrayed among you as crucified? This only I want to learn from you: Did you receive the Spirit by the works of the law, or by the hearing of faith? Are you so foolish? Having begun in the Spirit, are you now being made perfect by the flesh? Have you suffered so many things in vain—if indeed it was in vain? Therefore He who supplies the Spirit to you and works miracles among you, does He do it by the works of the law, or by the hearing of faith?*

Paul is speaking to Spirit-filled people who started in the Spirit but ended in the flesh. When we take our eyes off the finished work of the cross and Christ, we will be led by works, not by grace. This leads to carnality and legalism and is where sin sets in. When we talk about "the flesh," it means trying to do the works ourselves, and this always produces rules and regulations. The Galatians were trying to find favor with God by their works. In other words, they wanted to go back to the flesh and keep the law.

> *Jeremiah 17:5*
> *Thus says the LORD: "Cursed is the man who trusts in man and makes flesh his strength, whose heart departs from the LORD."*

> *Romans 6:14*
> *For sin shall not have dominion over you, for you are not under law but under grace.*

> *Romans 10:4*
> *For Christ is the end of the law for righteousness to everyone who believes.*

Trust in God, not in the flesh.

I am sure you have heard the word *occult*.

The occult includes:

- **Witchcraft**
- **Divination**
- **Sorcery**

1. Witchcraft

Witchcraft is imposing one's will upon another. It is mainly operated through the use of curses and spells.

The main aim of witchcraft is to try to take people's eyes off the cross of Calvary, because it is at the cross of Calvary that every work of witchcraft was broken.

2. Divination

Divination includes fortune-telling, tarot cards, and reading horoscopes.

Acts 16:16–18
Now it happened, as we went to prayer, that a certain slave girl possessed with a spirit of divination met us, who brought her masters much profit by fortune-telling. This girl followed Paul and us, and cried out, saying, "These men are the servants of the Most High God, who proclaim to us the way of salvation." And this she did for many days. But Paul, greatly annoyed, turned and said to the spirit, "I command you in the name of Jesus Christ to come out of her." And he came out that very hour.

The spirit of divination spoke through the slave girl and said the right things, but the apostle Paul perceived that the source of the spirit's manifestation was not God, but it was a demonic manifestation.

It is important for us to discern. That is why the Word of God tells us to be discerning.

1 John 4:1
Beloved, do not believe every spirit, but test the spirits, whether they are of God; because many false prophets have gone out into the world.

God is the only One who knows our future.

3. Sorcery

Sorcery includes charms, amulets, potions, drugs, music, etc.

Today, many young people are influenced by demonic music. The enemy has perverted the music world. The devil uses the music as a channel to transfer evil spirits into the lives of people. Be careful what type of music you allow in your home.

Paintings are the same. It is not the painting, but the spirit of the painter that comes into our homes. Our homes need to be cleansed and sanctified by the blood of Jesus.

Deuteronomy 18:10–12
There shall not be found among you anyone who makes his son or his daughter pass through the fire, or one who practices witchcraft, or a soothsayer, or one who interprets omens, or a sorcerer, or one who conjures spells, or a medium, or a spiritist, or one who calls up the dead. For all who do these things are an abomination to the LORD, and because of these abominations the LORD your God drives them out from before you.

Certain objects carry a demonic presence. When these objects are brought into the home, they bring a demonic spirit, similarly, the lyrics in some music opens the way for demonicactivity.

The occult always brings bondage and a curse to the individual. When you operate in the flesh, it opens the door for a demonic element to enter your life. People lose control and the demonic presence takes over. Witchcraft obscures the cross.

Hebrews 12:2
Looking unto Jesus, the author and finisher of our faith, who for the joy that was set before Him endured the cross, despising the shame, and has sat down at the right hand of the throne of God.

Do not take your eyes off the cross of Calvary, because it was at the cross that Jesus disarmed and defeated the enemy.

The apostle Paul asks the question: "Have you been bewitched?"

The occult includes witchcraft, divination, and sorcery. These things are very prevalent in today's society. If you have visited fortune-tellers or tarot card readers, these things must be renounced so God can break the evil consequences off your life.

Rebellion

The Word declares that rebellion is as witchcraft. Let us look at rebellion and stubbornness.

> *1 Samuel 15:23–24*
> *"For rebellion is as the sin of witchcraft, and stubbornness is as iniquity and idolatry. Because you have rejected the word of the LORD, He also has rejected you from being king." Then Saul said to Samuel, "I have sinned, for I have transgressed the commandment of the LORD and your words, because I feared the people and obeyed their voice."*

If you have seen rebellion, you have seen witchcraft. Rebellion is rebelling against God's righteous government. God is the One who gives us His authority and power to rule and reign righteously. When people want to rule but are not operating under God's government, they are forcing their will upon someone else. That is called rebelliousness.

Stubbornness

Stubbornness is a person making an idol out of their own opinion: *I will do it my way because my opinion is better than God's opinion and word.*

Galatians 5:19–21
Now the works of the flesh are evident, which are: adultery, fornication, uncleanness, lewdness, idolatry, sorcery, hatred, contentions, jealousies, outbursts of wrath, selfish ambitions, dissensions, heresies, envy, murders, drunkenness, revelries, and the like.

Witchcraft is described in the Word of God as:

1. Evil spiritual power

Galatians 3:1–5
O foolish Galatians! Who has bewitched you that you should not obey the truth, before whose eyes Jesus Christ was clearly portrayed among you as crucified? This only I want to learn from you: Did you receive the Spirit by the works of the law, or by the hearing of faith? Are you so foolish? Having begun in the Spirit, are you now being made perfect by the flesh? Have you suffered so many things in vain—if indeed it was in vain? Therefore He who supplies the Spirit to you and works miracles among you, does He do it by the works of the law, or by the hearing of faith?

2. Works of the flesh

Galatians 5:19–20
Now the works of the flesh are evident, which are: adultery, fornication, uncleanness, lewdness, idolatry, sorcery, hatred, contentions, jealousies, outbursts of wrath, selfish ambitions, dissensions, heresies.

Today many individuals operate in the realm of witchcraft through:

a. Manipulation

When parents manipulate their children, they break their self-confidence. Lead by example; do not manipulate. Manipulation becomes witchcraft because you are controlling someone else's will.

b. Intimidation

Intimidation can take various forms, including through words, acts, body language, etc.

Intimidation is a spirit that needs to be bound.

c. Domination

Many people dominate through not allowing others to participate or share.

One example is women not being allowed to do anything in the church. God made us equal, and the Word tells us to "submit to one another." If you have the fear of God, you will treat your spouse well, not dominate him or her, but speak in love and with grace.

We need to be very aware of the subtleties of the enemy.

Deliverance from Witchcraft

The only protection we have against witchcraft is the finished work of the cross of Calvary.

> **Romans 8:12–13** AMP
> *So then, brethren, we are debtors, but not to the flesh [we are not obligated to our carnal nature], to live [a life ruled by the standards set up by the dictates] of the flesh. For if you live according to [the dictates of] the flesh, you will surely die. But if through the power of the [Holy] Spirit you are [habitually] putting to death (making extinct, deadening) the [evil] deeds prompted by the body, you shall [really and genuinely)] live forever.*

We should not allow the flesh to dictate to us, but we should lead a Spirit-led life. If you allow the flesh to dictate terms to you, you will surely die. Putting the flesh to death is a continual process.

> **Romans 8:8**
> *So then, those who are in the flesh cannot please God.*

The flesh has an appetite.

> **Galatians 5:19–21** AMP
> *Now the doings (practices) of the flesh are clear (obvious): they are immorality, impurity, indecency, idolatry, sorcery, enmity, strife, jealousy, anger (ill temper), selfishness, divisions (dissensions), party spirit (factions, sects with peculiar opinions, heresies), envy, drunkenness, carousing,*

*and the like. I warn you beforehand, just as I did previously,
that those who do such things shall not inherit the kingdom
of God.*

These things are all works of the flesh, and they open the door
for the enemy to enter. They include anger, fear, resentment,
self-pity, and mood swings. The only solution to these things is
the cross of Calvary.

Galatians 5:24 AMP
*And those who belong to Christ Jesus (the Messiah) have
crucified the flesh (the godless human nature) with its passions
and appetites and desires.*

We must crucify the flesh, its appetite, and its passions. It is the
application of the finished work of the cross in our daily life that
keeps us free from the work of the flesh.

Romans 6:6
*Knowing this, that our old man was crucified with Him, that
the body of sin might be done away with, that we should no
longer be slaves of sin.*

Galatians 2:20
*I have been crucified with Christ; it is no longer I who live,
but Christ lives in me; and the life which I now live in the
flesh I live by faith in the Son of God, who loved me and gave
Himself for me.*

Galatians 5:24
*And those who are Christ's have crucified the flesh with its
passions and desires.*

How to apply the cross

We protect ourselves from witchcraft through the cross of Calvary.

1. Reckon yourselves dead to sin.

Romans 6:11
Likewise you also, reckon yourselves to be dead indeed to sin, but alive to God in Christ Jesus our Lord.

This is your death certificate. You must accept that your old man died on the cross. We are buried with Christ, and the life we live is now in Christ.

2. Arm yourself with the right mind-set.

Apply the Word of God to your life daily.

1 Peter 4:1–2
Therefore since Christ suffered for us in the flesh, arm yourselves also with the same mind, for he who has suffered in the flesh has ceased from sin, that he no longer should live the rest of his time in the flesh for the lusts of men, but for the will of God.

Arm yourself with the right attitude and mind-set. You must spend time in the Word and fill your heart and mind with His Word.

3. Establish your legal ownership and know that Jesus Christ is the legal owner.

Matthew 12:43–45
When an unclean spirit goes out of a man, he goes through dry places, seeking rest, and finds none. Then he says, 'I will return to my house from which I came.' And when he comes, he finds it empty, swept, and put in order. Then he goes and takes with him seven other spirits more wicked than himself, and they enter and dwell there; and the last state of that man is worse than the first. So shall it also be with this wicked generation.

Know that when you accepted the Lord and allowed Him to be the Lord of your life, He became your legal owner.

Therefore, give no room for the enemy to do as this verse states: the spirit returns to see whether the house it was living in is vacant. Fill your vessel with the Word and with prayer.

You must declare that Jesus Christ is the owner of your life. You belong to Jesus. Jesus is your owner.

Colossians 1:13–14
He has delivered us from the power of darkness and conveyed us into the kingdom of the Son of His love, in whom we have redemption through His blood, the forgiveness of sins.

We must stand our ground and say, "This vessel belongs to Jesus."

James 4:7
Submit to God. Resist the devil and he will flee from you.

Do not allow the devil to dictate terms to you. When the devil comes resist him and say, "It is written."

Blessed man versus cursed man

Jeremiah 17:5–8
Thus says the Lord: "Cursed is the man who trusts in man and makes flesh his strength, whose heart departs from the Lord. For he shall be like a shrub in the desert, and shall not see when good comes, but shall inhabit the parched places in the wilderness, in a salt land which is not inhabited. Blessed is the man who trusts in the Lord, and whose hope is the Lord. For he shall be like a tree planted by the waters, which spreads out its roots by the river, and will not fear when heat comes; but its leaf will be green, and will not be anxious in the year of drought, nor will cease from yielding fruit."

If we trust in and depend on the flesh, we will be cursed. Fleshly living will bring you under a curse and bondage. This scripture shows the difference between a cursed man and a blessed man. Do not rely on the arm of the flesh; rely on God.

Isaiah 61:3
To console those who mourn in Zion, to give them beauty for ashes, the oil of joy for mourning, the garment of praise for the spirit of heaviness; that they may be called trees of righteousness, the planting of the Lord, that He may be glorified.

God wants to deliver you. Once you have been delivered, you must stay delivered.

Let me share with you certain truths that will help you stay delivered:

- **Ask the Holy Spirit to show you the root cause of your problem.**

If you treat the root cause all the branches will die. Uproot them by the Name and the blood of Jesus.

- ## Build a strong spiritual wall around yourself

Proverbs 25:28
Whoever has no rule over his own spirit is like a city broken down, without walls.

We build this wall by the Word of God, prayer, and walking in the Spirit. If fear comes, quote the following scripture:

1 John 4:18
There is no fear in love; but perfect love casts out fear, because fear involves torment. But he who fears has not been made perfect in love.

The opposite of fear is love.

This adds another brick to the wall you are building. Keep speaking the Word.

If anger is a problem, you must replace that anger with God's Word. You say, "It is written."

2 Timothy 2:24
And a servant of the Lord must not quarrel but be gentle to all, able to teach, patient.

The opposite of anger is patience.

If you feel like complaining, speak the Word.

Philippians 2:14
Do all things without complaining and disputing.

The opposite of complaining is contentment.

You must know how to use the Word of God to build the wall around you.

When you walk in freedom and liberty through what Jesus has accomplished for you on the cross, it will produce divine worship in your life.

Philippians 3:3
For we are the circumcision, who worship God in the Spirit, rejoice in Christ Jesus, and have no confidence in the flesh.

Worship produces fellowship with God, and fellowship with God produces revelation.

Only those who have fellowship with God receive revelation. The only way to have fellowship is to worship God, and the only way you are going to worship God is when you have no confidence in the flesh.

Your protection from witchcraft only comes through the cross of Calvary. When you move away from the cross, you open yourself up to witchcraft. When you come to the cross, the blood of Jesus, the name of Jesus, and what Jesus has done on the cross protect you and watch over you.

Deliverance from
the Present Evil Age

The cross of Calvary not only gives us protection from witchcraft, but it gives us protection in the present evil age.

Galatians 1:4
Who gave Himself for our sins, that He might deliver us from this present evil age, according to the will of our God and Father.

1 John 4:3
And every spirit that does not confess that Jesus Christ has come in the flesh is not of God. And this is the spirit of the Antichrist, which you have heard was coming, and is now already in the world.

The spirit of antichrist is already in the world. Antichrist means "against the Anointed One."

1 John 2:15
Do not love the world or the things in the world. If anyone loves the world, the love of the Father is not in him.

Your eyes need to be on Jesus, not the things of the world.

James 4:4
Adulterers and adulteresses! Do you not know that friendship with the world is enmity with God? Whoever therefore wants to be a friend of the world makes himself an enemy of God.

The world cannot give you anything. Only God can give you what you need.

The word translated world means "ordered system", or "this order of things", thus, "the world".

> *Galatians 1:4*
> *Who gave Himself for our sins, that He might deliver us from this present evil age, according to the will of our God and Father.*

The word translated age means "period of time."

Why does God want to protect us from this world?

- ## Satan is the god of this world or age.

    > *2 Corinthians 4:3–4*
    > *But even if our gospel is veiled, it is veiled to those who are perishing, whose minds the god of this age has blinded, who do not believe, lest the light of the gospel of the glory of Christ, who is the image of God, should shine on them.*

- ## This age is coming to an end.

    > *Matthew 13:39–40*
    > *The enemy who sowed them is the devil, the harvest is the end of the age, and the reapers are the angels. Therefore as the tares are gathered and burned in the fire, so it will be at the end of this age.*

    > *Matthew 13:49*
    > *So it will be at the end of the age. The angels will come forth, separate the wicked from among the just.*

    > *Matthew 24:14*
    > *"And this gospel of the kingdom will be preached in all the world as a witness to all the nations, and then the end will come."*

James 5:7-8
Therefore be patient, brethren, until the coming of the Lord.
See how the farmer waits for the precious fruit of the earth,
waiting patiently for it until it receives the early and latter
rain. You also be patient. Establish your hearts, for the
coming of the Lord is at hand.

The Word clearly states this age is coming to a close. That is why we must share the good news with every human being on the face of the earth.

As we journey through this world we must know that:

a) Jesus died on the cross for us to cross over into His Kingdom.

b) We have not received the spirit of the world.

1 Corinthians 2:12
Now we have received, not the spirit of the world, but the
Spirit who is from God, that we might know the things that
have been freely given to us by God.

You must know that you have not received the spirit of the world, but the Spirit of God.

c) We have tasted the power of the next age.

Hebrews 6:4–6
For it is impossible for those who were once enlightened, and
have tasted the heavenly gift, and have become partakers of
the Holy Spirit, and have tasted the good word of God and
the powers of the age to come, if they fall away, to renew them
again to repentance, since they crucify again for themselves
the Son of God, and put Him to an open shame.

When you come to a knowledge of Christ and the finished work of Calvary, you will be enlightened because you are seated in heavenly places. God tells us that we are a "royal priesthood, a holy nation, a citizen of heaven" and have tasted the powers of the next age.

The cross of Calvary also protects us from self-centeredness.

The manifestations of self-centeredness are:

1. Pride

James 4:6
But He gives more grace. Therefore He says: "God resists the proud, but gives grace to the humble."

God hates pride, but when you are humble, God pours in His grace.

2. Ego

Denying yourself will rid you of ego.

3. Me and I

It should always be about Jesus, not us.

4. Nationalism

When you come to the cross, nationality does not matter, because you now belong to the Kingdom of God.

5. Racism

When people talk about racism, it is coming from self-centeredness. There is no place for it in the Kingdom of God. God is colorblind! The anointing has no color.

6. Heritage

God can use anyone for His glory. Heritage and education mean nothing to God because God sees the heart.

7. Attitude

Attitude is expressed through body language. You do not have to say much for people to know where you stand.

Let us look at an incident in the Word of God.

Luke 22:24–26
Now there was also a dispute among them, as to which of them should be considered the greatest. And He said to them, "The kings of the Gentiles exercise lordship over them, and those who exercise authority over them are called 'benefactors.' But not so among you; on the contrary, he who is greatest among you, let him be as the younger, and he who governs as he who serves.

We are here to serve. Jesus went where the need was not where it was comfortable. When God sees your servant heart He will bless you.

Matthew 20:22–26
But Jesus answered and said, "You do not what you ask. Are you able to drink, the cup that I am about to drink and be baptized with the baptism that I am baptized with?" They said to Him, "We are able." So He said to them, "You will indeed drink My cup, and be baptized with the baptism that I

*am baptized with; but to sit on My right hand and on My left
is not Mine to give, but it is for those for whom it is prepared
by My Father." And when the ten heard it, they were greatly
displeased with the two brothers. But Jesus called them to
Himself and said, "You know that the rulers of the Gentiles
lord it over them, and those who are great exercise authority
over them. Yet it shall not be so among you; but whoever
desires to become great among you, let him be your servant."*

Whenever we apply the cross of Calvary to our lives, the self-centeredness disappears. As you walk with God, He begins to bless you.

Genesis 22:16–17
*By Myself I have sworn, says the Lord, because you have done
this thing, and have not withheld your son, your only son—
blessing I will bless you, and multiplying I will multiply your
descendants as the stars of the heaven and as the sand which
is on the seashore; and your descendants shall possess the gate
of their enemies.*

God required Abraham's son of promise. Everything God gives us belongs to God, not to us.

Abraham did not have any fear because he knew that the same God who gave Him Isaac would raise his son again. God said He would bless Abraham in the midst of blessing.

Deuteronomy 7:14
*You shall be blessed above all peoples; there shall not be a
male or female barren among you or among your livestock.*

When you bring something back to God that He gave you, He will bless you in that blessing.

Self-centeredness holds you back from receiving God's blessing.

Let me take you to a statement that Paul the apostle made:

Galatians 2:20
I have been crucified with Christ; it is no longer I who live,
but Christ lives in me; and the life which I now live in the
flesh I live by faith in the Son of God, who loved me and gave
Himself for me.

How do we apply this scripture to our lives?

The apostle Paul had already made a decision. He was crucified with Christ, he had died to himself, and now it was Christ that lived in him by faith. When we apply this to our lives, strife will go and rest will come. Remember, we have nothing to prove— the proof is Calvary. When the enemy came to Jesus, He never defended who He was; He just said "..it is written."

We must live by the faith of the Son of God and know that He lives within us.

When you see, you see with His eyes; when you touch, you touch with His hands; when you walk, you walk with His feet; when you feel, you feel with His heart; when you speak, you speak His words.

The difference between the Spirit of God and the spirit of the world

1. **The Spirit of God brings truth.** The spirit of the world brings error.

2. **The Spirit of God will only glorify Jesus.** The spirit of the world will glorify the flesh.

    John 16:14
    He will glorify Me, for He will take of what is Mine and declare it to you.

    John 15:26
    But when the Helper comes, whom I shall send to you from the Father, the Spirit of truth who proceeds from the Father, He will testify of Me.

3. **The Spirit of God reveals the things of God**—the spirit of the world cannot comprehend anything of God.

    1 Corinthians 2: 12–14
    Now we have received, not the spirit of the world, but the Spirit who is from God, that we might know the things that have been freely given to us by God. These things we also speak, not in words which man's wisdom teaches but which the Holy Spirit teaches, comparing spiritual things with spiritual. But the natural man does not receive the things of the Spirit of God, for they are foolishness to him; nor can he know them, because they are spiritually discerned.

4. The Spirit of God will change you from glory to glory—the spirit of the world will make you more self-centered.

2 Corinthians 3:18
But we all, with unveiled face, beholding as in a mirror the glory of the Lord, are being transformed into the same image from glory to glory, just as by the Spirit of the Lord.

5. The Spirit of God does things that are eternal—the spirit of the world does things that are temporary.

2 Corinthians 4:17
For our light affliction, which is but for a moment, is working for us a far more exceeding and eternal weight of glory.

The cross of Calvary protects us from the spirit of the world by showing us that we belong to another kingdom; our King is Jesus Christ, the Son of the living God.

Matthew 4:17
From that time Jesus began to preach and to say, "Repent, for the kingdom of heaven is at hand."

This was the first message that Jesus preached.

Matthew 6:10
Your kingdom come. Your will be done on earth as it is in heaven.

God wants us to pray that His Kingdom will manifest in and through us here on earth.

Matthew 6:33
But seek first the kingdom of God and His righteousness, and all these things shall be added to you.

These verses show us the importance of belonging to the Kingdom of God.

> *Matthew 24:14*
> *And this gospel of the kingdom will be preached in all the world as a witness to all the nations, and then the end will come.*

The gospel of the kingdom must be preached because people must know the Kingdom of God and be citizens of that Kingdom.

> *John 18:36*
> *Jesus answered, "My kingdom is not of this world. If My kingdom were of this world, My servants would fight, so that I should not be delivered to the Jews; but now My kingdom is not from here."*

Jesus says that His kingdom is not of this world, and yet we embrace the things of the world. Everything in this world is temporal, but what God gives is eternal.

In the Kingdom of God, there is no sickness or disease.

> *Matthew 10:5–8*
> *These twelve Jesus sent out and commanded them, saying: "Do not go into the way of the Gentiles, and do not enter a city of the Samaritans. But go rather to the lost sheep of the house of Israel. And as you go, preach, saying, 'The kingdom of heaven is at hand.' Heal the sick, cleanse the lepers, raise the dead, cast out demons. Freely you have received, freely give."*

This is what the kingdom of God is all about.

Where the Kingdom of God is there is healing, liberty, and freedom.

Luke 9:1–2
Then He called His twelve disciples together and gave them
power and authority over all demons, and to cure diseases.
He sent them to preach the kingdom of God and to heal the
sick.

Let me share with you some Kingdom principles.

The Kingdom of God has:

1. Currency   → The name of the currency
                      is faith

2. Constitution   → Word of God

3. Communication   → Prayer

4. Coach   → Holy Spirit

5. Captain   → Jesus Christ

6. Conduct   → Beatitudes

7. Confession   → Citizens' profession
                      is confession

Let us look at a situation in which God protected His children in
the Old Covenant.

Daniel 3:14–18
Nebuchadnezzar spoke, saying to them, "Is it true, Shadrach,
Meshach, and Abed-Nego, that you do not serve my gods
or worship the golden image which I have set up? Now if
you are ready at the time you hear the sound of the horn,
flute, harp, lyre and psaltery, in symphony with all kinds of
music, and you fall down and worship the image which I
have made; good! But if you do not worship, you shall be
cast immediately into the midst of a burning fiery furnace.
And who is the god who will deliver you from my hands?

Shadrach, Meshach, and Abed-Nego answered and said to the king, "O Nebuchadnezzar, we have no need to answer you in this matter. If that is the case, our God whom we serve is able to deliver us from the burning fiery furnace, and He will deliver us from your hand, O king. But if not, let it be known to you, O king, that we do not serve your gods, nor will we worship the gold image which you have set up."

The results of not bowing to Nebuchadnezzar are found later in Daniel 3.

Daniel 3:23–25
And these three men, Shadrach, Meshach, and Abed-Nego, fell down bound into the midst of the burning fiery furnace. Then King Nebuchadnezzar was astonished, and he rose in haste and spoke, saying unto his counselors, "Did not we cast three men bound into the midst of the fire?" They answered and said to the king, "True, O king.""Look!" he answered, "I see four men loose, walking in the midst of the fire; and they are not hurt, and the form of the fourth is like the Son of God."

Nebuchadnezzar had his own world system, and he wanted the Hebrew young men to dance to the music of that world system. These men refused to bow down to the system of the world; they knew that God would deliver them. We have to be people of conviction who have seen and heard from God. When you do not bow to the world's system, God will walk with you. This is how the cross of Calvary protects us from the spirit of the world.

Finished Work of the Cross of Calvary

- Disarmed and Defeated Satan

- Protects Us From:
  - Flesh
  - Witchcraft
  - Present Evil Age
  - Self-Centeredness
  - Spirit of the World

Pesach - Faster than Time

Before we go any further, I would like you to understand the significance of the Passover. Everything in the Old Covenant is a type and shadow of what is to come in Christ Jesus.

Pesach or Passover

Both Rosh Hashanah and Pesach are celebrated at the beginning of the year. Many Jews believe Rosh Hashanah is the occasion of the new creation of the human as an individual and Pesach as a new creation of the Jewish people.

The psalmist described the events that took place after Pesach.

> *Psalm 105:37*
> *He also brought them out with silver and gold, and there was none feeble among His tribes.*

God brought the children of Israel out from slavery and bondage with silver and gold. There was not one person sick or feeble among them. Whatever condition they previously had was healed.

> *Exodus 12:1–14*
> *Now the LORD spoke to Moses and Aaron in the land of Egypt, saying, "This month shall be your beginning of months; it shall be the first month of the year to you. Speak to all the congregation of Israel, saying: On the tenth of this month every man shall take for himself a lamb, according to the house of*

his father, a lamb for a household. And if the household is too small for the lamb, let him and his neighbor next to his house take it according to the number of the persons; according to each man's need you shall make your count for the lamb. Your lamb shall be without blemish, a male of the first year. You may take it from the sheep or from the goats. Now you shall keep it until the fourteenth day of the same month. Then the whole assembly of the congregation of Israel shall kill it at twilight. And they shall take some of the blood and put it on the two doorposts and on the lintel of the houses where they eat it. Then they shall eat the flesh on that night; roasted in fire, with unleavened bread and with bitter herbs they shall eat it. Do not eat it raw, nor boiled at all with water, but roasted in fire—its head with its legs and its entrails. You shall let none of it remain until morning, and what remains of it until morning you shall burn with fire. And thus you shall eat it: with a belt on your waist, your sandals on your feet, and your staff in your hands. So you shall eat it in haste. It is the LORD's Passover. For I will pass through the land of Egypt on that night, and will strike all the firstborn in the land of Egypt, both man and beast; and against all the gods of Egypt I will execute judgment: I am the LORD. Now the blood shall be a sign for you on the houses where you are. And when I see the blood, I will pass over you; and the plague shall not be on you to destroy you when I strike the land of Egypt. So this day shall be to you a memorial; and you shall keep it as a feast to the LORD throughout your generations. you shall keep it as a feast by an everlasting ordinance.

Jesus fulfilled exactly what was written in Exodus 12. He became the Passover Lamb for you and for me.

The Passover is a unique and very significant feast. God ordained the Passover, the children of Israel observed it, Christ Jesus came and fulfilled it, but you and I must appropriate it.

1 Corinthians 5:7
Therefore purge out the old leaven, that you may be a new lump, since you truly are unleavened. For indeed Christ, our Passover, was sacrificed for us.

Even to this day, the Jews believe that during Passover a divine supernatural power is released for individuals who believe in God.

Why was this Passover night more significant than any other night? Because approximately three million Jews came out of slavery and bondage in a twinkling of an eye. They had been in slavery for four hundred years and had never known freedom in their lives. In just one night, God brought them out of bondage and slavery; debt and poverty were broken, and they began to walk in freedom and liberty.

God Himself carried them out of Egypt. All the other nights, they needed human protection, but that night they did not need protection because God Himself protected them.

Exodus 12:29
And it came to pass at midnight that the LORD struck all the firstborn in the land of Egypt, from the firstborn of Pharaoh who sat on his throne to the firstborn of the captive who was in the dungeon, and all the firstborn of livestock.

God Almighty did not send an angel to smite the firstborn; He Himself smote the firstborn of Egypt.

The events that took place during Passover occurred very quickly - "faster than time" according to a Jewish saying. The leaven did not have time to rise.

Exodus 12:39
And they baked unleavened cakes of the dough which they had brought out of Egypt; for it was not leavened, because they were driven out of Egypt and could not wait, nor had they prepared provisions for themselves.

Every time God struck Egypt with a plague and performed miracles, faith was growing in the hearts of the children of Israel. When they walked out of Egypt, they were able to believe because of the miracles they had seen, and they found it easy to walk in the supernatural. It should be natural for us to live in the supernatural.

Three things happened when they came out of Egypt:

→ God broke the spirit of slavery.

→ God broke the spirit of poverty.

→ God broke the spirit of sickness and disease.

Let us look at Jesus our Lord, the Passover Lamb.

> *Matthew 26:26–28*
> *And as they were eating, Jesus took bread, blessed, and broke it, and gave it to the disciples and said, "Take, eat; this is My body." Then He took the cup, and gave thanks, and gave it to them, saying, "Drink from it all of you. For this is My blood of the new covenant, which is shed for many for the remission of sins."*

Jesus Christ, our Passover Lamb, instructed His disciples to take and eat His body and then partake of His blood.

In the Old Covenant, the blood was applied first, pointing to the coming Redeemer. Jesus came and said, "Take eat of My body (first) and then take the blood." Why? When the Redeemer came, He was saying, "Come and feast on Me, and when you feast on Me, you will have My blood." In the Old Covenant, they celebrated Passover every year. Today we can celebrate Passover every day because we have Jesus living in us and He is the Passover Lamb.

Hebrews 8:6
But now He has obtained a more excellent ministry, inasmuch as He is also Mediator of a better covenant, which was established on better promises.

We have a better covenant based upon better promises.

Results of celebrating the Passover in the Old Covenant:

1. They had divine protection for their homes.

Exodus 12:13
Now the blood shall be a sign for you on the houses where you are. And when I see the blood, I will pass over you; and the plague shall not be on you to destroy you when I strike the land of Egypt.

2. There was not one feeble person in their house.

Psalm 105:37
He also brought them out with silver and gold, and there was none feeble among His tribes.

3. God's judgment was removed.

Exodus 12:29
And it came to pass at midnight that the LORD struck all the firstborn in the land of Egypt, from the firstborn of Pharaoh who sat on his throne to the firstborn of the captive who was in the dungeon, and all the firstborn of livestock.

God judged Egypt by smiting the firstborn of Egypt and not the firstborn Israelite, because the Passover blood protected the Israelites.

4. Divine deliverance for their homes was accomplished.

Exodus 12:27
*That you shall say, "It is the Passover sacrifice of the LORD,
who passed over the houses of the children of Israel in Egypt
when He struck the Egyptians and <u>delivered our households</u>.
So the people bowed their heads and worshiped.*

5. There was worship and adoration in their hearts.

Exodus 12:27
*That you shall say, "It is the Passover sacrifice of the LORD,
who passed over the houses of the children of Israel in Egypt
when He struck the Egyptians and delivered our households.
So <u>the people bowed their heads and worshiped</u>.*

6. His presence was with them.

Exodus 12:32
*Also take your flocks and your herds, as you have said, and be
gone; and bless me also.*

Pharaoh recognized that God was with Moses.

7. Transference of wealth took place from the Egyptians to the children of Israel.

Exodus 12:35–36
*Now the children of Israel had done according to the word
of Moses, and they had asked from the Egyptians articles of
silver, articles of gold, and clothing. And the LORD had given
the people favor in the sight of the Egyptians, so that they
granted them what they requested. Thus they plundered the
Egyptians.*

The children of Israel were asking their masters for their goods. The Egyptians had been through all the plagues by now, and all they wanted was to be left alone. They gave their neighbors everything they asked for.

If God can do all this under the Old Covenant, how much more will He do these things for us under the New Covenant?

The children of Israel were thrust out of Egypt very quickly: Even the leaven did not have time to rise.

Exodus 12:39
   And they baked unleavened cakes of the dough which they had brought out of Egypt; for it was not leavened, because they were driven out of Egypt, and could not wait, nor had they prepared provisions for themselves.

I would like to bring this to your notice: After they celebrated the Passover, the events that took place by the hand of God for the children of Israel happened "faster than time". God has not changed. In Christ He can do the same for you.

When the children of Israel celebrated the Passover:

1. Supernatural energy was released from the hand of God.
2. There was not one feeble person among them.
3. There was a brand-new opportunity given to the children of God.
4. There was a time of new beginning, from slavery to freedom.
5. It was a time for a new spiritual life.
6. It was a time to be inspired.
7. It was a time to reach out for impossible things.
8. Things happened faster than time.

Every time we partake of the body and the blood of our Lord Jesus Christ, who is our Passover Lamb, we must and should expect these things to take place in our lives.

Communion in His body and blood, and tithing

> *Genesis 14:18–20*
> *Then Melchizedek king of Salem brought out bread and wine, he was the priest of the Most High God. And he blessed him and said: "Blessed be Abram of God Most High, Possessor of heaven and earth; and blessed be God Most High, who has delivered Your enemies into Your hand." And he gave him a tithe of all.*

Just like our Passover Lamb, Christ Jesus, Melchizedek offers bread and wine to Abram. The Word of God says that Jesus Christ is after the order of Melchizedek.

> *Hebrews 5:6*
> *As He also says in another place: "You are a priest forever according to the order of Melchizedek."*

After partaking of the bread and wine, Abram gave Melchizedek tithes of all. Communion and tithing go hand in hand. Abraham not only celebrated a type of Passover, but that day he began investing in the highest investment opportunity known to mankind.

There is a link between communion and the tithe. Every time you feast on the Passover, you say, "Here I am, Lord. I bring everything to You."

Likewise, when we celebrate Jesus Christ as our Passover Lamb, we should expect to walk in divine health and to be free from bondage and poverty. This is part of the exchange that took place at the cross of Calvary.

*Consider Calvary,
It Is Perfect in Every
Aspect and Respect.*

The Cross of Calvary
Provides Us
with a Challenge

The Challenge
of the Cross

The cross of Calvary provides us with a challenge. When God is on the throne all is well but there are some things that we must do.

> *Matthew 16:24–26*
> *Then Jesus said to His disciples, "If anyone desires to come after Me, let him deny himself, and take up his cross, and follow Me. For whoever desires to save his life will lose it, but whoever loses his life for My sake will find it. For what profit is it to a man if he gains the whole world, and loses his own soul? Or what will a man give in exchange for his soul?"*

The word translated life is the Greek word for "soul."

> *John 12:24–25*
> *Most assuredly, I say to you, Unless a grain of wheat falls into the ground and dies, it remains alone; but if it dies, it produces much grain. He who loves his life will lose it, and he who hates his life in this world will keep it for eternal life.*

We need to let go of all the things that are holding us back and let God be God. As long as we hold on to things, life cannot come out and God can do nothing.

> *Luke 14:26–27, 33*
> *If anyone comes to Me and does not hate his father and mother, wife and children, brothers and sisters ,yes, and his own life also, he cannot be My disciple. And whoever does not bear his cross and come after Me cannot be My disciple.*

So likewise, whoever of you does not forsake all that he has cannot be My disciple.

There are no exceptions to what Jesus says in this verse. Every day we have the choice to pick up our cross. Jesus said we must forsake all if we want to be His disciple.

Matthew 10:34–39
"Do not think that I came to bring peace on earth. I did not come to bring peace but a sword. For I have come to "set a man against his father, a daughter against her mother, and a daughter-in-law against her mother-in-law'; and 'a man's enemies will be those of his own household.' He who loves father or mother more than Me is not worthy of Me. And he who loves son or daughter more than Me is not worthy of Me. And he who does not take his cross and follow after Me is not worthy of Me. He who finds his life will lose it, and he who loses his life for My sake will find it."

When you give your life to Christ, many times the first people who will come against you are those in your household. When you decide to follow Jesus, there is a clear division between those who walk with the Lord and those who do not. There is already coming a division between the churches, between those who preach Christ crucified and His blood and those who compromise and preach the spirit of the world.

Jesus is not asking you to literally hate your father or mother. Jesus is saying that the love you have for others is to be insignificant when compared to the love that you have for Him, because your loyalty must be with Christ alone. The love for the Lord must be so intense and so great that when you compare the love that you have for your husband, wife, or anyone else, it is insignificant. When you make an idol out of anything, God will destroy it. But when you put God first He will give you everything.

Give your soul to Jesus, and you will find life. Your soul is comprised of your will, emotions, and reason. To lose your soul for Jesus' sake means to say, "Not my will, but God's will." We must bring everything under subjection to His ways. When you lose your soul in Him, you will find life, and when you surrender to His will, His ways, and His Word, then He will lead you to life more abundantly.

> *Romans 14:17*
> *For the kingdom of God is not eating and drinking, but righteousness and peace and joy in the Holy Spirit.*

> *Romans 5:11*
> *And not only that, but we also rejoice in God through our Lord Jesus Christ, through whom we have now received the reconciliation.*

> *Habakkuk 3:17–18*
> *Though the fig tree may not blossom, nor fruit be on the vines; though the labor of the olive may fail, and the fields yield no food; though the flock may be cut off from the fold, and there be no herd in the stalls—yet I will rejoice in the Lord, I will joy in the God of my salvation.*

There is nothing to be happy about in verse 17. Circumstances were grim, but Habakkuk made a decision to rejoice in the Lord and to draw his joy from the God of his salvation. The decision must be made to draw from that well that never runs dry, regardless of the situation or circumstances. It is all about choices and decisions.

> *Luke 9:23*
> *Then He said to them all, "If anyone desires to come after Me, let him deny himself, and take up his cross daily, and follow Me."*

To deny yourself means to say "no" to yourself. The cross is where your will and God's will intersect. The cross is an instrument of death. Again, it is about choice.

Genesis 22:16–17
By Myself I have sworn, says the LORD, because you have done this thing, and have not withheld your son, your only son— blessing I will bless you, and multiplying I will multiply your descendants as the stars of the heaven and as the sand which is on the seashore; and your descendants shall possess the gate of their enemies.

In these verses we see that God blessed and multiplied the seed of Abraham because he placed his only son on the altar.

Everything must be put on the altar, because God cannot anoint what we hold on to.

The cross of Calvary will cost you everything. It is not my will; it is His will. Keep your eyes on Jesus in order to have life. The challenge of the cross is the love we have for Jesus—it must be greater than any other love that we have.

*Consider Calvary,
It Is Perfect in Every
Aspect and Respect.*

Section Four

The Cross of Calvary
Reveals God's
Unconditional Love to Us

The cross of Calvary demonstrates and reveals the love of God.

The cross of Calvary provides us with a challenge that we must appropriate every day to walk in His life.

> **John 3:16**
> *For God so loved the world that He gave His only begotten Son, that whoever believes in Him should not perish but have everlasting life.*

Jesus is different from any other person who has ever walked the face of the earth. He did not just talk about love, but He acted out love on the cross of Calvary.

> **Deuteronomy 7:6–8**
> *For you are a holy people to the LORD your God. The LORD your God has chosen you to be a people for Himself, a special treasure above all the peoples on the face of the earth. The LORD did not set His love on you nor choose you because you were more in number than any other people, for you were the least of all peoples; but because the LORD loves you, and because He would keep the oath which He swore to your fathers, the LORD has brought you out with a mighty hand, and redeemed you from the house of bondage, from the hand of Pharaoh king of Egypt.*

We have been chosen by God, and we are special.

Matthew 13:44–46
Again, the kingdom of heaven is like treasure hidden in a
field, which a man found and hid; and for joy over it he
goes and sells all that he has and buys that field. Again,
the kingdom of heaven is like a merchant seeking beautiful
pearls, who, when he had found one pearl of great price, went
and sold all that he had and bought it.

In this parable, the man is Christ Jesus, the field is the world, and the treasure is you and me. What the parable is describing is that God paid a price with His life to purchase us, whom God calls treasures.

When God looks at you, He sees the treasure that He has placed inside of you. You may think that you are worthless, but God knows there is treasure there. When God redeemed you, He purchased everything your life contained; past, present, and future. He bought everything. That is how much value God has put on your life.

We measure love and affection by what others say, but we need to acknowledge God's love. A merchant knows the value of the goods he is going to buy. You are that pearl of great price. God gave His very best on the cross of Calvary to buy that pearl. He is able to keep you, nourish you, protect you, and provide for you.

Hebrews 12:2
Looking unto Jesus, the author and finisher of our faith,
who for the joy that was set before Him endured the cross,
despising the shame, and has sat down at the right hand of
the throne of God.

This scripture verse talks about "the joy that was set before Him." What was that joy? The joy was to see us redeemed and made the children of the Most High God.

When He was on the cross of Calvary, He was saying, "I am buying the pearl." That is how valuable you are. A pearl is not only precious, but it is beautiful, formed and fashioned by the hand of God. Remember, you are that pearl of great price.

> *Acts 20:28*
> *Therefore take heed to yourselves and to all the flock, among which the Holy Spirit has made you overseers, to shepherd the church of God which He purchased with His own blood.*

The price He paid to purchase you was His own blood.

> *Psalm 130:7*
> *O Israel, hope in the LORD; for with the LORD there is mercy, and with Him is abundant redemption.*

The redemption that Jesus brought is so much greater than what we can comprehend. The price of it was high. It cost God's Son His life. He suffered and died to purchase you and me.

Let me give you a picture of the cost of redemption, which demonstrates His love for us.

1. He suffered in the Garden of Gethsemane.

> *Luke 22:44*
> *And being in agony, He prayed more earnestly. Then His sweat became like great drops of blood falling down to the ground.*

2. They placed upon Him a crown of thorns.

> *Matthew 27:29*
> *When they had twisted a crown of thorns, they put it on His head, and a reed in His right hand. And they bowed the knee before Him and mocked Him, saying, "Hail, King of the Jews!"*

3. They smote Him with a reed.

Matthew 27:30
Then they spat on Him, and took the reed and struck Him on the head.

4. They scourged Him.

Matthew 27:26
Then he released Barabbas to them; and when he had scourged Jesus, he delivered Him to be crucified.

5. They pierced His hands.

Matthew 27:35
Then they crucified Him, and divided His garments, casting lots, that it might be fulfilled which was spoken by the prophet: "They divided My garments among them, and for My clothing they cast lots."

6. They pierced His feet.

Matthew 27:35
Then they crucified Him, and divided His garments, casting lots, that it might be fulfilled which was spoken by the prophet: "They divided My garments among them, and for My clothing they cast lots."

7. The soldiers pierced His side.

John 19:34
But one of the soldiers pierced His side with a spear, and immediately blood and water came out.

The cross of Calvary revealed to us God's great love. Remember, you are the pearl of great price.

Consider Calvary,
It Is Perfect in Every
Aspect and Respect.

The Cross of Calvary Provides Us with a New Covenant

The Blessing of the New Covenant

~ THE POWER OF THE COVENANT ~

The cross of Calvary provides us with a better covenant based upon better promises.

> *Hebrews 8:6*
> *But now He has obtained a more excellent ministry, insomuch as He is also Mediator of a better covenant, which was established on better promises.*

The Bible has two covenants—the Old Covenant and the New Covenant. There are sixty-six books in the Bible. They are divided between thirty-nine books in the Old Covenant and twenty-seven books in the New Covenant. Therefore the Word of God is a book of covenants. The New Covenant was hidden in the Old Covenant and the New Covenant reveals to us the Old Covenant.

God is the only One who can reveal the covenant because the covenant is sacred and holy.

> *Psalm 25:8–14*
> *Good and upright is the LORD; therefore He teaches sinners in the way. The humble He guides in justice, and the humble He teaches His way. All the paths of the LORD are mercy and truth, to such as keep His covenant and His testimonies. For Your name's sake, O LORD, pardon my iniquity, for it is great. Who is the man that fears the LORD? Him shall He teach in the way He chooses. He Himself shall dwell in prosperity, and his descendants shall inherit the earth. The secret of the*

LORD *is with those who fear Him, and He will show them His covenant.*

Those who know their covenant with God will walk in victory, because we know that we have an agreement that cannot be broken. Psalm 25 clearly states that the secret that lies within the covenant is only revealed to those people who are meek, who are humble, and who fear God. Meek people are those who depend on God for everything. We must be humble according to His ways. When you understand the covenant, you will never be defeated.

Four basic principles of a covenant:

1. The covenant requires two parties.

2. A covenant is binding.

3. A covenant is holy and sacred.

4. A covenant is ratified by a sacrifice.

The world breaks agreements, but when God makes an agreement with us, He stands by us and makes a covenant with us forever. The word covenant means "strong agreement."

Psalm 50:5
"Gather My saints together to Me, those who have made a covenant with Me by sacrifice."

God will gather all those who have made a covenant based upon sacrifice.

Let me explain to you about the power of the covenant.

Genesis 15:7–18
*Then He said to him, "I am the L*ORD*, who brought you out of Ur of the Chaldeans, to give you this land to inherit it." And he said, "L*ORD *God, how shall I know that I will inherit it?" So He said to him, "Bring Me a three-year-old heifer, a three-year-old female goat, a three-year-old ram, a turtledove, and young pigeon." Then he brought all these to Him and cut them in two, down the middle, placed each piece opposite the other, but he did not cut the birds in two. And when the vultures came down on the carcasses, Abram drove them away. Now when the sun was going down, a deep sleep fell upon Abram; and behold, horror and great darkness fell upon him. Then He said to Abram: "Know certainly that your descendants will be strangers in a land that is not theirs, and will serve them, and they will afflict them four hundred years. And also the nation whom they serve I will judge; afterward they shall come out with great possessions. Now as for you, you shall go to your fathers in peace; you shall be buried at a good old age. But in the fourth generation they shall return here, for the iniquity of the Amorites is not yet complete. And it came to pass, when the sun went down and it was dark, that behold, there appeared a smoking oven and a burning torch that passed between those pieces. On the same day the L*ORD *made a covenant with Abram, saying: "To your descendants I have given this land, from the river of Egypt to the great river, the River Euphrates."*

In Genesis 15:7 God told Abram that He would give him this land. Abram's reaction was to ask God how he would know that God would give it to him. God answered by entering into a covenant with Abram, and at that moment the covenant was established. After the covenant was established, God stated in

Genesis 15:18 that He had given Abram the land. This is the power of covenant.

Christ invites us to accept Him and enter a new covenant with Him. He invites us with great promises such as eternal life and healing. The moment we receive Him and enter into the new covenant, the Word states that we have received eternal life and we are healed.

> *1 John 5:13*
> *These things I have written to you who believe in the name of the Son of God, that you may know that you have eternal life, and that you may continue to believe in the name of the Son of God.*

> *1 Peter 2:24*
> *Who Himself bore our sins in His own body on the tree, that we, having died to sins, might live for righteousness—by whose stripes you were healed.*

I want you to see the power of the covenant.

When we ask God when it will happen, we need to look to the cross. Covenant establishes the fact that He has already given it to you.

> *Hebrews 12:2*
> *Looking unto Jesus, the author and finisher of our faith, who for the joy that was set before Him endured the cross, despising the shame, and has sat down at the right hand of the throne of God.*

When two people make a covenant, they say, "All that I have is yours, and all that you have is mine." Abraham realized that everything he had belonged to God because he had a covenant with God. We also must walk in that truth.

The Blessing of
the New Covenant

~ THE COVENANT REMINDS GOD OF US ~

Covenant changed the name.

Genesis 15:18
On the same day the LORD made a covenant with Abram, saying, "To your descendants I have given this land, from the river of Egypt to the great river, the River Euphrates."

The Word of God states it is a "covenant."

In Genesis 17:4 the Word of God states it is "My covenant."

Genesis 17:1–8
When Abram was ninety-nine years old, the LORD appeared to Abram and said to him, "I am Almighty God; walk before Me and be blameless. And I will make My covenant between Me and you, and will multiply you exceedingly." Then Abram fell on his face, and God talked with him, saying: "As for Me, behold, My covenant is with you, and you shalt be a father or many nations. No longer shall your name be called Abram, but your name shall be Abraham; for I have made you a father of many nations. I will make you exceedingly fruitful; and I will make nations of you, and kings shall come from you. And I will establish My covenant between Me and you and your descendants after you in their generations, for an everlasting covenant, to be God to you and your descendants after you. Also I give to you and your descendants after you the land in which you are a stranger, all the land of Canaan, as an everlasting possession; and I will be their God."

In Genesis 15, God talks about **a** covenant, but in Genesis 17, He is talking about **My** covenant. What has happened? **My** covenant becomes an everlasting covenant that lasts forever. God has established **My** covenant to be our God and He wants us to be His people. Covenant establishes relationship.

When God established the covenant with Abram, He changed his name to Abraham. The name change was important. Abram means "exalted father," but Abraham means "father of many nations."

> *2 Corinthians 5:17*
> *Therefore, if anyone is in Christ, he is a new creation; old things have passed away; behold, all things have become new.*

God gives you a new identity when you give your life to Him, because His covenant changes your name.

Let me explain the concept of the covenant.

> *Genesis 17:9–11*
> *And God said to Abraham: "As for you, you shall keep My covenant, you and your descendants after you throughout their generations. This is My covenant which you shall keep, between Me and you and your descendants after you: Every male child among you shall be circumcised; and you shall be circumcised in the flesh of your foreskins, and it shall be a sign of the covenant between Me and you."*

Where there is a covenant, there has to be a sacrifice. Circumcision is a sign; the blood has been shed through circumcision, but there is no sacrifice. Where is the sacrifice? Sacrifice would come through the seed of Abraham, the perfect sacrifice made by God's Son, Jesus. He would establish the New Covenant.

Covenant reminds the parties who have entered into the covenant of each other. Covenant reminds God of us.

Genesis 9:16
The rainbow shall be in the cloud, and I will look on it to remember the everlasting covenant between God and every living creature of all flesh that is on the earth.

Every time God sees the covenant, He remembers whom He made the covenant with.

Exodus 2:24
So God heard their groaning, and God remembered His covenant with Abraham, with Isaac, and with Jacob.

Exodus 6:5
And I have also heard the groaning of the children of Israel whom the Egyptians keep in bondage, and I have remembered My covenant.

When the children of Israel were afflicted in Egypt, God remembered His covenant with them.

It was the covenant that made Him act.

Psalm 105:8
He remembers His covenant forever, the word which He commanded, for a thousand generations.

Psalm 106:45
And for their sake He remembered His covenant, and relented according to the multitude of His mercies.

These scriptures clearly indicate that the covenant makes God remember us.

The covenant causes you and me to remember God.

Deuteronomy 8:18
And you shall remember the Lord *thy God, for it is He who*
gives you power to get wealth, that He may establish His
covenant which He swore to your fathers, as it is this day.

This reminds us not to forget God. God blesses us because of
the covenant.

1 Corinthians 11:25
In the same manner He also took the cup after supper, saying,
"This cup is the new covenant in My blood. This do, as often
as you drink it, in remembrance of Me."

When we partake in communion of the New Covenant, we
remember the great God of heaven who has entered into a
covenant with you and me.

The strength of the covenant depends on the commitment.

Psalm 89:34
My covenant I will not break, nor alter the word that has
gone out of My lips.

God will not break or alter the words that He has spoken,
because He has made a covenant. Our trust must be in almighty
God, not in things of this world.

Psalm 89:28
My mercy I will keep for him forever, and My covenant shall
stand firm with him.

The next scripture explains the strong commitment of the parties
to the covenant they have entered into.

Exodus 32:10–14
"Now therefore, let Me alone, that My wrath may burn hot
against them and I may consume them. And I will make of
you a great nation." Then Moses pleaded with the LORD *his*
God, and said: "LORD, *why does Your wrath burn hot against*
Your people whom You have brought out of the land of Egypt
with great power and with a mighty hand? Why should the
Egyptians speak, and say, 'He brought them out to harm
them, to kill them in the mountains, and to consume them
from the face of the earth'? Turn from Your fierce wrath, and
relent from this harm to Your people. Remember Abraham,
Isaac, and Israel, Your servants, to whom You swore by Your
own self, and said to them, 'I will multiply your descendants
as the stars of heaven; and all this land that I have spoken
of I will give to your descendants, and they shall inherit it
forever.'" So the LORD *relented from the harm which He said*
He would do to His people.

We see that God was angry and He wanted to consume the
children of Israel and begin again with Moses. Moses brought to
His attention the covenant that God had made with Abraham,
Isaac, and Israel. The result was that the Lord repented. I
want you to see the strength of the covenant. Remember, the
covenant you and I have with God will stand fast.

The New Covenant

Hebrews 9:14–17
How much more shall the blood of Christ, who through the
eternal Spirit offered Himself without spot to God, cleanse
your conscience from dead works to serve the living God?
And for this reason He is the Mediator of the new covenant,
by means of death, for the redemption of the transgressions
under the first covenant, that those who are called may receive
the promise of the eternal inheritance. For where there is a
testament, there must also of necessity be the death of the

> *testator. For a testament is in force after men are dead, since it has no power at all while the testator lives.*

This is the New Covenant that we have entered into through the cross of Calvary. There is the eternal Spirit and eternal inheritance in the covenant. The eternal inheritance means that it does not stop. We not only have everlasting life, but all that belongs to Jesus is ours!

The Heavenly Will

The **will** cannot be enforced unless the person who made the **will** dies.

Hebrews 9:17
For a testament is in force after men are dead, since it has no power at all while the testator lives.

Christ died on the cross of Calvary so that we can enjoy the "new will" or "new covenant."

I want to share an incident that took place a number of years ago, so that you will understand the benefits of a "new covenant" or "new will."

There was a man who lived in England. His dream was to sail to the United States. He worked hard to earn enough money to buy a ticket to sail to New York City. The day came and he boarded the ship, and the ship began to sail. Every day he would walk around the ship, and when he came to a certain spot where a large room was located, he would stop and look. He saw many passengers enjoying a wonderful selection of food in this room at different times. He was sad because all he had to eat was crackers and cheese, which he was carrying on board. Now the ship arrived at her destination, and the passengers were disembarking. Finally his turn came. The captain of the ship asked him if everything had been to his satisfaction. He answered, "Yes, sir."

Then the captain said, "We never saw you in that large room. You never came to enjoy a meal with us." He was a bit embarrassed, and replied, "I am sorry. I did not have sufficient funds to purchase any food." The captain was somewhat perplexed. "Sir, did you not know that when you purchased the ticket to sail, it included all the meals?"

There are many Christians who do not realize that all the promises in Christ are ours to enjoy because we have a "new will" or a "new covenant" that is enforced through the death of Christ on the cross of Calvary.

The Blessing of
the New Covenant

~ THE BLESSINGS OF THE ABRAHAMIC COVENANT ~

Let us look at certain covenants in the Word.

The Abrahamic Covenant

Genesis 1:26–28
Then God said, "Let Us make man in Our image, according
to Our likeness, let them have dominion over the fish of the
sea, over the birds of the air, and over the cattle, over all the
earth and over every creeping thing that creeps on the earth."
So God created man in His own image; in the image of God
He created him; male and female He created them. Then
God blessed them, and God said to them, "Be fruitful and
multiply; fill the earth and subdue it; have dominion over the
fish of the sea, over the birds of the air, and over every living
thing that moves on the earth."

God gave Adam dominion and authority, but Adam committed
treason and handed over this dominion and authority to the
enemy.

Matthew 4:8
Again, the devil took Him up on an exceedingly high
mountain, and showed Him all the kingdoms of the world
and their glory.

Here the enemy confirms what Adam gave him. God had to choose a man to bring back divine order to mankind, and He chose Abraham, who simply believed God and began to walk on the journey. God established a covenant with Abraham and bestowed blessings on him.

The Abrahamic Covenant has no curses, only blessings.

Genesis 17:5–8
"No longer shall your name be called Abram, but your name shall be Abraham; for I have made you a father of many nations. I will make you exceedingly fruitful; and I will make nations of you, and kings shall come from you. And I will establish My covenant between Me and you and your descendants after you in their generations, for an everlasting covenant, to be God to you and your descendants after you. Also I give to you and your descendants after you the land in which you are a stranger, all the land of Canaan, as an everlasting possession; and I will be their God."

Genesis 22:16–17
And said: "By Myself I have sworn, says the LORD, because you have done this thing, and have not withheld your son, your only son—blessing I will bless you, and multiplying I will multiply your descendants as the stars of the heaven and as the sand which is on the seashore; and your descendants shall possess the gate of their enemies."

Remember, covenant always gives and never withholds anything.

Descendants of Abraham, Isaac, Jacob, and the next generations walked under this covenant until God had to step in because of their transgressions.

Galatians 3:13–19
Christ has redeemed us from the curse of the law, having become a curse for us (for it is written, "Cursed is everyone who hangs on a tree"), that the blessing of Abraham might come upon the Gentiles in Christ Jesus, that we might receive

*the promise of the Spirit through faith. Brethren, I speak in
the manner of men: Though it is only a man's covenant, yet if
it is confirmed, no one annuls or adds to it. Now to Abraham
and his Seed were the promises made. He does not say, "And
to seeds," as of many, but as of one, "And to your Seed,"
who is Christ. And this I say, that the law, which was four
hundred and thirty years later, cannot annul the covenant
that was confirmed before by God in Christ, that it should
make the promise of no effect. For if the inheritance is of the
law, it is no longer of promise; but God gave it to Abraham by
promise. What purpose then does the law serve? It was added
because of transgressions, till the Seed should come to whom
the promise was made; and it was appointed through angels
by the hand of the mediator.*

The Law was added because of wrong living. God had to
introduce the Law to make them aware that they were sinning,
so He made a covenant with Moses.

Covenant with Moses

The Law that God gave to Moses includes Deuteronomy 28,
which has sixty-eight verses. The first fourteen verses are
blessings, and the rest of the fifty-four verses are curses.

Thus, the covenant that God made with Moses contains
blessings and curses.

The New Covenant

Galatians 3:22–29
*But the Scripture has confined all under sin, that the promise
by faith in Jesus Christ might be given to those who believe.
But before faith came, we were kept under guard by the
law, kept for the faith which would afterward be revealed.
Therefore the law was our tutor to bring us to Christ, that we*

might be justified by faith. But after faith has come, we are no longer under a tutor. For you are all sons of God through faith in Christ Jesus. For as many of you as were baptized into Christ have put on Christ. There is neither Jew nor Greek, there is neither slave nor free, there is neither male nor female; for you are all one in Christ Jesus. And if you are Christ's, then you are Abraham's seed, and heirs according to the promise.

Every time a person violated the covenant, they were punished. Jesus came and fulfilled the law and bore the punishment at Calvary.

Thereby He made available, for all those who would enter into the New Covenant through His death and resurrection, the enjoyment of all the blessings of Abraham.

Galatians 3:9
So then those who are of faith are blessed with believing Abraham.

Galatians 3:29
And if you are Christ's, then you are Abraham's seed, and heirs according to the promise.

Everything that God blessed Abraham with is ours in Christ Jesus. We now walk in a new covenant.

The New Covenant not only gives us the blessing of Abraham, but much more.

Before we look at the benefits of the New Covenant, I would like to bring the last verse of the Old Testament to your attention.

Malachi 4:6
And he will turn the hearts of the fathers to the children, and the hearts of the children to their fathers, lest I come and strike the earth with a curse.

The last word in the last verse of the Old Covenant is "curse."

By contrast, the last verse in the New Covenant is about grace.

Revelation 22:21
The grace of our Lord Jesus Christ be with you all. Amen.

The last verse in the New Covenant is about grace.

Grace never fails, grace is rich, and grace holds us up. The New Covenant is a covenant of grace and mercy.

The Blessing of
the New Covenant

Benefits of the New Covenant

The new covenant has blessed us with all spiritual blessings in heavenly places.

As I mentioned earlier, Deuteronomy 28 contains fourteen blessings. In Christ we have more than fourteen blessings; we are blessed with unlimited blessings.

1. We have unlimited blessings.

Let us comprehend the eternal blessings that are ours.

Ephesians 1:1–9
Paul, an apostle of Jesus Christ by the will of God, to the saints who are in Ephesus, and the faithful in Christ Jesus: Grace to you and peace from God our Father and the Lord Jesus Christ. Blessed be the God and Father of our Lord Jesus Christ, who has blessed us with every spiritual blessing in the heavenly places in Christ, just as He chose us in Him before the foundation of the world, that we should be holy and without blame before Him in love, having predestined us to the adoption as sons by Jesus Christ to Himself, according to the good pleasure of His will, to the praise of the glory of His grace, by which He made us accepted in the Beloved. In Him we have redemption through His blood, the forgiveness of sins, according to the riches of His grace which He made to abound toward us in all wisdom and prudence, having made

known to us the mystery of His will, according to His good pleasure which He purposed in Himself.

- He has blessed us with all spiritual blessings.
- He has chosen us.
- That we should be holy.
- We are without blame before Him in love.
- We have been adopted by Jesus Christ as the children of the most High God according to His will.
- We are accepted in the Beloved.
- We are redeemed.
- We have His wisdom and prudence.
- He has made known to us the mystery of His will.

2. We are joint heirs with Jesus.

James 2:23
And the Scripture was fulfilled which says, "Abraham believed God, and it was accounted to him for righteousness." And he was called the friend of God.

In Christ we are more than a friend to God—we are an heir of God.

Galatians 4:6–7
And because you are sons, God has sent forth the Spirit of His Son into your hearts, crying out, "Abba, Father!" Therefore you are no longer a slave but a son, and if a son, then an heir of God through Christ.

3. He has made us a new creature.

2 Corinthians 5:17
Therefore, if anyone is in Christ, he is a new creation; old things have passed away; behold, all things have become new.

We are a new species in Christ Jesus.

4. We have a Great High Priest over our covenant.

Hebrews 8:1
Now this is the main point of the things we are saying: We have such a High Priest, who is seated at the right hand of the throne of the Majesty in the heavens.

This High Priest lives forevermore.

5. The New Covenant has a mediator.

Hebrews 8:6–8
But now He has obtained a more excellent ministry, inasmuch as He is also Mediator of a better covenant, which was established on better promises. For if that first covenant had been faultless, then no place would have been sought for a second. Because finding fault with them, He says: "Behold, the days are coming, says the LORD, when I will make a new covenant with the house of Israel and with the house of Judah."

6. The New Covenant is based upon a new relationship.

Hebrews 8:9–10
"Not according to the covenant that I made with their fathers in the day when I took them by the hand to lead them out

of the land of Egypt; because they did not continue in My covenant, and I disregarded them, says the LORD. For this is the covenant that I will make with the house of Israel after those days, says the LORD: I will put My laws in their mind and write them on their hearts; and I will be their God, and they shall My people."

In this new relationship with God, He has written His laws in our hearts.

7. This covenant is guaranteed.

Hebrews 7:22
By so much more Jesus has become a surety of a better covenant.

Nothing in this world is guaranteed, because the world has no surety. There is only one covenant that is guaranteed because it is ratified by the blood of Jesus. God will do what He said He will do.

8. The blood of the Mediator of this covenant speaks for those who have entered into covenant with God.

Hebrews 12:24
To Jesus the Mediator of the new covenant, and to the blood of sprinkling that speaks better things than that of Abel.

The blood of Jesus speaks for us.

9. The New Covenant has made a way for us to walk into the Holy of Holies.

Hebrews 9:8
The Holy Spirit indicating this, that the way into the Holiest of All was not yet made manifest while the first tabernacle was still standing.

Hebrews 10:19
Therefore, brethren, having boldness to enter the Holiest by the blood of Jesus.

You can enter boldly into the Holy of Holies at any time and in any place.

10. We have an everlasting covenant.

Hebrews 13:20–21
Now may the God of peace who brought up our Lord Jesus from the dead, that great Shepherd of the sheep, through the blood of the everlasting covenant, make you complete in every good work to do His will, working in you what is well pleasing in His sight, through Jesus Christ, to whom be glory forever and ever. Amen.

To obtain the promises in the New Covenant, we must listen, learn, and obey

In order to appropriate the blessings of the New Covenant, we must walk by faith just like Abraham did.

Genesis 15:6
And he believed in the LORD, and He accounted it to him for righteousness.

Romans 10:17
So then faith comes by hearing, and hearing by the word of God.

Every time you hear, faith is being built into your heart. Faith is a person, and His name is Jesus.

Matthew 11:29
Take My yoke upon you and learn from Me, for I am gentle and lowly in heart, and you will find rest for your souls.

The more you learn of Jesus, the more you are going to have faith. Now you have to put faith into action and obey.

Romans 1:17
For in it the righteousness of God is revealed from faith to faith; as it is written, "The just shall live by faith."

God wants us to go from faith to faith. Faith must grow in us. We can only appropriate the promises of the covenant by faith.

Different Aspects of Faith

Common faith

Titus 1:4
To Titus, a true son in our common faith: Grace, mercy, and peace from God the Father and the Lord Jesus Christ our Savior.

Before you accepted Jesus, God had to give you faith to believe.

Ephesians 2:8
For by grace you have been saved through faith, and that not of yourselves; it is the gift of God.

God gave you supernatural faith, placed inside of you for you to be able to believe. Everyone who comes to Jesus has saving faith, the faith common to all believers. But saving faith must grow.

Little faith

Matthew 8:23–26
Now when He got into a boat, His disciples followed Him.
And suddenly a great tempest arose on the sea, so that the
boat was covered with the waves. But He was asleep. Then
His disciples came to Him and awoke Him, saying, "Lord,
save us! We are perishing! But He said to them, "Why are you
fearful, O you of little faith?" Then He arose and rebuked the
winds and the sea, and there was a great calm.

Jesus was in the boat with His disciples, just as He is in our boat
with us. Faith was right next to them in the boat, but still they
could not believe. Initially we might have little faith, but we must
grow in faith.

Faith for a while

Luke 8:13
But the ones on the rock are those who, when they hear,
receive the word with joy; and these have no root, who believe
for a while and in time of temptation fall away.

Many people have faith till they face a difficult situation. God
wants us to be consistent.

Strong in faith

Romans 4:17–20
(As it is written, "I have made you a father of many nations")
in the presence of Him whom he believed—God, who gives
life to the dead and calls those things which do not exist as
though they did; who contrary to hope, in hope believed, so
that he became the father of many nations, according to what
was spoken, "So shall your descendants be." And not being
weak in faith, he did not consider his own body, already dead
(since he was about a hundred years old), and the deadness

of Sarah's womb. He did not waver at the promise of God through unbelief, but was strengthened in faith, giving glory to God.

God sees everything before it happens. This had already happened in the spiritual realm. Abraham believed the impossible and believed against all hope that the promise would be appropriated. That means everything he could see with his natural eye was hopeless, but he chose to trust in the hope of God because he had a covenant with God. He did not look at the circumstances, but he looked at what God could do. That is what strong faith is all about.

Great faith

Matthew 8:5–10
Now when Jesus had entered Capernaum, a centurion came to Him, pleading with Him, saying, "Lord, my servant is lying at home paralyzed, dreadfully tormented." And Jesus said to him, "I will come and heal him." The centurion answered and said, "Lord, I am not worthy that You should come under my roof. But only speak a word, and my servant will be healed. For I also am a man under authority, having soldiers under me. And I say to this one, 'Go,' and he goes; and to another, 'Come,' and he comes; and to my servant, 'Do this,' and he does it." When Jesus heard it, He marveled, and said to those who followed, "Assuredly, I say to you, I have not found such great faith, not even in Israel!"

This man knew all about authority. He said to Jesus, "You speak the word, and it will be done". He did not limit Jesus. Great faith is when we take all the limits off our minds and allow God to be God.

Matthew 15:22–28
And behold, a woman of Canaan came from that region, and cried out to Him, saying, "Have mercy on me, O Lord, Son of David! My daughter is severely demon-possessed." But He answered her not a word. And His disciples came and urged Him, saying, "Send her away, for she cries out after us." But He answered and said, "I was not sent except to the lost sheep of the house of Israel." Then she came and worshiped Him, saying, "Lord, help me!" But He answered and said, "It is not good to take the children's bread and throw it to the little dogs." And she said, "Yes, Lord, yet even the little dogs eat the crumbs which fall from their masters' table." Then Jesus answered and said to her, "O woman, great is your faith! Let it be to you as you desire." And her daughter was made whole from that very hour.

Here we see that Jesus, our Lord, commended her on her faith and said, "Great is thy faith."

Have you realized that the centurion and this woman both were Gentiles? They were not accustomed to any Jewish customs or laws. Their faith was not based on the rituals or the laws of the Jews, but on Jesus. The object of their faith was Jesus. That is why they had great faith.

Faith must act

James 2:14–17
What does it profit, my brethren, if someone says he has faith but does not have works? Can faith save him? If a brother or sister is naked and destitute of daily food, and one of you says to them, "Depart in peace, be warmed and filled," but you do not give them the things which are needed for the body, what does it profit? Thus also faith by itself, if it does not have works, is dead.

Faith must be active. If it does not act, it is dead.

Consistent faith

Galatians 2:20
I have been crucified with Christ; it is no longer I who live,
but Christ lives in me; and the life which I now live in the
flesh I live by faith in the Son of God, who loved me and gave
Himself for me.

Paul shows us that he lived by consistent faith. He was not one day up and the next day down. He lived by divine, consistent faith in Jesus.

2 Timothy 1:13
Hold fast the pattern of sound words which you have heard
from me, in faith and love which are in Christ Jesus.

When you hear the word, hold it fast in faith and in love.

Hebrews 12:2
Looking unto Jesus, the author and finisher of our faith,
who for the joy that was set before Him endured the cross,
despising the shame, and has sat down at the right hand of
the throne of God.

Always look to Jesus for your faith—what He has started He will finish.

The word faith and faithfulness go hand in hand.

2 Timothy 2:2
And the things that you have heard from me among many
witnesses, commit these to faithful men who will be able to
teach others also.

You may not make an able man faithful, but you can make a faithful man able.

Faithfulness is an important ingredient in the Kingdom of God.

*Consider Calvary,
It Is Perfect in Every
Aspect and Respect.*

Section Six

The Cross of Calvary
Provides Us with
the Blood of God's Son

The Power of the Blood

~ THE IMPORTANCE OF THE BLOOD OF JESUS ~

The cross of Calvary has given us the blood of God's Son, Jesus.

We must know why the blood is so important

1. The blood has the ability to speak

> *Genesis 4:10*
> *And He said, "What have you done? The voice of your brother's blood cries out to Me from the ground."*

The blood of Jesus Christ speaks for us. The blood of Abel cried out for vengeance, but the blood of Jesus cries for mercy. The book of Revelation says that the martyrs' blood speaks.

One day I was in India and I could not pray in my room. God took me to this scripture, and I realized that the blood of Jesus speaks for me. As soon as I declared what the blood does for me, the powers of darkness were broken.

2. The blood has the ability to protect

> *Exodus 12: 13*
> *Now the blood shall be a sign for you on the houses where you are. And when I see the blood, I will pass over you, and the plague shall not be on you to destroy you when I strike the land of Egypt.*

The blood was applied for protection. If the blood of goats and calves can protect under the Old Covenant, how much more can the blood of Jesus protect you today?

3. The blood has the ability to cleanse

Exodus 29:20
Then you shall kill the ram, and take some of its blood and put it on the tip of the right ear of Aaron and on the tip of the right ear of his sons, on the thumb of their right hand and on the big toe of their right foot, and sprinkle the blood all around on the altar.

Leviticus 14:6
As for the living bird, he shall take it, the cedar wood and the scarlet and the hyssop, and dip them and the living bird in the blood of the bird that was killed over the running water.

Leviticus 14:14
The priest shall take some of the blood of the trespass offering, and the priest shall put it on the tip of the right ear of him who is to be cleansed, on the thumb of his right hand, and on the big toe of his right foot.

The blood of the bird and the animal was used to cleanse in the Old Covenant. Today God has given us the blood of Jesus, which has the ability to cleanse. If the blood of a bird has the ability to cleanse a leper, how much more will the blood of Jesus cleanse us from all plagues and sickness?

4. The blood has the ability to consecrate

Exodus 29:21
And you shall take some of the blood that is on the altar, and some of the anointing oil, and sprinkle it on Aaron and on

his garments, on his sons and on the garments of his sons with him; and he and his garments shall be hallowed, and his sons and his sons' garments with him.

The blood was applied to dedicate Aaron and his sons for God's service. When you are under the blood of Jesus, you are already dedicated and consecrated for His call.

Leviticus 8:30
Then Moses took some of the anointing oil and some of the blood which was on the altar, and sprinkled it on Aaron, on his garments, on his sons, and on the garments of his sons with him; and he consecrated Aaron, his garments, his sons, and the garments of his sons with him.

5. The blood has the ability to give us access to God's sanctuary

Leviticus 4:6
The priest shall dip his finger in the blood and sprinkle some of the blood seven times before the LORD, in front of the veil of the sanctuary.

Without the blood, they could not enter into the Holy of Holies. Today, we can enter the Holy of Holies any time and any place because of the blood of Jesus.

6. The blood brings the oil

Leviticus 14:17
And of the rest of the oil in his hand, the priest shall put some on the tip of the right ear of him who is to be cleansed, on the thumb of his right hand, and on the big toe of his right foot, on the blood of the trespass offering.

The blood was applied first, and then oil was placed upon it. If you want the anointing, declare the blood. It is the blood of Jesus that brings the anointing of God. Never do anything without first applying the blood of Jesus.

7. The blood has the ability to cleanse the dwelling places

Leviticus 14:51–53
And he shall take the cedar wood, the hyssop, the scarlet, and the living bird, and dip them in the blood of the slain bird and in the running water, and sprinkle the house seven times. And he shall cleanse the house with the blood of the bird and with the running water and the living bird, with the cedar wood, the hyssop, and the scarlet. Then he shall let the living bird loose outside the city in the open field, and make atonement for the house, and it shall be clean.

The blood of Jesus has the ability to cleanse your home. When you cleanse your home, sickness cannot remain. God brings the anointing into that place.

8. The soul of the flesh is in the blood

Leviticus 17:11–12
For the life of the flesh is in the blood, and I have given it to you upon the altar to make atonement for your souls; for it is the blood that makes atonement for the soul. Therefore I said to the children of Israel, "No one among you shall eat blood, nor shall any stranger who dwells among you eat blood."

The reason they were instructed not to eat the blood was because the life of the flesh is in the blood. The blood was to be treated as sacred.

9. The blood has the power to deliver

Zechariah 9:11, 16–17
"As for you also, because of the blood of your covenant, I will set your prisoners free from the waterless pit. The LORD their God will save them in that day, as the flock of His people. For they shall be like the jewels of a crown, lifted like a banner over His land—for how great is its goodness and how great its beauty! Grain shall make the young men thrive, and new wine the young women.

The blood of the covenant has the power to deliver you out of the pit.

We must have faith in the blood

Romans 3:25
Whom God set forth as a propitiation by His blood, through faith, to demonstrate His righteousness, because in His forbearance God had passed over the sins that were previously committed.

You must know and believe that the blood of Jesus is powerful, and when you apply the blood, by declaring what the Word says it will do for you, forgiveness will happen.

Hebrews 11:28
By faith he kept the Passover and the sprinkling of blood, lest he who destroyed the firstborn should touch them.

They had to have faith in the blood so that the plague would not touch their house or anyone that was inside. If you have faith in the blood, it will do whatever God has promised.

The Power of the Blood

~ THE BLOOD OF THE COVENANT ~

Let us look at the blood of the New Covenant

Matthew 26:26–28
And as they were eating, Jesus took bread, blessed and broke
it, and gave it to the disciples and said, "Take, eat; this is My
body." Then He took the cup, and gave thanks, and gave it to
them, saying, "Drink from it, all of you. For this is My blood
of the new covenant, which is shed for many for the remission
of sins."

Whenever you declare the blood of Jesus, you are declaring the
blood of the New Covenant.

What the blood of the New Covenant has done for us

1. The blood of the New Covenant has redeemed us

Ephesians 1:7
In Him we have redemption through His blood, the
forgiveness of sins, according to the riches of His grace.

His blood has given us redemption. The word redemption
means "bought back." Jesus paid with His blood to legally
purchase you back, and He is now your legal owner.

Acts 20:28

Therefore take heed to yourselves and to all the flock, among which the Holy Spirit has made you overseers, to shepherd the church of God which He purchased with His own blood.

God purchased every part of you at the cross—your strengths and your weaknesses.

Hebrews 9:12

Not with the blood of goats and calves, but with His own blood He entered the Most Holy Place once for all, having obtained eternal redemption.

Jesus redeemed us with His own blood. It is time for us to declare and appropriate the blood of Jesus, because He gave His own blood to give us eternal redemption.

Colossians 1:13–14

He has delivered us from the power of darkness and conveyed us into the kingdom of the Son of His love, in whom we have redemption through His blood, the forgiveness of sins.

The blood has brought us out of the kingdom of darkness into the Kingdom of Light. God will honor those who are in His Kingdom.

Jeremiah 15:21

"I will deliver you from the hand of the wicked, and I will redeem you from the grip of the terrible."

The enemy comes to rob, to destroy, and to kill, but God promised He would taken you out of his hand. The enemy has no legal authority over you because you have been redeemed by the blood of Jesus.

Isaiah 43:1

But now, thus says the LORD, who created you, O Jacob, and He who formed you, O Israel: "Fear not, for I have redeemed you; I have called you by your name; you are Mine."

God knows your name because He redeemed you. He takes legal ownership of us and says, "You are Mine." God knows you are His—and the enemy knows you belong to God.

We have a blood covenant with God, and He will honor that covenant. God heals the sinner because of His mercy, but He heals the child of God because of the covenant.

2. The blood of the New Covenant has forgiven us

The difference between man and God is that man may forgive but not forget, and when someone remembers what you have done, they will not trust you. When God forgives, He forgets, too.

Remember, forgiveness was obtained by the blood of Jesus.

Psalm 51:1–3
Have mercy upon me, O God, according to Your lovingkindness; according to the multitude of Your tender mercies, blot out my transgressions. Wash me thoroughly from my iniquity, and cleanse me from my sin. For I acknowledge my transgressions, and my sin is always before me.

David mentions three things—sin, iniquity, and transgressions. Sin is the evil thought of. For example, the moment a person lusts after a woman in his heart or mind, he has already sinned. Transgression is the act of sin. A person goes and acts out what they have thought about. Iniquity is living in sin. Now that sin becomes their lifestyle.

David asks God to blot out his transgressions. The blood has the power to go to the root cause of the sin and destroy that root. The blood has the power to cleanse you from your iniquity and sin.

Romans 3:25
Whom God set forth as a propitiation by His blood, through faith, to demonstrate His righteousness, because in His forbearance God passed over the sins that were previously committed.

Micah 7:19
He will again have compassion on us, and will subdue our iniquities. You will cast all our sins into the depths of the sea.

When God throws your sins into the depths of the sea, you should not go fishing anymore. If God does not want to remember, why do you want to remind yourself? When the enemy tries to bring guilt upon you, say, "It is written."

Isaiah 38:17
Indeed it was for my own peace that I had great bitterness; but You have lovingly delivered my soul it from the pit of corruption, for You have cast all my sins behind Your back.

When God forgives, God forgets.

1 John 1:7–9
But if we walk in the light as He is in the light, we have fellowship with one another, and the blood of Jesus Christ His Son cleanses us from all sin. If we say that we have no sin, we deceive ourselves, and the truth is not in us. If we confess our sins, He is faithful and just to forgive us our sins and to cleanse us from all unrighteousness.

3. The New Covenant blood has brought us near to God

Ephesians 2:13–19
But now in Christ Jesus you who once were far off have been brought near by the blood of Christ. For He Himself is our peace, who has made both one, and has broken down the middle wall of separation between us; having abolished in His flesh the enmity, that is the law of commandments contained in ordinances so as to create in Himself one new man from the two, thus making peace, and that He might reconcile them both to God in one body through the cross, thereby putting to death the enmity. And He came and preached peace to you who were afar off and to those who were near. For through Him we both have access by one Spirit to the Father. Now, therefore, you are no longer strangers and foreigners, but fellow citizens with the saints and members of the household of God.

You can now enjoy everything in God's house because you belong to that household. You have the legal right.

4. The blood of the New Covenant has reconciled us

Colossians 1:20
And by Him to reconcile all things to Himself, by Him, whether things on earth or things in heaven, having made peace through the blood of His cross.

We have been reconciled through the blood of His cross. The word reconciled means to bring you back to the same place or position that you previously had, a position of righteousness in God.

5. The blood of the New Covenant has sanctified you

1 Peter 1:2
Elect according to the foreknowledge of God the Father, in sanctification of the Spirit, for obedience and sprinkling of the blood of Jesus Christ: Grace to you and peace be multiplied.

Hebrews 13:12
Therefore Jesus also, that He might sanctify the people with His own blood, suffered outside the gate.

The word sanctification means separation in order to honor, worship and serve God.

6. The blood of the New Covenant cleanses

1 John 1:7
But if we walk in the light as He is in the light, we have fellowship with one another, and the blood of Jesus Christ His Son cleanses us from all sin.

As long as we walk in the light, the blood cleanses twenty-four hours a day.

7. The blood of the New Covenant justifies

Romans 5:9
Much more then, having now been justified by His blood, we shall be saved from wrath through Him.

8. The blood of the New Covenant has made us perfect

Hebrews 10:14
For by one offering He has perfected forever those who are being sanctified.

When God looks at His covenant people, He looks at you through the blood and sees you as perfect.

9. The blood of the New Covenant has made our conscience clean

Hebrews 9:14
How much more shall the blood of Christ, who through the eternal Spirit offered Himself without spot to God, cleanse your conscience from dead works to serve the living God?

The blood has made a way for us to serve God. Nothing can purge your conscience except the blood of Jesus. His blood is able to cleanse our conscious and subconscious minds.

Hebrews 10:19
Therefore, brethren, having boldness to enter the Holiest by the blood of Jesus.

You can enter into the Holy of Holies with boldness and confidence.

10. The blood of the New Covenant has great power

Hebrews 13:20–21
Now may the God of peace who brought up our Lord Jesus from the dead, that great Shepherd of the sheep, through the blood of the everlasting covenant, make you complete in every good work to do His will, working in you what is well pleasing in His sight, through Jesus Christ, to whom be glory forever and ever. Amen.

God raised Jesus from the dead, the sacrifice of the blood having sealed the eternal covenant with power. Because of what that sacrifice achieved, He now works in us do His good will.

239

11. The blood of the New Covenant has made us kings and priests

Revelation 1:5–6
And from Jesus Christ, the faithful witness, the firstborn from the dead, and the ruler over the kings of the earth. To Him who loved us and washed us from our sins in His own blood, and has made us kings and priests to His God and Father, to Him be glory and dominion forever and ever. Amen.

It is time to rise up and act like the kings and priests we have been made through the blood of Jesus. We often put ourselves down, but when we know who we are, we will stand tall and serve God as kings and priests.

12. The blood of the New Covenant makes way for the eternal Spirit

Hebrews 9:14
How much more shall the blood of Christ, who through the eternal Spirit offered Himself without spot to God, cleanse your conscience from dead works to serve the living God?

Hebrews 10:29
Of how much worse punishment, do you suppose, will he be thought worthy who has trampled the Son of God underfoot, counted the blood of the covenant by which he was sanctified a common thing, and insulted the Spirit of grace?

When you reject the blood, the Holy Spirit is grieved. When you declare the blood of Jesus in faith, the blessed Holy Spirit will be present.

13. The Holy Spirit bears witness to the blood of the New Covenant

1 John 5:6
This is He who came by water and blood—Jesus Christ; not only by water, but by water and blood. And it is the Spirit who bears witness, because the Spirit is truth.

The blood of the New Covenant brings heaven's power to act upon a situation in which the blood has been applied, appropriated, proclaimed, and confessed.

14. The blood of the New Covenant speaks when it hears the redeemed speak

Psalm 107:2
Let the redeemed of the LORD say so, whom He has redeemed from the hand of the enemy.

The moment you speak, God's blood speaks for you.

Revelation 12:11
And they overcame him by the blood of the Lamb and by the word of their testimony, and they did not love their lives to the death.

We overcome Satan by personally testifying to what the Word says the blood does for us.

Hebrews 12:24
To Jesus the Mediator of the new covenant, and to the blood of sprinkling that speaks better things than that of Abel.

The blood speaks when it hears the redeemed speak.

Build a Hedge

Ecclesiastes 10:8
He who digs a pit will fall into it, and whoever breaks through a wall will be bitten by a serpent.

Hebrews 9:19–20
For when Moses had spoken every precept to all the people according to the law, he took the blood of calves and goats, with water, scarlet wool, and hyssop, and sprinkled both the book itself and all the people, saying, "This is the blood of the covenant which God has commanded you."

It is important to build a hedge around you. This hedge is built by the blood of Jesus.

Serpents are biting Christians because they do not know how to build a hedge. Today we have the blood of Jesus and water, which is symbolic of the Word of God. Scarlet symbolizes the covenant, and hyssop is a weed they used for applying the blood. Today the hyssop is symbolic of our tongues. We apply the blood of Jesus by declaring it with our mouth.

We build a hedge by declaring what the Word says the blood will do for us. Every day we need to build this hedge around our home, family, children, finances, jobs, possessions, etc. When God saw the blood, He did not allow the plagues to touch His people.

Psalm 107:2
Let the redeemed of the LORD say so, whom He has redeemed from the hand of the enemy.

Revelation 12:11
And they overcame him by the blood of the Lamb and by the word of their testimony, and they did not love their lives to the death.

The blood of **Abel** was spilt on the earth—he did not give his life willingly.

The blood of **Jesus** was shed on the earth—He gave His life willingly.

The blood of **Abel** was spilt on earth.

The blood of **Jesus** was offered in heaven.

The blood of **Abel** cries out for vengeance.

The blood of **Jesus** cries out for mercy and intercedes for us.

When we speak and declare the blood of Jesus, it affects the atmosphere around us.

There are three heavens: The first heaven is the atmosphere; the second heaven is where the principalities and powers dwell, and the third heaven is where God dwells. Today we have the blood of Jesus to cleanse the heavens.

One day while in prayer, the blessed Holy Spirit began to teach me how to pray. I felt in my heart that I should place this prayer in your hands so that you will learn how to build a hedge in prayer and so that you and your household will prosper.

Prayer

1. Always start with the Word of God. The Word of God will set your heart and mind on the things of God.

2. As the Holy Spirit leads, sanctify the heavens by the blood of Jesus.

    E.g.: "Lord, thank You for Your blood that is able to cleanse, purify, and sanctify. I take Your precious blood and cleanse, purify, and sanctify the heavens."

3. Cleanse and sanctify the atmosphere around you by the blood of Jesus. This will remove every oppressive spirit in the atmosphere.

    E.g.: "I take the blood of Jesus and cleanse and sanctify the atmosphere where I am and also the places my family and I may enter this day and night."

4. It is important that you bring the path of your travel daily under the blood of Jesus.

    E.g.: "Lord, I bring the vehicles in which I and my family will be travelling and the path of our travel under the protection of the blood of Jesus. I also bring the vehicles and the drivers that will come across our path under the precious blood. Let Your hands and eyes be upon me and my household day and night so that no harm will come to us or our property in Jesus' name. Amen."

5. Declare and proclaim that the blood of Jesus Christ speaks for you and your household.

    E.g.: "I thank You, Lord, that the blood of Jesus intercedes and speaks for me and my household. It speaks:

    *   Total provision, total protection, divine health, and all spiritual blessings for me and my household.

- Mercy and grace for me and my household day and night.
- Our names before the throne of grace day and night."

6. Cover your name and the names of your family members by the blood of Jesus. Remember, names represent the person, so many will be using your name. That is why the name must be protected by the blood of Jesus.

   E.g.: "Lord, I thank You for the protection that we have in the blood of Jesus. I cover my name and the names of my family members under the precious blood of Jesus for protection."

7. It is important to proclaim that we have been redeemed by the blood of Jesus from the powers of darkness into the Kingdom of His Son, Jesus.

   E.g.: "Lord, I thank You the blood of Jesus has redeemed me and my household from the powers of darkness into the Kingdom of His Son, Jesus. The blood of Jesus has redeemed me and my household from sickness, disease, and plagues and into divine health; from poverty to prosperity; from curses to the blessing of Abraham."

8. Finally, do not forget to bring your mind, memory, conscious, and subconscious under the blood of Jesus. As the Word says in Hebrews 9:14, only the blood of Jesus is able to cleanse our conscience from dead works to serve the living God.

   E.g.: "I cleanse my mind, memory, conscious, and subconscious by the blood of Jesus from all dead works to serve the living God. I have the mind of Christ, and my imagination will be inspired by the Holy Spirit in Jesus' name. Amen."

The Shed Blood
and the Broken Body

Leviticus 17:11–12
For the life of the flesh is in the blood, and I have given it to
you upon the altar to make atonement for your souls; for it is
the blood that makes atonement for the soul. Therefore I said
to the children of Israel, "No one among you shall eat blood,
nor shall any stranger who dwells among you eat blood."

The soul of the flesh is in the blood. We need to understand
the importance of the blood. When Jesus died on the cross of
Calvary, He gave His blood to redeem our souls.

Isaiah 53:10–12
Yet it pleased the LORD to bruise Him; He has put Him to
grief. When You make His soul an offering for sin, He shall
see His seed, He shall prolong His days, and the pleasure of
the LORD shall prosper in His hand. He shall see the labor of
His soul, and be satisfied. By His knowledge My righteous
Servant shall justify many, for He shall bear their iniquities.
Therefore I will divide Him a portion with the great,
and He shall divide the spoil with the strong, because He
poured out His soul unto death, and He was numbered with
the transgressors, and He bore the sin of many, and made
intercession for the transgressors.

Jesus did not spill His blood for us; He said, "I shed My blood
for you." There is a difference between spilling and shedding.
Spilling is by accident, but Jesus purposely shed His blood for
us.

Matthew 26:28
"For this is My blood of the new covenant, which is shed for many for the remission of sins."

Not only was His blood shed, but he took the blood and offered it in heaven. The Word of God says that when He entered into the Holy of Holies through His own blood, His blood paid the price for eternal redemption.

Hebrews 9:12
Not with the blood of goats and calves, but with His own blood He entered the Most Holy Place once for all, having obtained eternal redemption.

Because of the blood of Jesus, throughout eternity, we are able to enjoy the presence of God.

Remember, before that blood was offered in heaven we could not touch God because of our sin nature.

John 20:15–17
Jesus said to her, "Woman why are you weeping? Whom are you seeking?" She, supposing Him to be the gardener, said to Him, "Sir, if You have carried Him away, tell me where You have laid Him, and I will take Him away." Jesus said to her, "Mary!" She turned and said to Him, "Rabboni!" (which is to say, Teacher). Jesus said to her, "Do not cling to Me, for I have not yet ascended to My Father; but go to My brethren and say to them, 'I am ascending to My Father and your Father, and to My God and your God.'"

Jesus told Mary not to touch Him because He had not yet offered His blood in heaven. The sin nature cannot touch God. After He had offered His blood, He appeared to His disciples.

John 20:26–27

And after eight days His disciples were again inside, and Thomas with them. Jesus came, the doors being shut, and stood in the midst, and said, "Peace to you!" Then He said to Thomas, "Reach your finger here, and look at My hands; and reach your hand here, and put it into My side. Do not be unbelieving, but believing."

This time He tells Thomas to touch Him because he had already entered into heaven through His own blood, and because of His blood we can touch God and have communion with Him.

Hebrews 10:19–23

Therefore, brethren, having boldness to enter the Holiest by the blood of Jesus, by a new and living way which He consecrated for us, through the veil, that is, His flesh, and having a High Priest over the house of God, let us draw near with a true heart in full assurance of faith, having our hearts sprinkled from an evil conscience and our bodies washed with pure water. Let us hold fast the confession of our hope without wavering, for He who promised is faithful.

We have the confidence and boldness that has been given to us through the blood of Jesus; God has given us a new and living way. The old ways have passed away but all things have become new. Now we have a High Priest over our house and life because of the blood of Jesus. We just have to accept and have faith in the blood.

Psalm 89:28

My mercy I will keep for him forever, and My covenant shall stand firm with him.

Every time He sees the blood He remembers you and He is faithful to the covenant.

Hebrews 10:24

And let us consider one another in order to stir up love and good works.

We must consider each other and provoke one another to do good because we are washed in the same blood and born of the same Spirit.

Hebrews 10:25
Not forsaking the assembling of ourselves together, as is the manner of some, but exhorting one another, and so much the more as you see the Day approaching.

When we come together, we edify one another, encourage one another, and the Word washes, cleanses, and nourishes us. God loves His Church.

John 6:50–58
"This is the bread which comes down from heaven, that one may eat of it and not die. I am the living bread which came down from heaven. If anyone eats of this bread, he will live forever; and the bread that I shall give is My flesh, which I shall give for the life of the world." The Jews therefore quarrelled among themselves, saying, "How can this Man give us His flesh to eat?" Then Jesus said to them, "Most assuredly, I say to you, unless you eat the flesh of the Son of Man and drink His blood, you have no life in you. Whoever eats My flesh and drinks My blood has eternal life, and I will raise him up at the last day. For My flesh is food indeed, and My blood is drink indeed. He who eats My flesh and drinks My blood abides in Me, and I in him. As the living Father sent Me, and I live because of the Father, so he who feeds on Me will live because of Me. This is the bread which came down from heaven—not as your fathers ate the manna, and are dead. He who eats this bread will live forever."

The Jews could not understand what Jesus was saying. Jesus was talking about union and communion when we partake of His body. There is power in His blood and His body. When we partake of Him, we will live by Him and have eternal life. God has given us the Bread of Life.

Matthew 26:26–28
And as they were eating, Jesus took bread, blessed and broke it, and gave it to the disciples and said, "Take, eat; this is my body." Then He took the cup, and gave thanks, and gave it to them, saying, "Drink from it, all of you. For this is My blood of the new covenant, which is shed for many for the remission of sins."

Jesus wanted the disciples to partake in the union and communion. There is power in the Lord's blood and body. He establishes a new covenant.

1 Peter 1:19
But with the precious blood of Christ, as of a lamb without blemish and without spot.

The blood is precious and perfect.

1 Corinthians 5:7
Therefore purge out the old leaven, that you may be a new lump, since you truly are unleavened. For indeed Christ, our Passover, was sacrificed for us.

Exodus 12:7–13
And they shall take some of the blood and put it on the two doorposts and on the lintel of the houses where they eat it. Then they shall eat the flesh on that night; roasted in fire, with unleavened bread and with bitter herbs they shall eat it. Do not eat it raw, nor boiled at all with water, but roasted in fire—its head with its legs and its entrails. You shall let none of it remain until morning, and what remains of it until morning you shall burn with fire. And thus you shall eat it: with a belt on your waist, your sandals on your feet, and your staff in your hand. So you shall eat it in haste. It is the LORD's Passover. For I will pass through the land of Egypt on that night, and will strike all the firstborn in the land of Egypt, both man and beast; and against all the gods of Egypt I will execute judgment: I am the LORD. Now the blood shall

*be a sign for you on the houses where you are. And when I see
the blood, I will pass over you; and the plague shall not be on
you to destroy you when I strike the land of Egypt.*

Everything in the Old Covenant is a type, but today we do not
walk in the old; we walk in the new. The blood shall be for you
as a sign. The word translated sign also means "evidence." All
they did was to take part in the Passover for protection. Today,
Jesus is our Passover Lamb, so whenever you take communion,
you are saying "Jesus, You are my Passover."

When they took part in the Passover they had:

- Divine protection

- Healing

- Favor on their lives

- Divine deliverance in their homes

- The presence of God with them

- The transfer of wealth into their hands

If the Old Covenant can do this, how much more will the New
Covenant do for us?

The Importance of Communion

The apostles knew the power of the Passover, of Jesus' blood and Jesus' body.

> *Acts 2:42–47*
> *And they continued steadfastly in the apostles' doctrine and fellowship, in the breaking of bread, and in prayers. Then fear came upon every soul, and many wonders and signs were done through the apostles. Now all who believed were together, and had all things in common, and sold their possessions and goods, and divided them among all, as anyone had need. So continuing daily with one accord in the temple, and breaking bread from house to house, they ate their food with gladness and simplicity of heart, praising God and having favor with all the people. And the Lord added to the church daily those who were being saved.*

They were firm in their conviction. When they met they broke bread and although this was a common term for sharing a meal, it is also what was done when partaking in the body and the blood of the Lord. Something happens when you do that; something divine takes place.

When the apostles and disciples broke bread together, the Word says the following took place:

1. The fear of God was present.

2. Many wonders and signs were done.

3. People were of one heart and one mind.

4. Every need was met.

5. Gladness and praise was evident.

6. There was favour with all people.

7. God added to the Church.

The union and communion in His body and blood will do the same for us today.

When you know the power of the blood, you will not neglect breaking bread.

> *1 Corinthians 11:24–30*
> *And when He had given thanks, He broke it and said, "Take, eat; this is My body which is broken for you; do this in remembrance of Me. In the same manner He also took the cup after supper, saying, "This cup is the new covenant in My blood. This do, as often as you drink it, in remembrance of Me." For as often as you eat this bread and drink this cup, you proclaim the Lord's death till He comes. Therefore whoever eats this bread or drinks this cup of the Lord in an unworthy manner will be guilty of the body and blood of the Lord. But let a man examine himself, and so let him eat of the bread and drink of the cup. For he who eats and drinks in an unworthy manner eats and drinks judgment to himself, not discerning the Lord's body. For this reason many are weak and sick among you, and many sleep.*

Paul was not there when Jesus introduced communion. He was given this by divine revelation to share with the Church. Every time we eat and drink communion, we remember what Christ has done on the cross of Calvary. If we take part in communion not comprehending or understanding what the blood and the body has done, we will be guilty. We must examine ourselves in the light of the finished work of Calvary and appropriate and apply what Jesus did on the cross. We must acknowledge and accept what Jesus has done for us on the cross of Calvary. Paul goes on to explain why so many are weak and sick. It is because they have been careless and taken part in communion with wrong motives.

John 6:50–58

"This is the bread which comes down from heaven, that one may eat of it and not die. I am the living bread which came down from heaven. If anyone eats of this bread, he will live forever; and the bread that I shall give is My flesh, which I shall give for the life of the world." The Jews therefore quarrelled among themselves, saying, "How can this Man give us His flesh to eat?" Then Jesus said to them, "Most assuredly, I say to you, unless you eat the flesh of the Son of Man and drink His blood, you have no life in you. Whoever eats My flesh and drinks My blood has eternal life, and I will raise him up at the last day. For My flesh is food indeed, and My blood is drink indeed. He who eats My flesh and drinks My blood abides in Me, and I in him. As the living Father sent Me, and I live because of the Father, so he who feeds on Me will live because of Me. This is the bread which came down from heaven—not as your fathers ate the manna, and are dead. He who eats this bread will live forever."

Many partake without knowing what communion is all about, and so they bring guilt upon themselves. God says that His people perish because of lack of knowledge.

Matthew 4:23

And Jesus went about all Galilee, teaching in their synagogues, preaching the gospel of the kingdom, and healing all kinds of sickness and all kinds of disease among the people.

Exodus 12:13
Now the blood shall be a sign for you on the houses where you are. And when I see the blood, I will pass over you; and the plague shall not be on you to destroy you when I strike the land of Egypt.

God will not only remove sickness and disease, but He will remove every plague from your household when you understand what Jesus accomplished for you on the cross of Calvary and when you partake in His body and blood.

I would like to bring to your attention that we are governed by three laws:

1. God's law

2. Man's law

3. Natural law

If you break any of these laws, you will face the consequences and pay the price. The natural law was established by God. Often people are sick because they violate a natural law, such as not eating the correct food or not sleeping enough or not resting. Which is better—healing or divine health? We need to repent and walk right before God because God wants us healthy. The Word declares that our bodies are the temple of the Holy Spirit.

Exodus 15:23–26
Now when they came to Marah, they could not drink the waters of Marah, for they were bitter. Therefore the name of it was called Marah. And the people complained against Moses, saying, "What shall we drink?" So he cried out to the LORD, and the LORD showed him a tree. When he cast it into the waters, the waters were made sweet. There He made a statute and an ordinance for them, and there He tested

them, and said, "If you diligently heed the voice of the LORD your God and do what is right in His sight, give ear to His commandments and keep all His statutes, I will put none of the diseases on you which I have brought on the Egyptians. For I am the LORD who heals you."

We should be the healthiest people on the face of the earth because we know God's law.

Exodus 23:25
So you shall serve the LORD your God, and He will bless your bread and your water. And I will take sickness away from the midst of you.

God gave them a condition for their healing—they were to serve Him and He would heal them.

Deuteronomy 7:13–15
And He will love you and bless you and multiply you; He will also bless the fruit of your womb and the fruit of your land, your grain and your new wine and your oil, the increase of your cattle and the offspring of your flock, in the land of which He swore to your fathers to give you. You shall be blessed above all peoples; there shall not be a male or female barren among you or among your livestock. And the LORD will take away from you all sickness, and will afflict you with none of the terrible diseases of Egypt which you have known, but will lay them on all those who hate you.

Whatever you have will be blessed because you have communion and union with the Lord. All the sicknesses of the world will not touch you.

Luke 9:1–2
Then He called His twelve disciples together and gave them power and authority over all demons, and to cure diseases. He sent them to preach the kingdom of God and to heal the sick.

Acts 10:38
How God anointed Jesus of Nazareth with the Holy Spirit and with power, who went about doing good and healing all who were oppressed by the devil, for God was with Him.

God has provided healing in both the Old and the New Covenants. Healing means "restoring back to its rightful condition or position."

Job 42:10
And the LORD restored Job's losses when he prayed for his friends. Indeed the LORD gave Job twice as much as he had before.

God does not want you to be in captivity.

Luke 13:16
"So ought not this woman, being a daughter of Abraham, whom Satan has bound—think of it—for eighteen years, be loosed from this bond on the Sabbath?"

Sickness is bondage and is also called oppression.

Hebrews 4:14–16
Seeing then that we have a great High Priest who has passed through the heavens, Jesus the Son of God, let us hold fast our confession. For we do not have a High Priest who cannot sympathize with our weaknesses, but was in all points tempted as we are, yet without sin. Let us therefore come boldly to the throne of grace, that we may obtain mercy and find grace to help in time of need.

We have a Great High Priest who knows and understands us and our situation.

Luke 9:11
But when the multitudes knew it, they followed Him; and He received them and spoke to them about the kingdom of God, and healed those who had need of healing.

Matthew 12:15
But when Jesus knew it, He withdrew from there. And great multitudes followed Him, and He healed them all.

Jesus has all power, and all the natural elements are subject to Him. He healed Peter's mother-in-law; He healed the leper; He saw a blind man and He opened his eyes. Today Jesus is able to heal every sickness, disease, and plague, and He still raises the dead.

Remember, He is able and capable to do what He said He will do for you.

The cross of Calvary has provided us with the blood of God's Son.

Consider Calvary,
It Is Perfect in Every
Aspect and Respect.

The Cross of Calvary Provides Acceptance in the Beloved

Acceptance and Rejection

Jesus Christ, the Son of the living God, was rejected so that we could be accepted.

There are two forces that shape our souls in life:

1. Acceptance

2. Rejection

The opposite of rejection is acceptance. There are many people who have been hurt by rejection and still carry the scars. It may not only manifest in physical sickness, but they may also have mental problems. Jesus came to heal us from every rejection.

> *Luke 4:18*
> *The Spirit of the LORD is upon Me, because He has anointed Me to preach the gospel to the poor; He has sent Me to heal the brokenhearted, to proclaim liberty to the captives and recovery of sight to the blind, to set at liberty those who are oppressed.*

There is no earthly doctor who can heal a broken heart. Only Jesus can heal a broken heart.

> *Ephesians 1:7*
> *In Him we have redemption through His blood, the forgiveness of sins, according to the riches of His grace.*

Ephesians 1:5–6
Having predestined us to adoption as sons by Jesus Christ
to Himself, according to the good pleasure of His will, to the
praise of the glory of His grace, by which He made us accepted
in the beloved.

We have been adopted by God as His child. The cross of Calvary gave us the blood of His Son, Jesus, through which we are redeemed, whereby we have been reconciled and accepted in the Beloved.

Every human being is looking for five basic needs:

1. Love

2. Security

3. To be heard

4. To be recognized

5. An identity

Isaiah 43:1
But now, thus says the LORD, who created you, O Jacob, and
He who formed you, O Israel: "Fear not, for I have redeemed
you; I have called you by you name; you are Mine."

Remember, God has called you by your name. He knows your name. You are important to Him and very precious. Others may think that you are not important, but it is what God thinks that matters.

When you come to God, you have an eternal identity and belong to the Kingdom of God.

If rejection is not dealt with, people end up with low self-esteem, a lack of confidence, and they cannot focus.

Rejection always leads to a feeling of oppression. If you do not deal with oppression, it becomes depression. If you do not deal with depression, you come to a stage of illusion having believed a lie.

1. Many human beings are looking for love in the wrong places.

When they do not find love, they become discouraged.

Since it is God who created us, He knows our needs better than anyone else. Therefore when He decided to reach out to humanity, He reached out in love.

John 3:16
For God so loved the world that He gave His only begotten Son, that whoever believes in Him should not perish but have everlasting life.

1 John 4:16
And we have known and believed the love that God has for us. God is love, and he who abides in love abides in God, and God in him.

When God reveals Himself, He reveals His love. Love is a person—His Name is Jesus.

1 John 4:19
We love Him because He first loved us.

Every human being needs unconditional love. Man's love is conditional, and his love has limits. Only God's love is able to satisfy both your soul and your mind, and give you hope.

There is a difference between human love and God's love.

2. Let us look at human love.

   a. Human love is conditional.

   b. Human love wants to possess and control.

   c. Human love cannot and will not eliminate fear.

3. Let us look at God's love.

   a. God's love is unconditional.

> *Romans 5:8*
> *But God demonstrates His own love toward us, in that while we were still sinners, Christ died for us.*

   b. God's love provides us with freedom and liberty.

   c. God's love removes fear.

> *1 John 4:18*
> *There is no fear in love; but perfect love casts out fear, because fear involves torment. But he who fears has not been made perfect in love.*

I would like to bring to your attention three kinds of people

Most humans will fall into one or the other of these three categories:

1. People who have never been shown love

This is a group of people who were never told by their parents that they are loved. Many parents think if they do their duty as a parent, that is more than sufficient and they have no responsibility to say to their children that they love them.

The result is that the child grows up needing attention, and the way they express it is often through rebelling. A child who knows he or she is loved will grow up with stability.

Remember, worldly goods cannot replace love. Many parents think that because they have not spent enough time with their children or shown love, they can somehow replace this lack of time with money or goods.

When a girl has not been shown love by her father, she often grows up to hate men. All through her life she tries to compete with men. Sooner or later she acts like a man and it all started with rejection.

People who grow up not having received love are unable to love others, and they have unstable marriages.

2. People who have received conditional love

This group of people grow up constantly needing approval. They will always keep repeating, "Did I do it alright?" They want others to validate them constantly. They have low self-esteem, and they do not believe they can accomplish anything. When they are married, they find it difficult to receive love, since the love that was shown to them was conditional--something they had to earn.

The love that was given to them was conditional upon their achievement.

3. People who have been overprotected

Overprotecting children robs them of personality. They cannot focus and have no confidence or freedom to decide for themselves. All the decisions about their lives are made for them, and they are always looking for attention.

When a child is overprotected, they become either hypoactive or shy. They isolate themselves and cannot look anyone in the eye. Because no confidence has been put in them, their spirit is wounded. Their need for acceptance is great. Psychologists can tell you why, but they cannot provide the answer, because acceptance operates on the supernatural level. The spirit must be healed so the soul can flourish.

Only God can heal your spirit.

Romans 8:16
The Spirit Himself bears witness with our spirit that we are children of God.

Your spirit must know that you are a child of God and loved by God so that your spirit can be healed.

We need to let Jesus break every spirit of rejection upon our lives.

Acceptance and Rejection

~ BEGINS AT HOME ~

There are many who feel worthless. Worthlessness can come in two ways.

- The parents were very strict.

- The person had to buy love.

There are parents who constantly tell their children that they are no good. We have to allow our children to be who God has ordained them to be, whether that is a carpenter, a lawyer, a doctor, or something else. Discipline is good, but harshness is bad. When we speak negative words over our children, we are binding their souls, and those hurts last for a lifetime. Parents compare their children with others, and they grow up with social pressure from society. We must be the person God created us to be, not what someone else thinks we should be.

Everyone is unique, special, and loved by God.

Selling Love

Love equals performance: "If you become what I want, then I will love you." If you have to perform to earn love, then that is not love. This is not God's way, because God is gracious and merciful.

Love is not bought or sold through performance. God does not sell love; He gives it to you freely.

The Cross of Calvary
Provides Acceptance in the Beloved

Results of love based on performance

- They cannot love others because they feel they have nothing to give.

- They cannot receive love because they feel they are not good for anything because they have not performed.

- They become perfectionists.

- They are prone to depression.

- Some become workaholics.

It is important that parents live by way of example, because children learn from their parents. Make time for your family.

When people are brought up in this environment, they are often fearful to have children because they feel inadequate.

How do you know that the child is affected?

- The child begins to build a wall around them and will not allow anyone to come close to them.

- They will not allow anyone to love them.

- They have no close relationships.

- They develop psychological problems from a very early age.

- They are very unstable in their emotions.

- They cannot give or receive love.

- They find it hard to relate.

- Even when they are grown up and married, they tend to display symptoms in their marriages.

The root cause is rejection. Acceptance and rejection begin at home.

> *1 Thessalonians 5:23*
> *Now may the God of peace Himself sanctify you completely; and may your whole spirit, soul, and body be preserved blameless at the coming of our Lord Jesus Christ.*

We are spirit, soul, and body. Our soul is made up of our emotions, will, and much more. Research tells us that when a child is in the womb, it can actually feel the emotions the mother is feeling at any given time. The child can understand and perceive what is going on. They also tell us that the ages of five to seven years old is the most important time in a child's life. The child must know and must learn to have confidence and assurance from an early age.

Acceptance is in the spiritual realm, and rejection operates in the natural realm. Rejection manifests through your senses.

Some parents struggle to tell their children that they love them.

> *Matthew 3:17*
> *And suddenly a voice came from heaven, saying, "This is My beloved Son, in whom I am well pleased."*

The Son of God had to hear that His heavenly Father loved Him and was pleased with Him. The Father made sure that His Son knew that He was loved. We need to know that we are loved. Tell your children that you love them because it begins the healing process.

Jesus received love from His Father and was able to share that love with others.

> *John 15:9*
> *As the Father loved Me, I also have loved you; abide in My love.*

The Son of God needed His Father's love. The Son received the love of the Father and with that love, He loved us.

You cannot give what you do not have.

So you might be asking the question: What do I do as a parent? How do I rectify the situation?

1. Do not feel condemned.

In Christ there is hope. Ask the Lord Jesus to pour His love through His Spirit upon the situation.

2. Acknowledge that you have made mistakes.

The first step to recovery is acknowledging the mistakes.

3. Ask God to forgive you.

4. Invite the Holy Spirit to help you.

Jesus our Lord said that He is our helper and comforter.

John 14:26
But the Helper, the Holy Spirit, whom the Father will send in My name, He will teach you all things, and bring to your remembrance all things that I said to you.

5. Ask God for wisdom to handle the situation.

James 1:5
If any of you lacks wisdom, let him ask of God, who gives to all liberally and without reproach, and it will be given to him.

6. Gather your children together and talk it through with them.

Let them see the love of God. Assure them that you will be operating in accordance with God's love.

7. Allow the love of God to flow into the situation through daily prayer for the family.

You might be asking the question: What do I do if I am the affected child?

→ **Remove the spirit of rejection.**

Break its hold over you in the name of Jesus and through the blood of Jesus.

→ **Break the cycle of oppression and depression that comes from rejection in the name of Jesus and through the blood of Jesus.**

→ **Ask God to heal you. Jesus Christ came to heal us.**

Luke 4:18–19
The Spirit of the LORD is upon Me, because He has anointed Me to preach the gospel to the poor; He has sent Me to heal the brokenhearted, to proclaim liberty to the captives and recovery of sight to the blind, to set at liberty those who are oppressed; to proclaim the acceptable year of the LORD.

→ **Declare and proclaim that in Christ you are accepted in the Beloved and that the Lord Jesus has shed His love in your heart.**

Ephesians 1:6
To the praise of the glory of His grace, by which He made us accepted in the Beloved.

Romans 5:5
Now hope does not disappoint, because the love of God has been poured out in our hearts by the Holy Spirit who was given to us.

Rejection is a spirit, and it becomes a stronghold in our life and begins to manifest through our senses. When you renounce the spirit of rejection and you break its hold by the blood of Jesus and in the name of Jesus, you are binding the strong man. Then you allow God's love to flow through your life.

Acceptance and Rejection

~ In Marriage ~

Before we go any further, I want you to know that you are loved by Christ Jesus.

God's love for you never changes.

> *Ephesians 5:2*
> *And walk in love, as Christ also has loved us and has given Himself for us, an offering and a sacrifice to God for a sweet-smelling aroma.*

> *Galatians 2:20*
> *I have been crucified with Christ; it is no longer I who live, but Christ lives in me; and the life which I now live in the flesh I live by faith in the Son of God, who loved me and gave Himself for me.*

> *1 John 4:16*
> *And we have known and believed the love that God has for us. God is love, and he who abides in love abides in God, and God in him.*

It is important for you to know that you are loved by Christ; you were loved by Christ and you will be loved by Jesus Christ forever.

When you meet Jesus you have seen and experienced love.

> *John 13:1*
> *Now before the Feast of the Passover, when Jesus knew that His hour had come that He should depart from this world to*

the Father, having loved His own who were in the world, He loved them to the end.

John 14:21
"He who has My commandments and keeps them, it is he who loves Me. And he who loves Me will be loved by My Father, and I will love him and manifest Myself to him."

When God says He loves you, He backs it up with action.

The love of Christ is manifested in many ways.

1. He laid His life down for you.

John 15:13
Greater love has no one than this, than to lay down one's life for his friends.

2. He forgave you.

Revelation 1:5
And from Jesus Christ, the faithful witness, the firstborn from the dead, and the ruler over the kings of the earth. To him who loved us and washed us from our sins in His own blood.

3. He brings healing to all.

Matthew 8:17
That it might be fulfilled which was spoken by Isaiah the prophet, saying: "He Himself took our infirmities and bore our sicknesses."

4. He redeemed you.

Ephesians 1:7
In Him we have redemption through His blood, the forgiveness
of sins, according to the riches of His grace.

God has accepted us, loves us, and takes care of us.

When God deals with man, He deals with him through his spirit, because if you get the spirit of a man right, the soul will be right, and if you get the soul of a man right the body will be right. The world deals with the soul and ignores the spirit. Everything God does flows from spirit to spirit and then flows into the soul and body.

Romans 8:16
The Spirit Himself bears witness with our spirit that we are
children of God.

Our spirit has known, perceived, and received the acceptance of God, and from there it must flow to our soul.

Remember, the source of your acceptance is God's unconditional love.

Romans 5:5
Now hope does not disappoint, because the love of God has
been poured out in our hearts by the Holy Spirit, who was
given to us.

When God's love came into our heart, it came with the assurance of acceptance. This love of God has the power to destroy every stronghold of rejection.

Having learned about God's unconditional love, let us now look at marriage.

First of all, let me explain to you the three phases of marriage.

Stage 1:

They are getting to know each other.

During this period partners have greater tolerance for each other. They overlook each other's faults because they are romantically involved.

Stage 2:

The differences between each other become an issue.

They are no longer willing to tolerate. They become angry and impatient.

Stage 3:

They permit and allow God's love and His grace to work through their lives so that they have the love for each other to overcome differences and to mature in love.

Rejection in a Marriage

Rejection in a marriage leads to psychological problems, and the human spirit is affected.

1. A troubled spirit results.

Genesis 41:8
Now it came to pass in the morning that his spirit was troubled, and he sent and called for all the magicians of Egypt and all its wise men. And Pharaoh told them his dreams, but there was no one who could interpret them for Pharaoh.

2. An anguished spirit results.

Exodus 6:9
So Moses spoke thus to the children of Israel; but they did not heed Moses, because of <u>anguish of spirit</u> and cruel bondage.

The word here translated anguish means "shortness of spirit" or "impatience." Many people are subject to an anguished spirit.

3. A sorrowful spirit results.

Proverbs 18:14
The spirit of a man will sustain him in sickness, but who can bear a <u>broken spirit</u>?

Proverbs 15:13
A merry heart makes a cheerful countenance, but by <u>sorrow of the heart</u> the spirit is broken.

A troubled, anxious, and wounded spirit will cause problems in a person's physical body.

4. A spirit of suspicion results.

Proverbs 6:34
For <u>jealousy</u> is a husband's fury; therefore he will not spare in the day of vengeance.

Jealousy can often be accompanied by insecurity, anxiety and suspicion.

Many today are tormented by the spirit of jealousy and suspicion.

God wants us to live joyfully together and have joy in our marriage.

Ecclesiastes 9:9
Live joyfully with the wife whom you love all the days of your vain life which He has given you under the sun, all your days of vanity; for that is your portion in life, and in the labor which you perform under the sun.

Remember, if you are encountering any of the above, Jesus Christ, the Son of the living God, wants to set you free.

Malachi 2:14
Yet you say, "For what reason?" Because the LORD has been witness between you and the wife of your youth, with whom you have dealt treacherously; yet she is your companion and your wife by covenant.

We need to get our priorities right and not take each other for granted.

Children who are brought up in a house with disagreement, a broken marriage, or divorce

The child who comes from a home where there is no harmony between the parents will be affected. Research shows that when a divorce takes place in a family, the child usually feels that it is their fault, and guilt sets in even though the child is innocent. This leaves the door open for rejection. Researchers say that from rejection, the child will become fearful, not knowing what will happen. Their security is gone, and fear will lead to loneliness and insecurity, and they grow up with no confidence.

God did not put you together as husband and wife to get divorced. Marriage is a covenant and a lifetime commitment.

Therefore, if you are looking to get married do not marry the wrong person—listen to godly advice.

2 Corinthians 6:14
Do not be unequally yoked together with unbelievers. For what fellowship has righteousness with lawlessness? And what communion has light with darkness?

1 Peter 4:1
Therefore, since Christ suffered for us in the flesh, arm yourselves also with the same mind, for he who has suffered in the flesh has ceased from sin.

When God put you together, God ordained your marriage.

Prayer

In the name of Jesus, we come to You, Lord, and commit our marriage to You. We renounce and break every troubled spirit, anguished spirit, sorrowful spirit, suspicious spirit, and jealous spirit from our lives. We cover our marriage under the blood of Jesus. Lord, let the love of God be poured into our marriage by Your Spirit. We want to thank You and praise You in Jesus' name.

Amen

Acceptance and Rejection

~ HUSBAND'S ROLE ~

Acceptance and rejection within the household

It is the husband's responsibility to protect his wife from rejection. The Word of God says that the husband must take his rightful position because the husband is the head of the home, being a priest, prophet, and king.

A priest ministers to God and he ministers to others. A prophet seeks the face of God and brings direction for the household. A king protects and provides for the household. If the husband takes his rightful place in the home, the household will flourish.

> *Ephesians 5:23–29*
> *For the husband is head of the wife, as also Christ is head of the church; and He is the Savior of the body. Therefore, just as the church is subject to Christ, so let the wives be to their own husbands in everything. Husbands, love your wives, just as Christ also loved the church and gave Himself for her, that He might sanctify and cleanse her with the washing of water by the word, that He might present her to Himself a glorious church, not having spot or wrinkle or any such thing, but that she should be holy and without blemish. So husbands ought to love their own wives as their own bodies; he who loves his wife loves himself. For no one ever hated his own flesh, but nourishes and cherishes it, just as the Lord does the church.*

Let us look at a priest in the Word of God.

Leviticus 16:4
He shall put the holy linen tunic and the linen trousers on
his body; he shall be girded with a linen sash, and with the
linen turban he shall be attired. These are holy garments.
Therefore he shall wash his body in water, and put them on.

A priest had responsibilities. When a priest came before God,
there was preparation that took place before he approached the
altar. He washed himself and put on the garments to be ready to
fulfill his role as a priest.

The Role of a Priest in the Old Covenant

1. Wash yourself with the Word.

Leviticus 16:4
He shall put the holy linen tunic and the linen trousers on
his body; he shall be girded with a linen sash, and with the
linen turban he shall be attired. These are holy garments.
Therefore he shall wash his body in water, and put them on.

Psalm 119:9
How can a young man cleanse his way? By taking heed
according to Your word.

Husbands must wash themselves in the Word of God,
reading and applying the Word.

Ephesians 1:2–7
Grace to you and peace from God our Father and the Lord
Jesus Christ. Blessed be the God and Father of our Lord Jesus
Christ, who has blessed us with every spiritual blessing in
the heavenly places in Christ, just as He chose us in Him
before the foundation of the world, that we should be holy
and without blame before Him in love, having predestined
us to adoption as sons by Jesus Christ to Himself, according

to the good pleasure of His will, to the praise of the glory of His grace, by which He made us accepted in the Beloved. In Him we have redemption through His blood, the forgiveness of sins, according to the riches of His grace.

The Word of God needs to be confessed so you can appropriate it in your own life and know that you are accepted in the Beloved.

2. Clothe yourself with Jesus Christ.

Leviticus 16:4
He shall put the holy linen tunic and the linen trousers on his body; he shall be girded with a linen sash, and with the linen turban he shall be attired. These are holy garments. Therefore he shall wash his body in water, and put them on.

He did not put on the garment until he had washed himself. To us the garment represents the righteousness of Christ. The garment had four colors: white, scarlet, blue, and purple. White signifies that Jesus is the perfect man; scarlet symbolizes that Jesus is our Savior; blue symbolizes that Jesus is the Son of God; and purple symbolizes that Jesus is the King of all kings.

Galatians 3:26–27
For you are all sons of God through faith in Christ Jesus. For as many of you as were baptized into Christ have put on Christ.

We put on Christ by accepting, acknowledging, and appropriating what Christ has done for us on the cross of Calvary by faith.

3. Accept your household in your heart.

Leviticus 1:4
Then he shall <u>put his hand</u> on the head of the burnt offering, and it will be accepted on his behalf to make atonement for him.

As a husband, you must accept your wife in your heart, lay hands on her, and pray for her. If you get the heart right, the man will be right. Men need to rise to the position of husbands and fathers.

4. Wash your family in the Word.

Leviticus 1:9
But he shall wash its entrails and its legs with water. And the priest shall burn all on the altar as a burnt sacrifice, an offering made by fire, a sweet aroma to the LORD.

Psalm 34:1–4
I will bless the LORD at all times; His praise shall continually be in my mouth. My soul shall make its boast in the LORD; the humble shall hear of it and be glad. Oh, magnify the LORD with me, and let us exalt His name together. I sought the LORD, and He heard me, and delivered me from all my fears.

Psalm 1:1–3
Blessed is the man who walks not in the counsel of the ungodly, nor stands in the path of sinners, nor sits in the seat of the scornful; but his delight is in the law of the LORD, and in His law he meditates day and night. He shall be like a tree planted by the rivers of water, that brings forth its fruit in its season, whose leaf also shall not wither; and whatever he does shall prosper.

Declare the Word of God over your wife and family, especially these psalms, and begin to apply it and wash your wife and family in the Word of God.

When God's Word goes out of our mouths, it will not return to Him void. Every time we speak and apply the Word, it accomplishes something in our spirits.

5. Present your offering on the altar.

Leviticus 1:9 NIV
He is to wash the inner parts and the legs with water, and the priest is to burn all of it <u>on the altar</u>. It is a burnt offering, an offering made by fire, an aroma pleasing to the LORD.

Today, husbands should bring their prayer to the altar by giving thanks to the Lord for their wives and family every day.

6. Presented your family unto the Lord.

Leviticus 1:9
But he shall wash its entrails and its legs with water. And the priest shall burn all on the altar as a burnt sacrifice, an offering made by fire, a sweet aroma to the LORD.

The husband must intercede for his household. There is nowhere in scripture that says that women should be the intercessors. It is the husband's responsibility to present his family to God as a sweet savor.

7. It is the husband's responsibility to apply the blood over his household.

Leviticus 1:5
He shall kill the bull before the LORD; and the priests, Aaron's sons, shall bring the blood and <u>sprinkle the blood all around on the altar</u> that is by the door of the tabernacle of meeting.

Colossians 1:13–14
He has delivered us from the power of darkness and conveyed us into the kingdom of the Son of His love, in whom we have redemption through His blood, the forgiveness of sins.

Apply the blood by the Word of God, declaring what the blood of Jesus has done for you, your wife, your family, and your household.

Ephesians 5:23
For the husband is head of the wife, as also Christ is head of the church; and He is the Savior of the body.

1 Corinthians 11:3
But I want you to know that the head of every man is Christ, the head of woman is man, and the head of Christ is God.

God has placed the man in the position of authority. The head not only speaks of authority, but the head has the position to establish authority in the household.

Husband's styles of leadership that exist in homes today

1. Dictator

The dictatorial leadership style is the reason there is so much abuse in homes. There is no cooperation with this type of government. The children are terrorized and leave home as soon as they can.

2. President and Wife

This is where the husband takes his headship at home, recognizing the importance of his wife and her responsibility. This style will work well if it is administered in line with the

Word. There is a proper method of consultation in this household. There is discussion with the wife before decisions are made.

3. President and Vice President

The vice president gives the rightful position to the president and does things in her own right, but she always keeps in mind that the president is the head.

This style is more appropriate when both the husband and wife are career-minded.

In this household, too, there is a proper method of consultation. There is discussion with the wife before decisions are made.

4. Two Presidents

When two people are ruling in the same household, nothing constructive happens because both are headstrong. Or the man does not take his rightful place but hands everything over to the wife. Then she becomes the head and controls everything. This is out of God's order. There is no government in the house, and everyone does their own thing. There will always be lack of consultation and agreement.

5. No Government

There is no proper order in the household. When there is no government in a household, it opens the door for confusion, misunderstanding, and strife, which will result in family breakdown.

There must be the right kind of leadership in the household. The right kind is the godly kind where the husband establishes a leadership style that involves love, commitment, cooperation, and prayer. There will always be harmony, fruitfulness, and godliness in his family.

Ephesians 5:24–25
Therefore, just as the church is subject to Christ, so let the wives be to their own husbands in everything. Husbands, love your wives, just as Christ also loved the church and gave Himself for her.

God compares the love that a husband should have for his wife with Christ's love for the Church.

What the love of Christ did for the Church

Ephesians 5:23–33
For the husband is head of the wife, as also Christ is head of the church; and He is the Savior of the body. Therefore, just as the church is subject to Christ, so let the wives be to their own husbands in everything. Husbands, love your wives, just as Christ also loved the church and gave Himself for her, that He might sanctify and cleanse her with the washing of water by the word, that He might present her to Himself a glorious church, not having spot or wrinkle or any such thing, but that she should be holy and without blemish. So husbands ought to love their own wives as their own bodies; he who loves his wife loves himself. For no one ever hated his own flesh, but nourishes and cherishes it, just as the Lord does the church. For we are members of His body, of His flesh and of His bones. "For this reason a man shall leave his father and mother and be joined to his wife, and the two shall become one flesh." This is a great mystery, but I speak concerning Christ and the church. Nevertheless let each one of you in particular so love his own wife as himself, and let the wife see that she respects her husband.

- He sacrificed His life for His bride.

- His love made His bride whole.

- His love took care of the bride and He cherished her.

- His love united Him with His bride.

- His love is faithful until the end.

Proverbs 5:18–22
Let your fountain be blessed, and rejoice with the wife of
your youth. As a loving deer and a graceful doe, let her
breasts satisfy you at all times; and always be enraptured
with her love. For why should you, my son, be enraptured
by an immoral woman, and be embraced in the arms of a
seductress? For the ways of man are before the eyes of the
LORD, and He ponders all his paths. His own iniquities entrap
the wicked man, and he is caught in the cords of his sin.

Thank God for the wife He has given you. There is nothing called
"living together" in the Word of God; this is sin in the eyes of
God. For God, marriage is sacred and holy.

Proverbs 18:22
He who finds a wife finds a good thing, and obtains favor
from the LORD.

When you have God's favor, you are blessed.

Ecclesiastes 9:9
Live joyfully with the wife whom you love all the days of your
vain life which He has given you under the sun, all your days
of vanity; for that is your portion in life, and in the labor
which you perform under the sun.

Live joyfully with your wife, not complaining and grumbling.

Ephesians 5:21
Submitting to one another in the fear of God.

Psalm 128:1–3
Blessed is every one who fears the LORD, who walks in His ways. When you eat the labor of your hands, you shall be happy, and it shall be well with you. Your wife shall be like a fruitful vine in the very heart of your house, your children like olive plants all around your table.

The prophet

A prophet represents God to the people. When God speaks, it is the prophet who brings the message to the people. The husband is not only a priest but a prophet in the household. It is the responsibility of the husband to bring the message of God to his family.

Exodus 33:11–13
So the LORD spoke to Moses face to face, as a man speaks to his friend. And he would return to the camp, but his servant Joshua the son of Nun, a young man, did not depart from the tabernacle. Then Moses said to the LORD, "See, You say to me, 'Bring up this people.' But You have not let me know whom You will send with me. Yet You have said, 'I know you by name, and you have also found grace in My sight.' Now therefore, I pray, if I have found grace in Your sight, show me now Your way, that I may know You and that I may find grace in Your sight. And consider that this nation is Your people."

Here is an example of a prophet from the life of Moses.

1. He sought the face of God.

It was Moses' place to seek the face of God, just as it is the husband's role to seek God on behalf of his family. Moses asked God to show him His ways. Likewise, the husband must seek God and find God's ways so he can impart them to his household.

2. He had an encounter with God.

Exodus 34:6–7
And the LORD passed before him and proclaimed, "The LORD, the LORD God, merciful and gracious, longsuffering, and abounding in goodness and truth, keeping mercy for thousands, forgiving iniquity and transgression and sin, by no means clearing the guilty, visiting the iniquity of the fathers upon the children and the children's children to the third and the fourth generation."

If we seek God, we will find Him. God gave Moses a revelation, and He showed His attributes and nature to Moses. The husband must continually seek God.

3. He interceded for his household.

Exodus 34:9
Then he said, "If now I have found grace in Your sight, O LORD, let my LORD, I pray, go among us, even though we are a stiff-necked people; and pardon our iniquity and our sin, and take us as Your inheritance.".

This is intercession. Husbands must intercede for their households.

4. God gave him instructions.

Exodus 34:10–14
*And He said: "Behold, I make a covenant. Before all your
people I will do marvels such as have not been done in all the
earth, nor in any nation; and all the people among whom you
are shall see the work of the LORD. For it is an awesome thing
that I will do with you. Observe what I command you this
day. Behold, I am driving out from before you the Amorite
and the Canaanite and the Hittite and the Perizzite and the
Hivite and the Jebusite. Take heed to yourself, lest you make
a covenant with the inhabitants of the land where you are
going, lest it be a snare in your midst. But you shall destroy
their altars, break their sacred pillars, and cut down their
wooden images (for you shall worship no other god, for the
LORD, whose name is Jealous, is a jealous God)."*

God gave Moses clear instructions.

When you seek God and ask Him to show you the way, He
will give you instructions.

5. He consecrated himself to God.

Exodus 34:28
*So he was there with the LORD forty days and forty nights;
he neither ate bread nor drank water. And He wrote on the
tablets the words of the covenant, the Ten Commandments.*

Husbands must fast and pray for their households. Do not
wait until trouble comes; set time aside now. Fasting and
prayer does not change God, but it changes us and our
circumstances.

6. He gave God all the glory.

Exodus 34:29
Now it was so, when Moses came down from Mount Sinai
(and the two tablets of the Testimony were in Moses' hand
when he came down from the mountain), that Moses did not
know that the skin of his face shone while he talked with
Him.

God's countenance was all over him, but Moses did not want
the glory. Be careful of pride setting in when you have heard
from God. Instead give God all the glory.

7. He came and delivered the message.

Exodus 34:30-32
So when Aaron and all the children of Israel saw Moses,
behold, the skin of his face shone, and they were afraid to
come near him. Then Moses called to them, and Aaron and
all the rulers of the congregation returned to him; and Moses
talked with them. Afterward all the children of Israel came
near, and he gave them as commandments all that the LORD
had spoken with him on Mount Sinai.

This is the responsibility of a prophet. It is the husband's
responsibility to communicate the God-given message to
his family.

The King

The king does not sit on his throne and demand that everyone
serve him. Your wife is not your

1. Teach your household to walk by faith.

Hebrews 11:6
But without faith it is impossible to please Him, for he who comes to God must believe that He is, and that He is a rewarder of those who diligently seek Him.

Teach your household the currency of the Kingdom of God, which is faith.

2. Teach the Word of God to your family.

Matthew 4:4
But He answered and said, "It is written, 'Man shall not live by bread alone, but by every word that proceeds from the mouth of God.'"

It is the husband's responsibility to teach the Word of God to the household. The Word of God is the constitution of the Kingdom of God.

3. Teach your family Kingdom culture.

Romans 14:17
For the kingdom of God is not eating and drinking, but righteousness and peace and joy in the Holy Spirit.

When we try to establish our own culture, we bring all the negative things into our family from past generations. When Kingdom culture is established in your home, everyone will be whole and well.

Remember, all responsibility is given with accountability. You cannot have the God-given position without taking responsibility.

Acceptance and Rejection

~ WIFE'S ROLE ~

Rejection comes to the wife when she refuses to accept the husband's God-given position. This means she does not accept him as the prophet, priest, and king in her home, and she fails to cooperate in her God-given role as a helpmate.

Genesis 2:20–25
So Adam gave names to all cattle, to the birds of the air, and to every beast of the field. But for Adam there was not found a helper comparable to him. And the LORD God caused a deep sleep to fall on Adam, and he slept; and He took one of his ribs, and closed up the flesh in its place. Then the rib which the LORD God had taken from man He made into a woman, and He brought her to the man. And Adam said: "This is now bone of my bones and flesh of my flesh; she shall be called Woman, because she was taken out of Man." Therefore a man shall leave his father and mother and be joined to his wife, and they shall become one flesh. And they were both naked, the man and his wife, and were not ashamed.

Let us have a closer look at this passage of scripture.

→ God creates Adam.
→ God in His wisdom decides that Adam needs help.
→ God creates Eve.
→ God brings Eve to Adam.
→ God defines their relationship.

Marriage was instituted by God Himself. It is a reflection of the relationship between Christ and His Church, and of what is going to happen in heaven between Christ and His Church. God wanted the woman to walk by her spouse's side.

The word *help* means:

- Help
- Assist
- Encourage
- Complete
- Fulfill need
- Build
- Minister

God made husband and wife so they could build each other up. He placed in them a need for each other.

> *Ecclesiastes 4:9-12*
> *Two are better than one, because they have a good reward for their labor. For if they fall, one will lift up his companion. But woe to him who is alone when he falls, for he has no one to help him up. Again, if two lie down together, they will keep warm; but how can one be warm alone? Though one may be overpowered by another, two can withstand him. And a threefold cord is not quickly broken.*

When a woman does not take her rightful role, she opens the door for rejection and strife to come into the house.

Responsibility of the Wife

1. A loving wife will maintain her relationship with God.

God always comes first. The children will learn from their mother because she is the one the children spend the most time with.

Matthew 6:33
But seek first the kingdom of God and His righteousness, and all these things shall be added to you.

2. A loving wife will submit to her husband.

To submit means to come under, not to be inferior to. Jesus submitted to His Father.

Philippians 2:6
Who, being in the form of God, did not consider it robbery to be equal with God.

Jesus was equal with God, but He was not inferior in any way. A wife is not inferior to her husband, but she comes under his covering and protection.

Ephesians 5:21–24
Submitting to one another in the fear of God. Wives, submit to your own husbands, as to the Lord. For the husband is head of the wife, as also Christ is head of the church; and He is the Savior of the body. Therefore, just as the church is subject to Christ, so let the wives be to their own husbands in everything.

It is important to note in verse 21 that God instructs husbands and wives to submit to each other in the fear of God. This means they must have a mutual respect for each other. Then the wife submits to her husband because that is what God has instructed her to do and she has come under the protection of his divine position. Our relationship with Christ gives a comparison when explaining submission.

If Jesus is your Lord and Saviour how would you relate to Him?

- Respect Him

- Reverence Him

- Honor Him

- Please Him

- Follow Him

- Obey Him

This is what a wife ought to do to for her husband. If a man loves his wife as Christ loves the Church, then there will not be any problem for the wife to submit to her husband. The wife needs to recognize what the husband needs and fulfill that role.

1 Peter 2:13–17
Submit yourselves to every ordinance of man for the Lord's sake, whether to the king as supreme, or to governors, as to those who are sent by him for the punishment of evildoers and for the praise of those who do good. For this is the will of God, that by doing good you may put to silence the ignorance of foolish men—as free, yet not using liberty as a cloak for vice, but as bondservants of God. Honor all people. Love the brotherhood. Fear God. Honor the king.

Peter says we are to submit to authority. If your husband is not saved, through your good conduct he will be drawn to the Lord.

1 Peter 3:1
Wives, likewise, be submissive to your own husbands, that even if some do not obey the word, they, without a word, may be won by the conduct of their wives.

1 Peter 3:5–6
For in this manner, in former times, the holy women who trusted in God also adorned themselves, being submissive to their own husbands, as Sarah obeyed Abraham, calling him lord, whose daughters you are if you do good and are not afraid with any terror.

If you conduct yourself well, you will draw your unsaved husbands to Christ.

1 Corinthians 11:3, 7, 10
But I want you to know that the head of every man is Christ, the head of woman is man, and the head of Christ is God. For a man indeed ought not to cover his head, since he is the image and glory of God; but woman is the glory of man. For this reason the woman ought to have a symbol of authority on her head, because of the angels.

The woman draws her glory from the man. Just like the moon only shines because of the sun.

3. A loving wife will respect, honor, and admire her husband.

a) By not disagreeing with him in front of other people or the children

b) By not discussing his faults with others

When you discuss his faults with everyone, you are allowing the enemy to take those words and bind your household. Speak positively and do not concentrate on the negative.

c) By doing things that please him

d) By supporting his decisions and choices

There is communication when a decision is made together. Pray for him that everything will go well.

4. A loving wife will communicate with her husband.

Share your thoughts with your husband in love.

Before I go any further, let me share with you four things women do that bring strife in a marriage:

a. They give advice when the husband has not asked for it.

The man feels that his wife does not have trust in him to make decisions. If you want to discuss something with your husband, pick the right time.

b. They try to control the husband through feelings.

She stops talking to her husband and opens the door to manipulation through her feelings.

c. They complain about things that the husband has not done.

Get your facts right and know the truth.

d. They try to instruct and correct continuously.

Proverbs 25:24
It is better to dwell in a corner of a housetop, than in a house shared with a contentious woman.

Proverbs 27:15–16
A continual dripping on a very rainy day and a contentious woman are alike; whoever restrains her restrains the wind, and grasps oil with his right hand.

Know when, where, and how to talk. Be motivated by love and godliness.

5. A loving wife will let her husband be the head of the home.

She will accept and enhance his God-given roles and responsibilities.

6. A loving wife will care about being attractive to her husband.

Ruth 3:3
Therefore wash yourself and anoint yourself, put on your best garment and go down to the threshing floor; but do not make yourself known to the man until he has finished eating and drinking.

7. A loving wife will meet her husband's physical needs.

Acceptance
and Rejection

~ CONFLICT IN MARRIAGE ~

Why conflict arises in a marriage:

1. There are unmet needs.

Acts 6:1–7
Now in those days, when the number of the disciples was multiplying, there arose a complaint against the Hebrews by the Hellenists, because their widows were neglected in the daily distribution. Then the twelve summoned the multitude of the disciples and said, "It is not desirable that we should leave the word of God and serve tables. Therefore, brethren, seek out from among you seven men of good reputation, full of the Holy Spirit and wisdom, whom we may appoint over this business; but we will give ourselves continually to prayer and to the ministry of the word." And the saying pleased the whole multitude. And they chose Stephen, a man full of faith and the Holy Spirit, and Philip, Prochorus, Nicanor, Timon, Parmenas, and Nicolas, a proselyte from Antioch, whom they set before the apostles; and when they had prayed, they laid hands on them. Then the word of God spread, and the number of the disciples multiplied greatly in Jerusalem, and a great many of the priests were obedient to the faith.

This scripture passage indicates that there were unmet needs in the Church but because they resolved the issues, the Word of God spread and the number of disciples grew.

When there are unmet needs, there will always be conflict.

2. Emotions are being controlled by the flesh.

You talk before you think and afterward you say, "I wish I had not said that."

Ephesians 4:26
"Be angry, and do not sin": do not let the sun go down on your wrath.

Let your emotions always be controlled by the Spirit. If you let your emotions be controlled by the flesh, you create an atmosphere in the home that is not conducive to peace, and your children will be affected because they will learn from you. They observe how you react and behave in situations, and they will implement this in their own lives.

3. There is selfishness.

As long as there is selfishness in a marriage, there will always be conflict. Marriage should be about partnership and relationship.

James 4:1–4
Where do wars and fights come from among you? Do they not come from your desires for pleasure that war in your members? You lust and do not have. You murder and covet and cannot obtain. You fight and war. Yet you do not have because you do not ask. You ask and do not receive, because you ask amiss, that you may spend it on your pleasures. Adulterers and adulteresses! Do you not know that friendship with the world is enmity with God? Whoever therefore wants to be a friend of the world makes himself an enemy of God.

There should not be any conflict in your marriage if you are doing what is right in the Lord and each spouse is looking out for the other. Put your own house in order first.

4. One person is making quick judgments about what their spouse means.

Ecclesiastes 7:9
Do not hasten in your spirit to be angry, for anger rests in the bosom of fools.

Think before you speak. Do not jump to quick conclusions.

Joshua 22:10–12
And when they came to the region of the Jordan which is in the land of Canaan, the children of Reuben, the children of Gad, and half the tribe of Manasseh built an altar there by the Jordan—a great, impressive altar. Now the children of Israel heard someone say, "Behold, the children of Reuben, the children of Gad, and half the tribe of Manasseh have built an altar on the frontier of the land of Canaan, in the region of the Jordan—on the children of Israel's side. And when the children of Israel heard of it, the whole congregation of the children of Israel gathered together at Shiloh to go to war against them.

They heard gossiping and rumors, and these were very dangerous. They should have gone to the source to get the right information.

Joshua 22:15–22
Then they came to the children of Reuben, to the children of Gad, and to half the tribe of Manasseh, to the land of Gilead, and they spoke with them, saying, "Thus says the whole congregation of the LORD: 'What treachery is this that you have committed against the God of Israel, to turn away this day from following the LORD, in that you have built for yourselves an altar, that you might rebel this day against the LORD? Is the iniquity of Peor not enough for us, from which we are not cleansed till this day, although there was a plague in the congregation of the LORD, but that you must turn away this day from following the LORD? And it shall be, if you rebel

today against the LORD, that tomorrow He will be angry with the whole congregation of Israel. Nevertheless, if the land of your possession is unclean, then cross over to the land of the possession of the LORD, where the LORD's tabernacle stands, and take possession among us; but do not rebel against the LORD, nor rebel against us, by building yourselves an altar besides the altar of the LORD our God. Did not Achan the son of Zerah commit a trespass in the accursed thing, and wrath fell on all the congregation of Israel? And that man did not perish alone in his iniquity.'" Then the children of Reuben, the children of Gad, and half the tribe of Manasseh answered and said to the heads of the divisions of Israel: "The LORD God of gods, the LORD God of gods, He knows, and let Israel itself know—if it is in rebellion, or if in treachery against the LORD, do not save us this day."

They should have asked for an explanation. If they had received the correct information, they could have avoided any strife and misunderstanding. Do not act in haste. The problem is that we usually hear half of what a person is saying and then jump to the wrong conclusion. This is where conflict and rejection come into a marriage. Where there is conflict, there is rejection and strife. Think before you speak and get the facts straight.

5. There are different values.

Results of a survey of differences in values between husband and wife:

a. Protection and security

"A" is a very cautious person. "A" wants to act protectively and make sure that before anything is done, everything has been checked out. "B" is not a cautious person but rather a risk-taker. Now we have opposites in a marriage and there is going to be conflict.

b. Tradition and wanting to please others

"A" wants to keep their traditions and wants to please others. "B" is not loyal to tradition but is a very practical person and adapts easily. Here we have a husband and wife where one says, "I want to keep my tradition and please others," and the other says, "I am a practical person and I just want to get on with life." Now there is conflict.

c. Caring and concern

When one person is caring and concerned and the other is not, there will be conflict in the marriage.

d. One person is neat and tidy, and the other person throws things everywhere. This creates a conflict.

e. Social time

One wants to have friends around and socialize but the other spouse says no; this creates a conflict.

f. Decisions

One person wants to make a decision instantly, but the other person wants time to think about the decision. This creates conflict.

Five ways people react to conflict:

a. My way

"If you do not like my way—too bad. This is the way it is going to be." This reaction will make the conflict worse. This will not only bring hardship to your spouse but also to your children. There will not be joy and peace in the house.

b. No way

There are people who do not want to resolve issues at all. They just want to sweep it under the carpet.

c. Your way

Some people get to the point of saying, "I cannot do this anymore. Do whatever you like."

d. Halfway

Compromise does not always work because one spouse's needs have not been fully met. The resentment, pain, and hurt are still there because only half of the needs have been met.

Ephesians 4:3
Endeavouring to keep the unity of the Spirit in the bond of peace.

e. Our Way

When decisions are made "our way," there is a sense of togetherness and fulfillment. It has to be our way.

Seven ways to make decisions

1. Seek God's direction.

Psalm 119:105
Your word is a lamp to my feet and a light to my path.

2. Seek agreement from your spouse.

When there is agreement, there is power.

3. Give your spouse time to make their decision.

Some people can make decisions quickly, but others need more time.

4. Do not make decisions for the wrong reasons.

Right decisions make wealth, but a wrong decision brings poverty.

5. Commit the decision to the Lord.

When there is agreement between husband and wife, it touches heaven.

6. Both spouses must support each other on the decision that has been made.

7. Thank God for the answer.

Acceptance and Rejection

~ COMMUNICATION ~

Marriage

As I mentioned earlier, there are three stages in a marriage. Let me remind you of them.

1. Getting to know your spouse

Song of Solomon 2:2-3 NLT
Like a lily among thistles is my darling among young women.
Like the finest apple tree in the orchard is my lover among
other young men. I sit in his delightful shade and taste his
delicious fruit.

They are attracted to each other and see no wrong in each other, and they overlook all the faults that may be there.

2. Differences beginning to appear

This stage produces arguments and criticism, and the spouses begin to defend themselves because they are discovering that there are differences between them.

3. Maturing in love

There will still be differences, but how you handle the differences will determine the outcome of the relationship.

Now you learn to build on the rock, Christ Jesus, and allow the Holy Spirit to guide your marriage.

Rejection comes:

1. When the husband fails to take his rightful position

2. When he fails to love his wife as Christ loved the Church

3. When he fails to communicate properly

The Husband's love should:

Ephesians 5:25
Husbands, love your wives, just as Christ also loved the church and gave Himself for her.

- Sacrifice for his wife

- Make his bride better

- Care and nourish his bride

- Make him unite with his wife

- Remain faithful to the end

- Be gentle

- Not be rude

- Meet her needs

- Be honest

- Be patient

Communication

Communication is vitally important in a marriage.

Many marriages fall apart because of lack of communication or because couples do not know how to communicate properly with each other.

There are quite a few differences in the way men and women communicate. Let us look at some of these differences.

I would like to share with you five foundational steps in communication.

1. Thoughts come.

For example, the wife has a thought that she should cook a nice meal for her husband.

2. Thoughts must be put into words and communicated through words and meaning.

For example, as soon as the husband comes home, the wife asks him, "What would you like for dinner?"

3. Next, there has to be a mode or a method of delivering that communication.

For example, the wife chooses to use a soft, sweet voice to deliver her words with a smile to her husband. I want you to see the importance of the method of delivering a message.

4. Then the message must be received and interpreted.

For example, the husband must now receive the message and realize that his wife wants to please him by cooking dinner.

5. Feedback completes the cycle of communication.

A wise, considerate husband will encourage his wife and praise her for her effort.

Today, many couples do not complete the cycle of communication. They tend to ignore or focus on other things when there is a need to respond correctly. This is an area through which the enemy has brought rejection into the household.

Continuing on the subject of communication, the husband and wife should both realize that they express and communicate differently and that they should learn to understand each other.

In order to help you, I would like to share certain differences between men and women in the area of communication.

- Women want to talk about their feelings, but men want to fix the problem.

- Women can receive many messages at once, but men only focus on one thing at a time.

- Women are more aware of their emotions than men.

- Women expand information when they talk, but men want to condense information.

- Women talk to develop relationships, but men talk to share information.

One of the important keys concerning communication is not only knowing the different ways in which men and women communicate but also being a good listener.

A good listener must overcome temptation.

1. **As a listener, you may be tempted to think you know what the speaker is going to say before they finish.**

   Proverbs 18:13
   He who answers a matter before he hears it, it is folly and shame to him.

2. **You may be tempted to think about the answer without concentrating or listening first.**

3. **You may be tempted to react to certain words rather than listening to the entire conversation.**

4. **You may be tempted to stop listening because you are thinking of something else.**

5. **You may be tempted to listen poorly because you do not agree with the speaker.**

Acceptance and Rejection

~ CONCLUSION ~

Characteristics of a loving, godly wife

1. Loves her husband

Titus 2:4
That they admonish the young women to love their husbands, to love their children.

2. Reverences her husband

Ephesians 5:33
Nevertheless let each one of you in particular so love his own wife as himself, and let the wife see that she respects her husband.

3. Will be faithful

1 Corinthians 7:3–5
Let the husband render to his wife the affection due her, and likewise also the wife to her husband. The wife does not have authority over her own body, but the husband does. And likewise the husband does not have authority over his own body, but the wife does. Do not deprive one another except with consent for a time, that you may give yourselves to fasting and prayer; and come together again so that Satan does not tempt you because of your lack of self-control.

4. Obeys

1 Corinthians 14:34
Let your women keep silent in the churches, for they are not
permitted to speak; but they are to be submissive, as the law
also says.

5. Secures her husband's confidence

Proverbs 31:11
The heart of her husband safely trusts her; so he will have no
lack of gain.

6. Is her husband's crown

Proverbs 12:4
An excellent wife is the crown of her husband, but she who
causes shame is like rottenness in his bones.

7. Seeks ministry from her husband

1 Corinthians 14:35
And if they want to learn something, let them ask their own
husbands at home; for it is shameful for women to speak in
church.

8. Is virtuous

Proverbs 31:10–31
Who can find a virtuous wife? For her worth is far above
rubies. The heart of her husband safely trusts her; so he will
have no lack of gain. She does him good and not evil all the
days of her life. She seeks wool and flax, and willingly works
with her hands. She is like the merchant ships, she brings her
food from afar. She also rises while it is yet night, and provides

food for her household, and a portion for her maidservants. She considers a field and buys it; from her profits she plants a vineyard. She girds herself with strength, and strengthens her arms. She perceives that her merchandise is good, and her lamp does not go out by night. She stretches out her hands to the distaff, and her hand holds the spindle. She extends her hand to the poor, yes, she reaches out her hands to the needy. She is not afraid of snow for her household, for all her household is clothed with scarlet. She makes tapestry for herself; her clothing is fine linen and purple. Her husband is known in the gates, when he sits among the elders of the land. She makes linen garments and sells them, and supplies sashes for the merchants. Strength and honor are her clothing; she shall rejoice in time to come. She opens her mouth with wisdom, and on her tongue is the law of kindness. She watches over the ways of her household, and does not eat the bread of idleness. Her children rise up and call her blessed; her husband also, and he praises her: "Many daughters have done well, but you excel them all." Charm is deceitful and beauty is passing, but a woman who fears the LORD, she shall be praised. Give her of the fruit of her hands, and let her own works praise her in the gates.

Characteristics of a loving, godly husband

1. Respects his wife

1 Peter 3:7
Husbands, likewise, dwell with them with understanding, giving honor to the wife, as to the weaker vessel, and as being heirs together of the grace of life, that your prayers may not be hindered.

If your prayers are not answered, then check whether or not you are respecting your wife.

2. Loves his wife

Ephesians 5:25
Husbands, love your wives, just as Christ also loved the
church and gave Himself for her.

3. Is faithful to his wife

Proverbs 5:19
As a loving deer and a graceful doe, let her breasts satisfy you
at all times; and always be enraptured with her love.

4. Comforts his wife

1 Samuel 1:8
Then Elkanah her husband said to her, "Hannah, why do you
weep? Why do you not eat? And why is your heart grieved?
Am I not better to you than ten sons?"

5. Consults his wife

Genesis 31:4–7
So Jacob sent and called Rachel and Leah to the field, to his
flock, and said to them, "I see your father's countenance, that
it is not favorable toward me as before; but the God of my
father has been with me. And you know that with all my
might I have served your father. Yet your father has deceived
me and changed my wages ten times, but God did not allow
him to hurt me."

6. Does not interfere with his wife's godly duties

> **1 Corinthians 7:5**
> *Do not deprive one another except with consent for a time, that you may give yourselves to fasting and prayer; and come together again so that Satan does not tempt you because of your lack of self-control.*

7. Treats his wife as his own

> **Matthew 19:5**
> *For this reason a man shall leave his father and mother and be joined to his wife, and the two shall become one flesh.*

The Importance of the Family Altar

God created the institution of marriage, and every other institution has been built upon it. One day when I was in prayer the Lord asked me a question. "Where did all these people come from?" I said, "They all came from a home." Then He told me that whatever their profession might be, they all came from a home, whether they were a politician, a laborer, a doctor, an engineer, etc.

Then He told me, "Son, if you get the home right, the Church will be right. If you get the Church right, the nation will be right." Then I realized the importance of the home.

The family altar is an important aspect of the family. The word altar is a very important word in the Word of God. Altar in Hebrew is mizbeach. This word occurs about four hundred times in the Old Covenant. It means a raised place where a sacrifice was made.

When God instructed Israel to build an altar, He wanted it to be made of earth or natural stone. He did not want them to build an altar using hewn stone. The altar was to be a work of God and not man. Later, God gave Moses specific directions concerning building altars. These altars were sanctified according to God's instructions, and they were holy unto the Lord.

In the Old Covenant, we see some altars built to commemorate an event or encounter that the people had with God. The altar was considered a place where they received a revelation or a promise, where they made an agreement with God.

The word altar in Greek is thuciasterion. This word means to sacrifice. The altars of the Old Covenant are types and shadows that reveal key truths how we are to present our gifts, offerings, and sacrifices to God today.

In light of the above, I want you to consider the family altar. When the father gathers his family together and begins to pray and study the Word, he will begin to usher in the very presence of God into the household. Church begins at home. The father is the pastor, the wife is the elder, and the children are the congregation.

Remember, when a family unit comes together in the name of Jesus, they are building an altar in their home where God is able to direct and guide them. Now the home becomes the lighthouse for the neighbors.

I pray that you will consider the family altar and build an altar for God with your family in Jesus' name.

God wants you to spend time with your children. What you sow today is what you are going to reap tomorrow.

Isaiah 55:8–11
"For My thoughts are not your thoughts, nor are your ways My ways," says the LORD. "For as the heavens are higher than the earth, so are My ways higher than your ways, and My thoughts than your thoughts. For as the rain comes down, and the snow from heaven, and do not return there, but water the earth, and make it bring forth and bud, that it may give seed to the sower and bread to the eater, so shall My word be that

goes forth from My mouth; it shall not return to Me void, but it shall accomplish what I please, and it shall prosper in the thing for which I sent it."

We limit God with our thoughts, but God is greater than anything we can imagine. Whatever you put into the heart of your children, even though they may go astray, the Word will always work. Our children can never be lost if the Word is in their hearts. The Word will bring them back. There is power in the family altar, and we must build our families around the altar.

The relationship between husband and wife will set the atmosphere in the home.

The seed that you sow today is the harvest that you will reap tomorrow.

*Consider Calvary,
It Is Perfect in Every
Aspect and Respect.*

Section Eight

The Cross of Calvary
Provides Us with
the Indwelling Spirit

Indwelling Spirit

~ LIVING CONSCIOUSNESS OF THE HOLY SPIRIT ~

The cross of Calvary has provided us with the indwelling Spirit.

> *John 14:16–17*
> *And I will pray the Father, and He will give you another Helper, that He may abide with you forever—the Spirit of truth, whom the world cannot receive, because it neither sees Him nor knows Him; but you know Him, for He dwells with you and will be in you.*

The presence of God is known, but the power of God is felt. The presence of God is always with us, and Jesus said, "You will know Him."

Just before Jesus went to Calvary, He gathered His disciples and revealed to them a divine secret—that He would be in us. This is a secret He wanted them to know before He went to Calvary. He announced the great mystery of the indwelling Spirit, which is the crowning glory of the redemptive work of Christ.

> *Genesis 6:3*
> *And the LORD said, "My spirit shall not strive with man forever, for he is indeed flesh; yet his days shall be one hundred and twenty years."*

The Spirit has been striving with man throughout the ages.

Jesus lived and died so that we could have the indwelling Spirit. Without the indwelling Spirit, what the Father and Son have purposed and worked for could never be appropriated by any human being. To understand this, you must know the work of the Holy Spirit.

The indwelling Spirit produces a divine habitation. We are a habitation of heaven and carry heaven wherever we go.

In God the Father, we have the unseen God, the author of all.

In God the Son, the Father is revealed, made manifested, and brought near.

God at various times and in diverse ways spoke in time past to the forefathers by the prophets.

> **Hebrews 1:1–3**
> *God, who at various times and in various ways spoke in time past to the fathers by the prophets, has in these last days spoken to us by His Son, whom He has appointed heir of all things, through whom also He made the worlds; who being the brightness of His glory and the express image of His person, and upholding all things by the word of His power, when He had by Himself purged our sins, sat down at the right hand of the Majesty on high.*

In God the Spirit, we have the indwelling of God.

The glory is seen and is visible through God's Son, Jesus. If you see the Son, you see the Father. Today He is seated at the right hand of the Father.

The Spirit works in us what the Father has purposed and the Son has procured.

Ephesians 3:20 AMP
Now to Him Who, by (in consequence of) the [action of His] power that is at work within us, is able to [carry out His purpose and] do superabundantly, far over and above all that we [dare] ask or think [infinitely beyond our highest prayers, desires, thoughts, hopes or dreams]..

The power that works in us is the indwelling Spirit of God, and because of that power we are more than able. The Spirit is working in us to fulfill the Father's purpose. The indwelling Spirit has no limits.

God the Father is the source of love and blessing. In order for us to receive His love and His blessing, the Son and the Spirit have to work together. It is the Son of God who brings that love and blessing to us. Unless the Holy Spirit plays His part, we cannot receive what the Son brings from the Father.

The Holy Spirit quickens our spirits and prepares our souls to receive the love and the blessing. We have the indwelling Spirit inside of us.

The key to victorious Christian living is to have a continuous consciousness of the indwelling Spirit in our life.

The Apostle Paul told the people they were having problems because they did not have a continuous consciousness of the indwelling Spirit.

1 Corinthians 3:16
Do you not know that you are the temple of God and that the Spirit of God dwells in you?

1 Corinthians 3:1–7
And I, brethren, could not speak to you as to spiritual people but as to carnal, as to babes in Christ. I fed you with milk and not with solid food; for until now you were not able to receive it, and even now you are still not able; for you are still carnal. For where there are envy, strife, and divisions

among you, are you not carnal and behaving like mere men? For when one says, "I am of Paul," and another, "I am of Apollos," are you not carnal? Who then is Paul, and who is Apollos, but ministers through whom you believed, as the Lord gave to each one? I planted, Apollos watered, but God gave the increase. So then neither he who plants is anything, nor he who waters, but God who gives the increase.

There is division in the house and Paul puts the focus back on God. The reason for the division is that they have not walked in the continuous consciousness of the indwelling Spirit. So Paul reminds them that the Spirit of God dwells in them.

1 Corinthians 6:19
Or do you not know that your body is the temple of the Holy Spirit who is in you, whom you have from God, and you are not your own?

1 Corinthians 6:1–9
Dare any of you, having a matter against another, go to law before the unrighteous, and not before the saints? Do you not know that the saints will judge the world? And if the world will be judged by you, are you unworthy to judge the smallest matters? Do you not know that we shall judge angels? How much more, things that pertain to this life? If then you have judgments concerning things pertaining to this life, do you appoint those who are least esteemed by the church to judge? I say this to your shame. Is it so, that there is not a wise man among you, not even one, who will be able to judge between his brethren? But brother goes to law against brother, and that before unbelievers! Now therefore, it is already an utter failure for you that you go to law against one another. Why do you not rather accept wrong? Why do you not rather let yourselves be cheated? No, you yourselves do wrong and cheat, and you do these things to your brethren! Do you not know that the unrighteous will not inherit the kingdom of God? Do not be deceived. Neither fornicators, nor idolaters, nor adulterers, nor homosexuals, nor sodomites..

Paul reiterates in verses 15 and 19 that your bodies are members of Christ, temples of the Holy Spirit. When you know that the Spirit of God dwells in you, you will not get into strife and envy.

> *2 Corinthians 6:14–17*
> *Do not be unequally yoked together with unbelievers. For what fellowship has righteousness with lawlessness? And what communion has light with darkness? And what accord has Christ with Belial? Or what part has a believer with an unbeliever? And what agreement has the temple of God with idols? For you are the temple of the living God. As God has said: "I will dwell in them and walk among them. I will be their God, and they shall be My people." Therefore "Come out from among them and be separate, says the Lord. Do not touch what is unclean, and I will receive you."*

This does not apply only to marriage. What the apostle Paul is trying to tell us is to not put ourselves in the place where we become vulnerable. Worldly friends will not edify us but godly friends will edify us and speak the Word of God to us.

The world may see you as insignificant, but there is something great inside of you that is able to shake the world.

> *Romans 8:11*
> *But if the Spirit of Him who raised Jesus from the dead dwells in you, He who raised Christ from the dead will also give life to your mortal bodies through His Spirit who dwells in you.*

The indwelling Spirit is the same Holy Spirit who raised Jesus from the grave. That means He has the power to raise the dead. This power is greater than any other power.

> *Ephesians 2:22*
> *In whom you also are being built together for a dwelling place of God in the Spirit.*

You are a habitation of God. The indwelling Spirit gives you access to God's unsearchable riches.

Indwelling Spirit

~ ACCESS TO UNSEARCHABLE RICHES ~

The indwelling Spirit has access to all of God's unsearchable riches. If you have the indwelling Spirit inside you, you are exceedingly rich. Christ lives in us by and through the indwelling Spirit of God.

1. The indwelling Spirit imparts and brings to us all the promises of heaven.

2 Corinthians 1:20–22
For all the promises of God in Him are Yes, and in Him Amen, to the glory of God through us. Now He who establishes us with you in Christ and has anointed us is God, who also has sealed us and given us the Spirit in our hearts as a guarantee.

When you say "Amen," you seal it in heaven. The indwelling Spirit takes all the promises of heaven and imparts them to our life.

John 16:14
He will glorify Me, for He will take of what is mine and declare it to you.

Jesus is talking about the Holy Spirit in this verse. Everything of Christ He will take and give to us. Power, strength, glory, honor, riches, and victory belong to Him, and the Holy Spirit will take these from Jesus and reveal, disclose, and transmit them to you and me.

2. The indwelling Spirit imparts hope.

Hope is the divine, earnest expectation that God will do what He said He would do.

Colossians 1:27
> *To them God willed to make known what are the riches of the glory of this mystery among the Gentiles: which is Christ in you, the __hope__ of glory.*

Isaiah 55:11
> *So shall My word be that goes forth from My mouth; it shall not return to Me void, but it shall accomplish what I please, and it shall prosper in the thing for which I sent it.*

God is never late; He is always right on time. It is the indwelling Spirit that imparts hope.

3. The indwelling Spirit strengthens you with the might of heaven.

Ephesians 3:16
> *That He would grant you, according to the riches of His glory, to be __strengthened with might__ through His Spirit in the inner man.*

Colossians 1:11
> *__Strengthened with all might,__ according to His glorious power, for all patience and longsuffering with joy.*

Judges 6:11–14, 34–36
> *Now the Angel of the LORD came and sat under the terebinth tree which was in Ophrah, which belonged to Joash the Abiezrite, while his son Gideon threshed wheat in the winepress, in order to hide it from the Midianites. And the Angel of the LORD appeared to him, and said to him, "The LORD is with you, you mighty man of valor!" Gideon said to Him, "O my LORD, if the LORD is with us, why then has all*

*this happened to us? And where are all His miracles which our fathers told us about, saying, 'Did not the L*ORD *bring us up from Egypt?' But now the L*ORD *has forsaken us and delivered us into the hands of the Midianites." Then the L*ORD *turned to him and said, "Go in this might of yours, and you shall save Israel from the hand of the Midianites. Have I not sent you?"*

*But the Spirit of the L*ORD *came upon Gideon; then he blew the trumpet, and the Abiezerites gathered behind him. And he sent messengers throughout all Manasseh, who also gathered behind him. He also sent messengers to Asher, Zebulun, and Naphtali; and they came up to meet them. So Gideon said to God, "If you will save Israel by my hand as You have said."*

Judges 7:14
Then his companion answered and said, "This is nothing else but the sword of Gideon the son of Joash, a man of Israel! Into his hand God has delivered Midian and the whole camp."

God injected into Gideon the might of heaven, and the result was that he saved Israel.

The indwelling Spirit will impart God's might to you.

4. The indwelling Spirit imparts the fullness and love of God.

Ephesians 3:17–19
That Christ may dwell in your hearts through faith; that you, being rooted and grounded <u>in love</u>, may be able to comprehend with all the saints what is the width and length and depth and height—to know the love of Christ which passes knowledge; that you may be filled with all the <u>fullness of God</u>.

We have to know the love of Christ before we can pass it on to others and before we can be filled with the fullness of God. This is divine, supernatural, unconditional love.

Romans 5:5
Now hope does not disappoint, because the <u>love of God</u> has been poured out in our hearts by the Holy Spirit who was given to us.

Galatians 5:14
For all the law is fulfilled in one word, even in this: "You shall <u>love</u> your neighbour as yourself."

James 2:8
If you really fulfill the royal law according to the Scripture, "You shall <u>love</u> your neighbor as yourself," you do well.

God put this love inside you so you can walk in freedom and liberty.

Remember, God's love has no boundaries.

5. The indwelling Spirit bears witness to Christ.

John 15:26
But when the Helper comes, whom I shall send to you from the Father, the Spirit of truth who proceeds from the Father, He will <u>testify of Me</u>.

He is in you to testify of Jesus. He will bear witness of Jesus.

6. The indwelling Spirit bears witness to the truth.

1 Corinthians 12:3
Therefore I make known to you that no one speaking by the Spirit of God calls Jesus accursed, and no one can say that <u>Jesus is Lord except by the Holy Spirit</u>.

It is the work of the Holy Spirit to take that truth, to reveal it, and to impart it to us so that we will walk in freedom and liberty.

John 1:17
For the law was given through Moses, but grace and truth came through Jesus Christ.

Acts 5:32
And we are His witnesses to these things, and so also is the Holy Spirit whom God has given to those who obey Him.

The Holy Spirit is able to take the truth inside of us and reveal this truth to the unbeliever, convicting them of their sin.

7. The indwelling Spirit will regenerate you.

Titus 3:5
Not by works of righteousness which we have done, but according to His mercy He saved us, through the washing of regeneration and renewing of the Holy Spirit.

The indwelling Spirit washes, renews, restores, and regenerates.

2 Corinthians 5:17
Therefore, if anyone is in Christ, he is a new creation; old things have passed away; behold, all things have become new.

This divine power is able to dissolve diseases, restore tissue, and transmit heaven's power through our spirits to our souls and bodies.

8. The indwelling Spirit sets us free from the law of sin and death.

Romans 8:2
  For the law of the Spirit of life in Christ Jesus has made me free from the law of sin and death.

The indwelling Spirit of God connects us to a higher law so that we do not come under the law of sin and death. Now I have life in Christ Jesus and life more abundantly.

9. The indwelling Spirit leads us to a godly life.

Acts 10:38
  How God anointed Jesus of Nazareth with the Holy Spirit and with power, who went about <u>doing good and healing all who</u> were oppressed by the devil, for God was with Him.

Romans 8:16
  <u>The Spirit Himself bears</u> witness with our spirit that we are children of God.

Because we are the children of God, we are like our Father. Now the godly life flows in us.

Acts 17:28
  For in Him we live and move and have our being, as also some of your own poets have said, "For we are also His offspring."

Since we are His offspring, we should have His character, His nature, and His ability.

The only Bible that the world reads is your life and mine, and if they want to know God then they need to see your life. It is not difficult to live a holy life; you just have to yield to Him and His Spirit.

10. The indwelling Spirit makes us a spiritual man or woman possessing the mind of Christ.

1 Corinthians 2:12-16
Now we have received, not the spirit of the world, but the Spirit who is from God, that we might know the things that have been freely given to us by God. These things we also speak, not in words which man's wisdom teaches but which the Holy Spirit teaches, comparing spiritual things with spiritual. But the natural man does not receive the things of the Spirit of God, for they are foolishness to him; nor can he know them, because they are spiritually discerned. But he who is spiritual judges all things, yet he himself is rightly judged by no one. For "who has known the mind of the LORD that he may instruct Him?" But we have <u>the mind of Christ</u>.

Without the indwelling Spirit, we cannot discern, comprehend, or appreciate the things of God and get insight into God. We have access to all of God's wisdom through the indwelling Spirit.

John Wesley said, "Sanctification is to have all of Christ's mind."

Luke 12:12
"For the Holy Spirit will teach you in that very hour what you ought to say."

The mind of Christ connects us to the wisdom of heaven.

Protecting our heart and mind by the Spirit of God

Romans 7:23
But I see another law in my members, warring against the law of my mind, and bringing me into captivity to the law of sin which is in my members.

a. There is a war raging in the mind.

b. God has given us a way to overcome.

c. The mind has to be reset by the Holy Spirit.

Romans 8:5 NIV
Those who live according to the sinful nature have their minds set on what that nature desires; but those who live in accordance with the Spirit have their minds set on what the Spirit desires.

d. The reset mind must be controlled by the Spirit.

Romans 8:6
For to be carnally minded is death, but to be spiritually minded is life and peace.

e. The mind that is set and controlled by the Spirit will produce life and peace.

The sinful mind produces death and hostility to God.

f. Our minds must be renewed daily by His Word.

Romans 12:2
And do not be conformed to this world, but be transformed by the renewing of your mind, that you may prove what is that good and acceptable and perfect will of God.

When you have the mind of Christ, you have access to the thoughts of God.

I would like to take some time to talk to you about the importance of renewing your mind.

The indwelling Spirit who dwells in us is able to impart to us the spirit of discernment. The Lord shows us through the gift of discernment, the enemy's tactics, methods, and ways.

Some of the strategies that the enemy uses are:

- Temptation
- Depression
- Oppression
- Deception
- Delusion
- Obsession
- Fear
- Stress

The Lord told me to share with you that He is invading the hearts and minds of His people with a supernatural might and strength.

Romans 8:37
Yet in all these things we are more than conquerors through Him who loved us.

Matthew 11:12 AMP
And from the days of John the Baptist until the present time, the kingdom of heaven has endured violent assault, and violent men seize it by force [as a precious prize—a share in the heavenly kingdom is sought with most ardent zeal and intense exertion].

We have legal right to what belongs to us because Jesus has paid the price.

1 John 3:8
He who sins is of the devil, for the devil has sinned from the
beginning. For this purpose the Son of God was manifested,
that He might destroy the works of the devil.

2 Corinthians 10:4–5
For the weapons of our warfare are not carnal but mighty in
God for pulling down strongholds, casting down arguments
and every high thing that exalts itself against the knowledge
of God, bringing every thought into captivity to the obedience
of Christ.

Why is the mind so important to God and us?

What is in your heart and mind will determine what you are and
who you are.

God has given us the ability to walk with a pure, holy mind in
Christ Jesus by His indwelling Spirit.

The mind processes the thoughts that come out of our hearts
(our innermost being). Once it has processed it, the tongue
communicates it. The mind and the heart are closely connected.
All thoughts begin from within.

Mark 7:20–23 AMP
And He said, What comes out of a man is what makes a man
unclean and renders [him] unhallowed. For from within,
[that is] out of the heart of men, come base and wicked
thoughts, sexual immorality, stealing, murder, adultery,
coveting (a greedy desire to have more wealth), dangerous
and destructive wickedness, deceit; unrestrained (indecent)
conduct; an evil eye (envy), slander (evil speaking, malicious
misrepresentation, abusiveness), pride—(the sin of an
uplifted heart against God and man), foolishness (folly, lack
of sense, recklessness, thoughtlessness). All these evil [purposes
and desires] come from within, and they make the man
unclean and render him unhallowed.

Matthew 12:34–35 AMP
You offspring of vipers! How can you speak good things when
you are evil (wicked)? For out of the fullness (the overflow,
the superabundance of the heart the mouth speaks. The good
man from his inner good treasure flings forth good things,
and the evil man out of his inner evil storehouse flings forth
evil things.

The heart is the center of:

- Your thoughts

- Your existence

- Your beliefs

- Your doubt

- The issues of life

The meaning of the Greek word here translated heart
encompasses man's entire inner life and moral preference.

Let us look at what the Scriptures say about the heart.

Matthew 5:28
But I say to you that whoever looks at a woman to lust for her
has already committed adultery with her in his heart.

Ezekiel 28:14–17
You were the anointed cherub who covers; I established you;
you were on the holy mountain of God; you walked back
and forth in the midst of fiery stones. You were perfect in

your ways from the day you were created, till iniquity was found in you. By the abundance of your trading you became filled with violence within, and you sinned; therefore I cast you as a profane thing out of the mountain of God; and I destroyed you, O covering cherub, from the midst of the fiery stones. Your heart was lifted up because of your beauty; you corrupted your wisdom for the sake of your splendor; I cast you to the ground, I laid you before kings, that they might gaze at you.

Acts 5:3
But Peter said, "Ananias, why has Satan filled your heart to lie to the Holy Spirit and keep back part of the price of the land for yourself?"

The heart must be protected. That is why God says in His Word, "As a man thinketh in his heart, so is he."

Proverbs 23:7
For as he thinks in his heart, so is he, "Eat and drink!" he says to you, but his heart is not with you.

Proverbs 4:23
Keep your heart with all diligence, for out of it spring the issues of life.

Indwelling Spirit

~ A Victorious Mind through the Holy Spirit ~

1 Corinthians 2:16 AMP
For who has known or understood the mind (the counsels and purposes) of the Lord so as to guide and instruct Him and give Him knowledge? But we have the mind of Christ (the Messiah) and do hold the thoughts (feelings and purposes) of His heart.

We have the Messiah's mind! We can think like He thinks and we can talk like He talks.

The battle we face is in the mind and the heart. The enemy attacks us in our hearts and minds because that is where the Word of God is lodged and where faith is conceived. If Satan can attack your heart and mind with negative thoughts, he will uproot the Word of God in your heart. If he uproots the Word, faith cannot be born. If the Word is not there, you have nothing to hold on to. That is why Christians often walk a defeated life.

The Greek word here translated mind means "mental faculty of perception, understanding, knowing and feeling, judging and determining."

If someone controls your heart and mind, they are able to control your whole being. God has given us a victorious mind.

Ephesians 3:20 AMP
Now to Him Who, by (in consequence of) the [action of His]
power that is at work within us, is able to [carry out His
purpose and] do superabundantly, far over and above all
that we [dare] ask or think [infinitely beyond our highest
prayers, desires, thoughts, hopes or dreams]--

The same power that raised Jesus from the grave is working
inside of us. This indwelling Spirit is spiritually active.

2 Timothy 1:7
For God has not given us a spirit of fear, but of power and of
love and of a sound mind.

This sound mind is able to judge correctly, to discern and make
right decisions. So we must prepare our minds in and through
the Spirit of God.

To have a victorious mind:

1. We must have a sound mind.

2 Timothy 1:7
For God has not given us a spirit of fear, but of power and of
love and of a sound mind.

Take aggressive action against every thought that enters
into your mind; do not be passive. Recognize, resist, and
cast out all thoughts the enemy tries to plant into your heart
and mind.

2. Continually bring every thought into captivity.

You are in control of the thought; the thought is not in control
of you. Thoughts have the power to influence your future,
feelings, progress, and actions.

2 Corinthians 10:5
Casting down arguments and every high thing that exalts itself against the knowledge of God, bringing every thought into captivity to the obedience of Christ.

3. Continually renew your mind.

This means that we must conform our minds to the will of God.

Romans 12:2
And do not be conformed to this world, but be transformed by the <u>renewing of your mind</u>, that you may prove what is that good and acceptable and perfect will of God.

4. Fill your mind with the Word of God.

Joshua 1:8
This Book of the Law shall not depart from your mouth, but you shall <u>meditate in it day and night</u>, that you may observe to do according to all that is written in it. For then you will make your way prosperous, and then you will have good success.

a) This scripture states that we must confess the Word.

Romans 10:17
So then faith comes by hearing, and hearing by the word of God.

When you confess the Word of God, faith is born in your heart.

b) Meditate on the Word.

c) Observe the Word.

d) Act upon the Word.

Psalm 1:1–3

Blessed is the man who walks not in the counsel of the ungodly, nor stands in the path of sinners, nor sits in the seat of the scornful; but his delight is in the law of the LORD, and in His law he meditates day and night. He shall be like a tree planted by the rivers of water, that brings forth its fruit in its season, whose leaf also shall not wither; and whatever he does shall prosper.

God wants to change us into the image of His Son. He gave us the mind of Christ so we can walk a godly life.

Romans 8:29

For whom He foreknew, He also predestined to be conformed to the image of His Son, that He might be the firstborn among many brethren.

5. Every thought must be screened. Your Spirit man must be in control of your mind.

This must be a conscious effort—it is a discipline. We need to examine every thought that comes into our minds. When you allow a thought in, it will breed.

Thoughts have the power to influence your:

- Future

- Feelings

- Progress

- Actions

- Attitudes

You have legal rights to:

- Arrest every thought

- Choose every thought

- Develop positive thoughts

- Think good thoughts

Philippians 4:8
Finally, brethren, whatever things are true, whatever things
are noble, whatever things are just, whatever things are pure,
whatever things are lovely, whatever things are of good report,
if there is any virtue and if there is anything praiseworthy—
meditate on these things.

6. Guard your senses

Your senses are the gates to your heart and mind.

Your heart and mind are affected by:

- What you see

- What you say

- What you hear

It is our responsibility to protect our senses.

Romans 12:1
I beseech you therefore, brethren, by the mercies of God, that
you present your bodies a living sacrifice, holy, acceptable to
God, which is your reasonable service.

7. You have the mind of Christ.

1 Corinthians 2:16
For "who has known the mind of the LORD that he may instruct Him?" But we have the mind of Christ.

Set your mind in Christ for 100 percent:

- Freedom

- Cleanliness

- Health

- Renewal

- Victorious mind

I want to bring to your attention some of the thoughts the enemy tries to place in the hearts and minds of God's people.

1. He brings the thought that people are weak and cannot overcome.

There is a battle between the mind and the Word of God, but know this, the Word will prevail. The spies Moses sent into the Promised Land saw the giants, and it captured their thoughts. Thoughts of weakness took hold in their minds even though they had the promise of God.

The Word can do what God can do.

Romans 8:34–37
Who is he who condemns? It is Christ who died, and furthermore is also risen, who is even at the right hand of God, who also makes intercession for us. Who shall separate us from the love of Christ? Shall tribulation, or distress, or persecution, or famine, or nakedness, or peril, or sword? As it is written: "For Your sake we are killed all day long; we are accounted as sheep for the slaughter." Yet in all these things we are more than conquerors through Him who loved us.

There is no condemnation, and God is interceding for us. We have the power and ability to overcome because of the power working in us.

Nothing is impossible; we are more than conquerors.

Ephesians 3:16
That He would grant you, according to the riches of His glory, to be strengthened with might through His Spirit in the inner man.

We are strengthened supernaturally by His might through the indwelling Spirit.

Colossians 1:11
Strengthened with all might, according to His glorious power, for all patience and longsuffering with joy.

1 John 4:4
You are of God, little children, and have overcome them, because He who is in you is greater than he who is in the world.

His strength in us comes because of what Jesus did on the cross of Calvary and His indwelling Spirit.

Judges 6:11–12

> *Now the Angel of the LORD came and sat under the terebinth tree which was in Ophrah, which belonged to Joash the Abiezrite, while his son Gideon threshed wheat in the winepress, in order to hide it from the Midianites. And the Angel of the LORD appeared to him, and said to him, "The LORD is with you, you mighty man of valor!"*

The word *valor* means "boldness", "courage", "fearlessness." The key to having valor is realizing that the Lord is with you and in you.

Judges 6:13–14

> *Gideon said to Him, "O my LORD, if the LORD is with us, why then has all this happened to us? And where are all His miracles which our fathers told us about, saying, 'Did not the LORD bring us up from Egypt?' But now the LORD has forsaken us and delivered us into the hands of the Midianites." Then the LORD turned to him and said, "Go in this might of yours, and you shall save Israel from the hand of the Midianites. Have I not sent you?"*

In the weakness of Gideon, God saw an opportunity to reveal His might. In weakness God becomes strong. He wanted Gideon to discover the potential he had in God.

Judges 6:15–17

> *So he said to Him, "O my Lord, how can I save Israel? Indeed my clan is the weakest in Manasseh, and I am the least in my father's house." And the LORD said to him, "Surely I will be with you, and you shall defeat the Midianites as one man." Then he said to Him, "If now I have found favor in Your sight, then show me a sign that it is You who talk with me."*

You are the man or woman for this hour! God never makes a mistake.

Judges 7:1-2

Then Jerubbaal, (that is, Gideon) and all the people who were with him rose early and encamped beside the well of Harod, so that the camp of the Midianites was on the north side of them by the hill of Moreh in the valley. And the LORD said to Gideon, "The people who are with you are too many for Me to give the Midianites into their hands, lest Israel claim glory for itself against Me, saying, 'My own hand has saved me.'"

God placed the odds against Gideon because He wanted to show Gideon what He could do.

Judges 7:12–13

Now the Midianites and Amalekites, all the people of the East, were lying in the valley as numerous as locusts; and their camels were without number, as the sand by the seashore in multitude. And when Gideon had come, there was a man telling a dream to his companion. He said, "I have had a dream: To my surprise, a loaf of barley bread tumbled into the camp of Midian; it came to a tent and struck it so that it fell and overturned, and the tent collapsed." Then his companion answered and said, "This is nothing else but the sword of Gideon the son of Joash, a man of Israel! Into his hand God has delivered Midian and the whole camp."

With God's might we have the power to destroy every foe that comes against us because of the power of the indwelling Spirit of God.

God will never be late; He will be there for you.

Joshua 14:7–12

I was forty years old when Moses the servant of the LORD sent me from Kadesh Barnea to spy out the land, and I brought back word to him as it was in my heart. Nevertheless my brethren who went up with me made the heart of the people melt, but I wholly followed the LORD my God. So Moses swore on that day, saying, "Surely the land where your foot has trodden shall be your inheritance and your children's forever, because you have wholly followed the LORD my God." And now, behold, the LORD has kept me alive, as He said, these forty-five years, ever since the LORD spoke this word to Moses while Israel wandered in the wilderness; and now, here I am this day, eighty-five years old. As yet I am as strong this day as on the day that Moses sent me; just as my strength was then, so now is my strength for war, both for going out and for coming in. Now therefore, give me this mountain of which the LORD spoke in that day; for you heard in that day how the Anakim were there, and that the cities were great and fortified. It may be that the LORD will be with me, and I shall be able to drive them out as the LORD said."

Look at Caleb; even though he was eighty-five years old, his strength was that of a forty-year-old man. That is what the might of God can do.

Remember this truth: when you serve God, there is an anointing that touches you. The anointing will keep, transform, watch over, and provide for you.

Exodus 23:25
So you shall serve the LORD your God, and He will bless your bread and your water. And I will take sickness away from the midst of you.

This is the assurance we have when we serve God.

Deuteronomy 10:12-13
And now, Israel, what does the LORD your God require of you, but to fear the LORD your God, to walk in all His ways and to love Him, to serve the LORD your God with all your heart and with all your soul, and to keep the commandments of the LORD and His statutes which I command you today for your good?

1 Chronicles 28:9
And for you, my son Solomon, know the God of your father,
and serve Him with a loyal heart and with a willing mind;
for the LORD searches all hearts and understands all the intent
of the thoughts. If you seek Him, He will be found by you; but
if you forsake Him, He will cast you off forever.

Many of God's people have lost their peace and joy because they have allowed the enemy to put fear and doubt into their minds and hearts and they stopped serving and seeking the Lord.

The joy of the Lord is your strength.

2. The enemy brings thoughts that nobody cares.

Matthew 6:30 AMP
But if God so clothes the grass of the field, which today is
alive and green and tomorrow is tossed into the furnace, will
He not much more surely clothe you, O you of little faith?

Your heavenly Father knows and will give you what you need when you seek God and His righteousness. You will lack nothing!

Set your mind and thoughts on what Jesus Christ accomplished for you on the cross of Calvary.

Hebrews 12:2
Looking unto Jesus, the author and finisher of our faith,
who for the joy that was set before Him endured the cross,
despising the shame, and has sat down at the right hand of
the throne of God.

Jesus is the author of your faith.

Place your faith on:

a) The Word of God

It never changes.

Isaiah 55:8–11
"For My thoughts are not your thoughts, nor are your ways My ways," says the LORD. "For as the heavens are higher than the earth, so are My ways higher than your ways, and My thoughts than your thoughts. For as the rain comes down, and the snow from heaven, and do not return there, but water the earth, and make it bring forth and bud, that it may give seed to the sower and bread to the eater, so shall My word be that goes forth from My mouth; it shall not return to Me void, but it shall accomplish what I please, and it shall prosper in the thing for which I sent it."

God said His Word would not come back to Him until it accomplished what it was sent to do.

Luke 1:37–38
"For with God nothing will be impossible." Then Mary said, "Behold the maidservant of the Lord! Let it be to me according to your word." And the angel departed from her.

Mary did not place her faith on the experience with the angel, but she placed her faith on the Word of the living God.

b) The blood of Jesus

Romans 3:25
Whom God set forth as a propitiation by His blood, through faith, to demonstrate His righteousness, because in His forbearance God had passed over the sins that were previously committed.

In order to have faith in the blood of Jesus, we must know what the blood will do for us. The blood has sanctified, reconciled, and justified us.

c) The finished work of the cross of Calvary

Romans 5:11
And not only that, but we also rejoice in God through our Lord Jesus Christ, through whom we have now received the reconciliation.

The word reconciliation means the entire provision that the cross of Calvary has made for us.

d) The power of God that works inside of you

Ephesians 3:20
Now to Him who is able to do exceedingly abundantly above all that we ask or think, according to the power that works in us.

Matthew 6:25–34 AMP
Therefore I tell you, stop being perpetually uneasy (anxious and worried) about your life, what you shall eat or what you shall drink; or about your body, what you shall put on. Is not life greater [in quality] than food, and the body [far above and more excellent] than clothing? Look at the birds of the air; they neither sow nor reap nor gather into barns, and yet your heavenly Father keeps feeding them. Are you not worth more than they? And who of you by worrying and being anxious can add one unit of measure (cubit) to his stature or to the span of his life? And why should you be anxious about clothes? Consider the lilies of the field and learn thoroughly how they grow; they neither toil nor spin. Yet I tell you, even Solomon in all his magnificence (excellence, dignity, and grace) was not arrayed like one of these. But if God so clothes the grass of the field, which today is alive and green and tomorrow is tossed into the furnace, will He not much more

surely clothe you, O you men with little faith? Therefore do not worry and be anxious, saying, What are we going to have to eat? or, What are we going to have to drink? or, What are we going to have to wear? For the Gentiles (heathen) wish for and crave and diligently seek all these things, and your heavenly Father well knows that you need them all. But seek (aim at and strive after) first of all His Kingdom and His righteousness (His way of doing and being right), and then all these things taken together will be given you besides. So do not worry or be anxious about tomorrow, for tomorrow will have worries and anxieties of its own. Sufficient for each day is its own trouble.

God is in control of all things. Do not get concerned about the little things of life, but put your eyes on Jesus, who is more than able to meet all your needs. Nothing comes by our own efforts. We limit God by the way we think.

Mark 4:35–40
On the same day, when evening had come, He said to them, "Let us cross over to the other side." Now when they had left the multitude, they took Him along in the boat as He was. And other little boats were also with Him. And a great windstorm arose, and the waves beat into the boat, so that it was already filling. But He was in the stern, asleep on a pillow. And they awoke Him and said to Him, "Teacher, do You not care that we are perishing?" Then He arose and rebuked the wind, and said to the sea, "Peace, be still!" And the wind ceased and there was a great calm. But He said to them, "Why are you so fearful? How is it that you have no faith?"

The Word never said that the boat was sinking. As long as Jesus is in the boat, nothing will happen—He is in total control. The One who calms the storm walks with you. The disciples looked at the circumstances and forgot the truth of the word that God had spoken. Jesus has told us that He will never leave us or forsake us.

Matthew 10:29–31
Are not two sparrows sold for a copper coin? And not one of them falls to the ground apart from your Father's will. But the very hairs of your head are all numbered. Do not fear therefore, you are of more value than many sparrows.

This tells us how highly valued we are to God. He cares for every one of us.

1 Peter 5:7
Casting all your care upon Him, for He cares for you.

Jesus watches over you and cares about every aspect of your life.

Psalm 55:22
Cast your burden on the LORD, and He shall sustain you; He shall never permit the righteous to be moved.

He will never allow you to fail.

Psalm 121:1–4
I will lift up my eyes to the hills—from whence comes my help? My help comes from the LORD, who made heaven and earth. He will not allow your foot to be moved; He who keeps you will not slumber. Behold, He who keeps Israel shall neither slumber nor sleep.

God is not sleeping, He is continually watching over you.

3. Thoughts of fear

Ignorance and fear are very prevalent today.

2 Corinthians 3:17-18
Now the LORD is the Spirit; and where the Spirit of the Lord is, there is liberty. But we all, with unveiled face, beholding as in a mirror the glory of the Lord, are being transformed

into the same image from glory to glory, just as by the Spirit of the Lord.

Every spirit of fear needs to be broken over our lives.

Fear is real; it is not a figment of our imagination. There are two types of fear—godly fear and demonic fear.

Demonic fear torments.

1 John 4:18 AMP
There is no fear in love [dread does not exist], but full-grown (complete, perfect) love turns fear out of doors and expels every trace of terror! For fear brings with it the thought of punishment, and [so] he who is afraid has not reached the full maturity of love [is not yet grown into love's complete perfection].

Fear torments, terrorizes, and brings the thought of punishment.

How does fear torment people?

- It paralyzes.

- It makes people sick.

- Fear is a stronghold.

- It opens the door for other demonic spirits to enter.

Effects of Fear

Matthew 14:21–31
Now those who had eaten were about five thousand men, besides women and children. Immediately Jesus made His disciples get into the boat and go before Him to the other

side, while He sent the multitudes away. And when He had sent the multitudes away, He went up on the mountain by Himself to pray. Now when evening came, He was alone there. But the boat was now in the middle of the sea, tossed by the waves, for the wind was contrary. Now in the fourth watch of the night Jesus went to them, walking on the sea. And when the disciples saw Him walking on the sea, they were troubled, saying, "It is a ghost!" And they cried out for fear. But immediately Jesus spoke to them, saying, "Be of good cheer! It is I; do not be afraid." And Peter answered Him and said, "Lord, if it is You, command me to come to You on the water." So He said, "Come." And when Peter had come down out of the boat, he walked on the water to go to Jesus. But when he saw that the wind was boisterous, he was afraid; and beginning to sink he cried out, saying, "Lord, save me! And immediately Jesus stretched out His hand and caught him, and said to him, "O you of little faith, why did you doubt?"

Fear requires an atmosphere or situation to walk through in order to enter into the hearts and minds of people. The disciples looked at the situation and became fearful. Fear needs something to trigger it. Jesus said the same thing to the disciples as He says to us: "Be not afraid." Peter heard the Word of God and responded immediately as he fixed his eyes on Jesus. The moment he took his eyes off Jesus, he saw the situation and fear came into his heart and mind. His faith was replaced by fear.

The choice for us is whether to believe or doubt.

We have to be wary at all times because the enemy does not take breaks.

We must understand that fear is a spirit.

2 Timothy 1:7
For God has not given us a spirit of fear, but of power and of
love and of a sound mind.

There are many kinds of fear.

Psalm 34:4
I sought the LORD, and He heard me, and delivered me from
all my fears.

God does not want you to walk in bondage. He is able to deliver us from all our fears.

God has given us all we need to overcome and have a victorious mind through the wonderful, indwelling Spirit, the Holy Spirit.

Conclusion

The cross of Calvary made a way for us to cross over into the Kingdom of God. The person who made the difference for us is the One who died for us on the cross of Calvary. That is why the Word of God states:

> **Hebrews 12:2**
> *Looking unto Jesus, the author and finisher of our faith, who for the joy that was set before Him endured the cross, despising the shame, and has sat down at the right hand of the throne of God.*

We have a Savior who loves us and cares for us. He who was and is the Son of God became the Son of man that we, the sons of man, could become the sons of God. What a glorious exchange we have been given.

Walk in the victory that God's Son has provided for you in the cross of Calvary. All your needs have been taken care of on the cross of Calvary. The proof is that our Savior, our Lord, is alive.

> **Revelation 1:17–18**
> *And when I saw Him, I fell at His feet as dead. But He laid His right hand on me, saying to me, "Do not be afraid; I am the First and the Last. I am He who lives, and was dead, and behold, I am alive forevermore. Amen. And I have the keys of Hades and of Death."*

Finally, I want to remind you:

1. The cross of Calvary provides us with a divine exchange.

2. The cross of Calvary provides us with protection.

3. The cross of Calvary provides us with a challenge.

4. The cross of Calvary reveals God's unconditional love to us.

5. The cross of Calvary provides us with a New Covenant.

6. The cross of Calvary provides us with the blood of God's Son.

7. The cross of Calvary has provided us acceptance in the Beloved.

8. The cross of Calvary has provided us with the indwelling Spirit.

Therefore consider Calvary. It is perfect in every aspect and respect.

Amen!

Other resource material to enhance your spiritual growth and development.

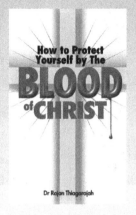

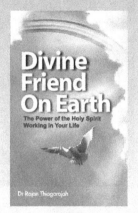

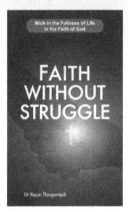

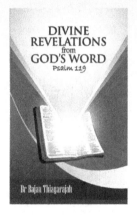

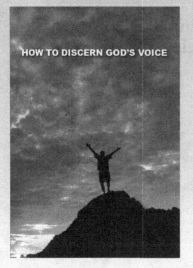

DVD

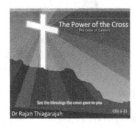

CD

You may order them from:

Mighty Living Waters Life Fellowship
P O Box 183, Willetton
Western Australia 6955
email : tv@lifeinthespirit.info
website : www.lifeinthespirit.info